Studies of the Americas

edited by

Maxine Molyneux
Institute for the Study of the Americas
University of London
School of Advanced Study

Titles in this series are multidisciplinary studies of aspects of the societies of the hemisphere, particularly in the areas of politics, economics, history, anthropology, sociology, and the environment. The series covers a comparative perspective across the Americas, including Canada and the Caribbean as well as the United States and Latin America.

Titles in this series published by Palgrave Macmillan:

Cuba's Military 1990–2005: Revolutionary Soldiers during Counter-Revolutionary Times
By Hal Klepak

The Judicialization of Politics in Latin America
Edited by Rachel Sieder, Line Schjolden, and Alan Angell

Latin America: A New Interpretation
By Laurence Whitehead

Appropriation as Practice: Art and Identity in Argentina
By Arnd Schneider

America and Enlightenment Constitutionalism
Edited by Gary L. McDowell and Johnathan O'Neill

Vargas and Brazil: New Perspectives
Edited by Jens R. Hentschke

When Was Latin America Modern?
Edited by Nicola Miller and Stephen Hart

Debating Cuban Exceptionalism
Edited by Bert Hoffman and Laurence Whitehead

Caribbean Land and Development Revisited
Edited by Jean Besson and Janet Momsen

Cultures of the Lusophone Black Atlantic
Edited by Nancy Priscilla Naro, Roger Sansi-Roca, and David H. Treece

Democratization, Development, and Legality: Chile, 1831–1973
By Julio Faundez

The Hispanic World and American Intellectual Life, 1820–1880
By Iván Jaksić

The Role of Mexico's Plural in Latin American Literary and Political Culture: From Tlatelolco to the "Philanthropic Ogre"
By John King

Faith and Impiety in Revolutionary Mexico
Edited by Matthew Butler

Reinventing Modernity in Latin America: Intellectuals Imagine the Future, 1900–1930
By Nicola Miller

The Republican Party and Immigration Politics: From Proposition 187 to George W. Bush
By Andrew Wroe

The Political Economy of Hemispheric Integration: Responding to Globalization in the Americas
Edited by Diego Sánchez-Ancochea and Kenneth C. Shadlen

Ronald Reagan and the 1980s: Perceptions, Policies, Legacies
Edited by Cheryl Hudson and Gareth Davies

Wellbeing and Development in Peru: Local and Universal Views Confronted
Edited by James Copestake

The Federal Nation: Perspectives on American Federalism
Edited by Iwan W. Morgan and Philip J. Davies

Base Colonies in the Western Hemisphere, 1940-1967
By Steven High

Beyond Neoliberalism in Latin America? Societies and Politics at the Crossroads
Edited by John Burdick, Philip Oxhorn, and Kenneth M. Roberts

Visual Synergies in Fiction and Documentary Film from Latin America
Edited by Miriam Haddu and Joanna Page

Cuban Medical Internationalism: Origins, Evolution, and Goals
By John M. Kirk and H. Michael Erisman

Governance after Neoliberalism in Latin America
Edited by Jean Grugel and Pía Riggirozzi

Modern Poetics and Hemispheric American Cultural Studies
By Justin Read

Youth Violence in Latin America: Gangs and Juvenile Justice in Perspective
Edited by Gareth A. Jones and Dennis Rodgers

The Origins of Mercosur
By Gian Luca Gardini

Belize's Independence & Decolonization in Latin America: Guatemala, Britain, and the UN
By Assad Shoman

Post-Colonial Trinidad: An Ethnographic Journal
By Colin Clarke and Gillian Clarke

The Nitrate King: A Biography of "Colonel" John Thomas North
By William Edmundson

Negotiating the Free Trade Area of the Americas
By Zuleika Arashiro

History and Language in the Andes
Edited by Paul Heggarty and Adrian J. Pearce

Cross-Border Migration among Latin Americans: European Perspectives and Beyond
Edited by Cathy McIlwaine

Native American Adoption, Captivity, and Slavery in Changing Contexts
Edited by Max Carocci and Stephanie Pratt

Struggle for Power in Post-Independence Colombia and Venezuela
By Matthew Brown

Taxation and Society in Twentieth-Century Argentina
By José Antonio Sánchez Román

Taxation and Society in Twentieth-Century Argentina

José Antonio Sánchez Román

palgrave
macmillan

TAXATION AND SOCIETY IN TWENTIETH-CENTURY ARGENTINA

Passages of my articles "Shaping Taxation: Economic Elites and Fiscal Decision-Making in Argentina, 1920–1945," *Journal of Latin American Studies* 40 (February 2008) and "Economic Elites, Regional Cleavages and the First Attempts at Introducing the Income Tax in Argentina," *Hispanic American Historical Review* 89, no. 2 (May 2009) are printed here with permission of *The Journal of Latin American Studies*/ Cambridge University Press and the *Hispanic American Historical Review*/ Duke University Press, respectively.

First published in 2012 by
PALGRAVE MACMILLAN®
in the United States—a division of St. Martin's Press LLC,
175 Fifth Avenue, New York, NY 10010.

Where this book is distributed in the UK, Europe and the rest of the world, this is by Palgrave Macmillan, a division of Macmillan Publishers Limited, registered in England, company number 785998, of Houndmills, Basingstoke, Hampshire RG21 6XS.

Palgrave Macmillan is the global academic imprint of the above companies and has companies and representatives throughout the world.

Palgrave® and Macmillan® are registered trademarks in the United States, the United Kingdom, Europe and other countries.

ISBN: 978–0–230–34126–5

Library of Congress Cataloging-in-Publication Data is available from the Library of Congress.

A catalogue record of the book is available from the British Library.

Design by Newgen Imaging Systems (P) Ltd., Chennai, India.

First edition: May 2012

10 9 8 7 6 5 4 3 2 1

Printed in the United States of America.

To David Webb
In memoriam

Contents

Figures and Tables

Figures

Tables

Acknowledgments

This book would not have been possible without the support of many people and institutions, which demonstrates the importance of trust and cooperation in any human enterprise. I would like to recognize that support. A postdoctoral grant of the Fulbright Commission/MECD and the hospitality of the Department of History at Ohio State University allowed me to begin this research. In Ohio, I found a stimulating and enviable atmosphere in which to develop my research. I wish to thank Ken Andrien and Donna Guy for their generous help during my two years in Ohio. I would like also to thank my colleagues and friends at Ohio State University for their support. I presented the first results of this research in the Brown Bag Seminar at the Department of History, Ohio State University. The comments I received were useful in guiding my investigation. Several colleagues and friends read drafts and made useful comments on different chapters of this book. I wish to mention Yovanna Pineda, Andrés Regalsky, Mariano Plotkin, Marcelo Rougier, Joel Horowitz, Liliana Da Orden, and Line Schjolden. Facundo Alvaredo made interesting suggestions on early drafts of different chapters and allowed me access to his own research before it was published. Roy Hora made a very careful reading of the entire manuscript and his comments were extremely valuable. I also thank, for their comments, the participants at different seminars in Argentina: the Seminars of the IDES held on several occasions; the Seminar on Nineteenth-Century History of the Instituto Ravignani; and the Seminar of Graduate Studies of the Universidad de San Andrés. I am grateful as well to Palgrave Macmillan's anonymous referee, who made important suggestions for improving the final result. Of course, I am solely responsible for any mistakes in this book.

During the process of transforming the research into a book, I enjoyed the wise guidance and friendship of Erick Langer. I want to thank Maxine Molineux and James Dunkerley for their availability.

My gratitude goes as well to Palgrave Macmillan for accepting this book for publication and to Sarah Nathan and Sara Doskow for being really helpful and patient editors. I have to express my gratitude as well to Iñaki Ibarra for his hospitality and generosity, in Buenos Aires and in Madrid. Javier Romero made an important contribution to the design of the cover. However, it is Mercedes who made the most important contribution. In a less-than-stimulating environment, it was she who kept my sanity afloat. Without her infinite generosity, this book would never have been finished. This book is hers.

Abbreviations

ACIEL	Asociación Coordinadora de Instituciones Empresariales Libres
AGN	Archivo General de la Nación (Argentina)
ASR	Anales de la Sociedad Rural
AUIA	Anales de la Unión Industrial Argentina
BDGI	Boletín de la Dirección General Impositiva
BUIA	Boletín de la Unión Industrial Argentina
CACIP	Confederación Argentina del Comercio, la Industria y la Producción (Argentine Confederation of Commerce, Industry and Production)
CGE	Confederación General Económica (Economic General Confederation)
CGT	Confederación General del Trabajo (Labor General Confederation)
CNP	Congreso Nacional de la Productividad (National Congress of Productivity)
DGI	Dirección General Impositiva
DGIR	Dirección General del Impuesto a los Réditos
DS Senado	Senado Diario de Sesiones del Honorable Senado de la Nación (Argentina)
DSCD	Diario de Sesiones de la Cámara de los Diputados (Argentina)
EIAL	Estudios Interdisciplinarios de América Latina y el Caribe
HAHR	Hispanic American Historical Review
IAPI	Instituto Argentino para la Promoción y el Intercambio (Argentine Institute for the Promotion of Trade)
ITDT	Instituto Torcuato di Tella (Buenos Aires)
NARA	National Archives and Records Administration (US)
REA	Revista de Economía Argentina
RRP	Review of the River Plate
RUIA	Revista de la Unión Industrial Argentina

SRA	Sociedad Rural Argentina (Argentina Rural Society)
UCR	Unión Cívica Radical (Civic Radical Union)
UCRI	Unión Cívica Radical Intransigente
UCRP	Unión Cívica Radical del Pueblo
UIA	Unión Industrial Argentina (Argentine Industrial Union)
VAT	Value-Added Tax

Introduction

In 2008, the Argentine national government became entangled in a bitter conflict with rural producers (the so-called *campo*) regarding the issue of the export retentions on soybeans. The government defended high levels of taxation as a distributive mechanism from affluent rural entrepreneurs to popular classes. This argument oversimplified the complexity of the rural world and hid the inability or unwillingness of the national government to carry out profound fiscal reform. But it also echoed an old tradition of social hostility toward big landowners who were traditionally considered inefficient *rentiers*, the most conspicuous representatives of the much-maligned oligarchy. Hence, this conflict had multiple links with past evolutions. There were others. The government chose the export tax rather than other duties because the latter were not part of the revenue-sharing regime with the provinces (the Argentine estates). This regime had been created in the 1930s as a way to appease the interior provinces amid a process of fiscal reform. Export withholdings—unlike most progressive and personal levies—were apparently easy to collect and did not require a great deal of cooperation. The lack of societal cooperation in tax matters is the product of a historical process that began in the 1920s. This book attempts to make this story understood by digging through the layers that have shaped Argentine tax culture in the twentieth century.

In Argentina, is not unusual to listen to someone naively confessing to being a tax dodger. Statements such as "I feel I am a sucker for having paid on due term. My impression is that nobody forces you to pay the tax; everyone does whatever he wants and nothing happens to the one who did not pay," made by a Buenos Aires taxi driver to the newspaper *La Nación,* are commonplace.[1] In fact, the most striking feature of Argentine lack of tax compliance is not its mere existence (tax fraud is a problem for states worldwide) but its level and the social sanction of evasion as a legitimate behavior.[2] Tax evasion seems to be a widespread behavior pattern in Argentina and in many other Latin American countries.[3] Reasons to avoid tax payment are not scarce: the government does not fulfill its role; politicians are corrupt and steal public monies, and so on. These are, indeed, real problems, but they are self-serving justifications as well.

What are the reasons for the legitimacy of this behavior? Since this seems to be a shared characteristic of Latin American nations, one is tempted to put the blame on common cultural or historical traits, such as Iberian roots or Catholicism. Yet, this kind of perspective many times reveals cultural prejudices rather than empirical analysis. This is not to say that some cultural aspects are not influential in the tax behavior of a society. Tax and budgetary cultures exist indeed.[4] But we have to explain how these cultures are shaped and how they evolve. To say that a common Spanish or Catholic matrix has made Argentineans—or Latin Americans—disrespectful of the law and distrustful of governments is to say everything and nothing at the same time. On the other hand, compliance and respect for the law might have segmentary qualities: citizens might be inclined to obey some kinds of laws and to comply with some kinds of rules, but not with others. Taxation is a particular field of rule and compliance; it has to be analyzed both within its own internal logic and without the broader frame of cultural patterns of respect for the law. We need a historical account of taxation in Argentina. The complexity of taxation in the twentieth century—in Argentina and elsewhere—made this century a peculiar one as far as tax matters were concerned. By exploring the twentieth century's own specificity, we will probably grasp the reasons behind the Argentineans' lack of fiscal compliance better than by resorting to cultural interpretations. This book aims to offer such an exploration.

At the turn of the century, the income tax in a graduated form was introduced in several European countries and in the United States. In the 1920s, Mexico and Brazil did so. In 1932, Argentina implemented her income tax. A graduated, progressive, income tax meant a break from what Martin Daunton has called the "principle of proportionality," that is, the idea that every taxpayer had to pay a similar proportion of their income. World wars, inflation and debt, social mobilization, which demanded greater equality, and increased state intervention in the economy strained the so-called "tax state."[5] The new types of taxes (income tax and other similar tools) accentuated the nineteenth-century trend toward a greater involvement of the state in its citizens' lives. It also meant a changing of gears in the relationship between the state and the civil society. These taxes were a challenge for both the state and the citizens, and ran parallel to the process of democratization and full-fledged development of a mass society in the twentieth century. The new taxes were sophisticated instruments that demanded from state bureaucrats an accurate knowledge of their national societies. These taxes were aimed at multiple and simultaneous goals, from helping the Treasury to distributing wealth. As the twentieth century went by, these goals, including economic development, became more complicated.[6] These goals were so important that one has to assume that rulers who implemented progressive duties believed in their feasibility. Besides, these taxes made citizens notably aware of their role as taxpayers. Hence, when introducing a progressive direct tax, a bureaucrat should be confident of the possibility of overcoming the difficulties in collection, among them, the resistance to payment of a society that is traditionally reluctant to do so due to cultural roots or for other reasons.

Cultural interpretations are mostly about social and moral issues; their main concern is the moral fabric of society. Another kind of interpretation focuses on economic performance. A state that does not collect money from its citizens is a state that does not work. Those preoccupied with economic efficiency addressed the issue of fiscal compliance. Many analyses drew on the so-called Virginia school of public economics or on some branch of the rational choice theory in order to understand individual behaviors vis-à-vis the tax. The focus of these "methodologically individualistic" theories is the way in which individuals make decisions. Although a simplification, it must be assumed that these perspectives emphasize that in the absence of coercion or punishments, individuals are prone to evade their taxes. Rulers always seek to maximize collection, while those ruled aim to pay less. According to the rational choice theory, evading taxes is a rational decision because it allows individuals to maximize profits. By calculating costs and benefits, a rational individual would contrast the cost of a fee—or the risk of a time in prison—with the benefits of noncompliance, and if the latter are greater than the former, they would probably take a decision to evade payment. On the same token, the success of a fiscal policy depends on the state's ability to collect taxes, in many instances, through coercion.[7]

As Richard Bonney puts it, "Coercion cannot be ignored in the historical development of the state."[8] However, his assertion that "taxation in a modern sense is a manifestation of the government's power to coerce, to take money from individuals" is a more arguable idea.[9] The rational agent approach does not take into account actual historical process in which tax compliance was successful with a minimum of coercion or threat. Most important, this approach does not seriously consider the issue of the social legitimacy of a behavior (paying or evading taxes) and the reasons for the development of this legitimacy. The idea of a "rational" individual in the rational choice approach is too narrow. Rationality is limited to the idea of maximizing some type of utility. As this book will show, the taxpayer is an individual who always thinks from a collective point of view. What other taxpayers (individuals or groups) think and do and what the state's representatives think and do are important matters for understanding the "rationality" of every taxpayer.[10] Moreover, this individualist methodology seems to reject the possibility of individuals sacrificing part of their interests for the sake of collective action. Thus, a rational individual would prefer more public goods than less of them. But if more public goods mean higher taxes, then the individual would prefer less collective activity.[11] However, this perspective neglects the possibility of renouncing to maximize individual utility for the sake of some public goods deemed essential by a community or when this sacrifice is seen as part of a broader commitment with a fair social or political agreement.[12] Lastly, rational choice approaches homogenize interests within a society and do not explain what allows the state to enforce credible threats during a long period in a particular community. Whereas cultural interpretations reify abstract values, rational choice perspectives miss the importance of specific contexts.

Therefore, we need to explore other issues that go beyond a mere calculus of cost and benefits to fully understand a state's capacities to tax their citizens. Institutionalist approaches or those focusing on the political dimension of economic policies provide better grounds to accomplish this task. (Here, "institutions" is a wide-ranging concept that includes not only a state's agencies, but also the set of rules and practices historically developed within a society). These approaches have emphasized issues such as the evolution of institutions, the formation of interest groups, social perceptions of the capacities of the state and, most important, the key role of state legitimacy in understanding the success of tax policies and reforms.[13] Within this framework, Margaret Levi developed an insightful theoretical reflection on the topic. Levi agrees with the idea that rulers seek to maximize revenue in order to maintain their positions (what she refers to as the theory of predatory rule). But their search for revenue is constrained by several institutional limits that force them to look for the "quasi voluntary" ("quasi," because coercion never disappears altogether) cooperation of those ruled.[14] Within these limits, the bargaining process with economic elites and interest groups plays a major role.

Institutions matter, and so does their history. When we pose questions about the ability of the state to collect taxes, we cannot escape the issue of the relationship between the state and the civil society in a particular community. Evan Lieberman's analysis of the cases of Brazil and South Africa is relevant here. Lieberman featured Brazil as an example of an adversarial tax state and South Africa as an example of a cooperative tax state. Adversarial and cooperative tax states are ideal types that encapsulate some of the main features of the relationship between state's apparatus and civil society as far as taxation is concerned. In a cooperative tax state, the tax bureau is an efficient collector of taxes. Here, the most important taxes are direct ones, and the civil society, in particular the upper classes, do not show stubborn resistance to fulfill their fiscal duties. In an adversarial state, however, direct or progressive taxes are more difficult to collect, and the civil society, particularly the economic elites, boycott the normal working of the tax system.[15]

This book argues that the main reason for the success or failure of a tax device is related to the ability of the state to gain the citizens' trust and their will to cooperate "voluntarily." Of course, this does not mean that taxpayers are happy about paying taxes, but rather that they consent to be taxed. In turn, cooperation depends on trust. To use Daunton's phrase, "Consent, trust and legitimacy are crucial to the history of taxation."[16] To obtain the citizens' trust, several issues must come into play. Of course, self-interest is part of the story: individuals trust the state because they believe that in doing so their interests are protected. Yet, individual interests are not enough to build and to maintain trust. One key factor is the perception of the tax system as fair, that is, as a contract in which all the parts fulfill their obligations. But it is not sufficient that citizens trust the state: they also must trust one other (although the state can also contribute to the development of trust within society).[17] If citizens, either individuals or a particular social segment, suspect that the state is not neutral or that other citizens are not fulfilling their duties, they would probably give up their compliant attitude.

What kind of tax state is Argentina? If we ask about recent times, the answer is, an adversarial tax state. Adversarial tax states are similar to the culture of noncompliance described by Marcelo Bergman for the Argentine case. Noncompliant societies are less prone to abide by norms, and even efficient and "modern" tax bureaucracies are unable to improve collection and tax compliance.[18] Yet, Argentina was not always an adversarial tax state characterized by her culture of noncompliance. Massive tax evasion and tax administration chaos were not permanent characteristics of Argentine society. In the 1930s, the national government was able to implement the income tax and to obtain the cooperation of economic elites in its collection and payment. The tax bureaucracy was modernized (in fact, it was almost created *ex novo*) and the national tax bureau—known originally as the *Dirección General del Impuesto a los Réditos* (General Bureau of the Income Tax) and later on as the *Dirección General Impositiva* (General Tax Bureau)—became one of the most successful bureaucracies within the Argentine state. Talking about the 1970s, a report of the World Bank stated: "[The DGI] was one of the most respected public agencies in Argentina 20 years ago. It was known for the high caliber of its technical personnel as well as high morale."[19] The transformation of Argentina from a cooperative tax state (in the 1930s) into an adversarial one (since the 1950s) deserves its own narrative, one focused on the dynamic of the relationship between state and society and on the process of institutionalization of these relations.

This book develops that narrative while focusing on wealth taxes (direct taxes),[20] such as the income tax, the tax on extraordinary profits, or the capital gains tax. There are at least two types of reasons that make worthy this endeavor. First, these taxes are relevant because they impose a heavy burden upon some citizens, which becomes a powerful incentive to evade their compliance. The income tax, unlike other kinds of taxation such as excises or a sales tax, implies a direct relation between civil society and the state and therefore allows us to pose questions about how the citizens perceive their duties toward the authorities. Second, the income tax and other forms of progressive taxation played a significant role in the Argentine fiscal regime for several decades. In the mid-twentieth century, the income tax became the single largest source of tax revenue for the Argentine Treasury. Later on, high levels of noncompliance led to the decline of the income tax revenues and forced rulers to search for alternative ways of financing the Treasury.

When Argentineans began to distrust their state; to think that the government was favoring some groups or social classes over others; to believe that the money they paid in taxes was wasted through corruption or graft; to consider that their fiscal treatment was unfair—that some people obtained undeserved privileges and exemptions; or to believe that their neighbors, friends, and fellow citizens cheated the Treasury, the virtuous circle of trust that keep together the tax regime started to crumble.[21] At this point, not even coercion was able to restore the former confidence.

Two questions arise: when did this happen and why? This book will attempt to answer both, but let's deal with the second one for the moment. Martin Daunton underlines four factors that influence taxpayers' willingness to cooperate: the institutional devices designed for collecting taxes; economic transformations; the introduction of major tax reforms; and the way in which the state spends the money collected.[22] The combination of these four factors in the Argentine case shows a particularly cumbersome outcome. Tax reform, especially the introduction of a new tax, mainly one as important as the income tax, always creates a difficult situation, that involves the state's ability to reinvent trust. In Argentina, the implementation of the income tax coincided with 1929's world depression. More important, it coincided—although of course this is something that contemporaries could not know—with the first decades of the secular process of decadence of the national economy.[23] The Argentine governments of the 1930s were able to create an efficient, modern, and trustworthy bureaucracy. Nonetheless, they did so at the same time in which the contested legitimacy of the national governments began to affect the very legitimacy of the state. Increasingly, the state became a territory of dispute. This question of political legitimacy is key, because a government that is deemed to be illegitimate is a government whose expenditures are automatically suspicious. The conservative governments of the 1930s gained a deserved reputation of electoral rigging that affected the general appreciation of the politics of the time. Later on, Juan Domingo Perón's popular regime was also tainted with the stain of corruption by those who opposed it to some extent due to the perception that the state had sided with some part of the society. The developments of the 1930s and the 1940s had momentous consequences for Argentine tax history. In fact, Argentina's tax evolution is almost a laboratory demonstration of the path dependency approach.

These four factors are part of the broader context in which the relationships of trust or distrust are built. In a more abstract perspective, one might assume that voluntary cooperation is based upon some ideological constructions, the idea that tax payment is a moral duty for citizens. This ideological factor is usually associated with the above-mentioned perception of the state's neutrality and the perception of taxes and public expenditures as fair. Beyond that, a state that wants to maximize voluntary compliance should consider its relative bargaining power in comparison to that of other actors.[24] In particular, Argentina's state was able to gain the economic elites' cooperation for its tax project, but was less successful in imposing an image of fairness among social classes. Besides, taxpayers' voluntary compliance and trust are hard to obtain and are unstable and fragile, as Argentina's case demonstrated.[25] Therefore, to explain how this precarious situation is achieved—or lost—becomes paramount.

This book is about taxes. But it is also about the relationship between the state and the civil society. A word or two about the state and society are due here. I will talk about individuals and about groups. Sometimes, I will refer to loose and broad collectives such as middle classes or economic elites; on other occasions, I will discuss professional associations or interest group representatives such as the Rural Society or the Industrial Union. These collectives, groups, associations, and classes developed interests and even their own tax culture. Hence, the dynamics of group identity are important factors in the shaping of tax institutions. Historians cannot believe in the "veil of ignorance"; we are not any longer in an "original position," *à la* Rawls: individuals know, or at least think they know, what their situation within society is.[26] Methodological individualistic theories assert that the "individual will not find it advantageous to vote for rules that may promote sectional, class or group interests because, by presupposition, he is unable to predict the role that he will be playing in the actual collective decision-making process at any particular time in the future."[27] My contention is quite the opposite. Even if individuals are unable to predict their place in future collective arrangements, they always try to do it to some extent on the basis of their collective identity.

Still, these interests and perceptions are interwoven with the state and the tax policy in an intimate way. Interests are not "natural" facts. Sven Steinmo states that institutions help individuals to "interpret their self-interest" by offering a context.[28] Interests and even class identities are sometimes created by or as a response to institutions in general and to tax regimes in particular.[29] Let's offer some examples.

Most scholars would agree today on the idea that Peronism, to some extent, (re)created working-class identity in Argentina. Taxation also contributed to this idea. Since an early date, the fourth category of taxpayers (wages and salaries) of the income tax scheme came to embody a positive image of labor, of those who deserved special tax treatment due to the origin of their incomes. Such was the appeal of this image that during the 1930s, Argentine manufacturers defended fourth category taxpayers and presented themselves as part of the *trabajo nacional* (national labor). A similar story could be told of the middle class. To some extent, middle-class identity was recast as a reaction to Peronist plebeian culture in the 1940s and the 1950s. Since the 1950s, middle-class identity, albeit that of a victim, was also built through the rhetoric of taxation. The middle class was that part of the society that saved, but it was punished by burdensome taxes. Big industrialists sided now with the middle classes. Facing a less sympathetic state than in the 1930s and a mobilized working class, the most affluent manufacturers changed their rhetoric, and the idea of saving and reinvestment became their mantra. These changes coincided with the growth of evasion and the beginning of the decline of the Argentine tax state.

The other actor in this play is the state. This is a natural consequence of being the creator and collector of taxes. The main purpose of taxes is to feed the Treasury. But even if it seems natural in a work like this one to talk about the *state*, it might be useful to briefly mention what this book understands by this word. To follow Max Weber's analysis, the state is an organization that controls a bounded territory and a population. This organization is a coercive one. It extracts resources from the territory and the people, but it also arranges the legal and administrative framework of society.[30] This does not mean that I believe the state to be a personal actor nor that I intend to neglect the complexities of bureaucratic formation and the conflictive and even incoherent features of the decision- making process. But a state is a corporate actor with its own peculiarities. A state is different from a community, in the sense that individuals feel that the state is an external entity. States are different from governments as well. Without any degree of institutional continuity, governments cannot work. This is evident as far as taxation is concerned. Governments inherit tax laws, bureaucracies that are in charge of collecting revenues and monitoring taxpayers. But also they receive from the past a complex institutional fabric that affects tax policies: for instance, the Senate and its working and composition, the federal organization of the state and the Constitution itself, and even working traditions. To speak of the state as an actor implies that one speaks about its relative autonomy. Today, this is probably a stale topic and even a pleonasm. But it is important to emphasize this: without state autonomy in some degree, distinguishing between state and civil society is futile, even if state autonomy is not a permanent condition and varies across time and space.[31] On the other hand, the societal impact on state's decisions has not vanished in this account of Argentine tax history: it is a central part of the narrative. Yet, the sources of societal reaction to taxation are more difficult to track beyond the usual responses of business associations, trade unions, and newspapers. In this sense, this book attempts to understand Argentineans bonds with taxes through the lens of public records. I hope future research will cast further light on this fascinating issue.

One of the most interesting aspects of the relationship between societal actors and the state in twentieth-century Argentina—as far as taxation is concerned—is the absence of tax revolts. Before the introduction of the income tax in the 1930s, there were episodes of resistance to taxation, especially among the upper classes, and particularly addressed to provincial governments rather than to national ones. Yet, these were embedded in a general framework of social consensus and an increased assertion of state autonomy.[32] The absence of tax revolts seems to be a common phenomenon in modern Latin America. According to Miguel Ángel Centeno, there were historical reasons for this. Nineteenth-century Latin American states did not resort to domestic taxes for building their treasuries. In many cases, these were lean treasuries. In others, the success of the export economy allowed rulers to maximize their revenues—either through customs duties or through the monopoly of some commodity—without forcing their citizens to directly contribute to public funds. The main consequence was the absence of an efficient tax bureaucracy and the building of a nonintrusive state ("weak," in Centeno's analysis).[33] Yet, it is possible to offer an alternative interpretation, at least for the Argentine case in the twentieth century. Peter Evans and Dietrich Rueschemeyer noticed that the very success of the state in intervening in society might have the paradoxical consequence of diminishing its efficiency by becoming "an arena of social conflict." In particular, attempts at changing the distribution of wealth are among the state's most resented intrusions in society.[34] In Argentina, the conservative governments of the 1930s increased the state's intervention in economy (including the income tax) and created multiple bureaucratic agencies to deal with economic matters. Under Perón's rule, major shifts of income distribution—from the countryside to the city and from capital to labor—were carried out. These public undertakings were possible because the Argentine state had been consolidating and growing since the 1880s.[35] At the same time, this success brought about societal attempts to erode state autonomy.

Nonetheless, and regardless of our position on the capacities of the Argentine state, the absence of tax revolts is related to the fact that the possibility of evading payment was a real one. To put it in Hirschman's words, "voice" is only an option when "exit" is unavailable.[36] For Argentine taxpayers, exit was available. The long-term consequences of these are significant: Argentineans renounce the collectively shaping any coherent tax system whatsoever. Civil society shares with the state the responsibility for the fiscal failure of the nation.

The book begins (chapter 1) with the origins of the public discussion about the income tax in Argentina. These discussions were related to the fiscal problems caused by World War I and by the expansion of public expenditures since the beginning of the century. The chapter deals with the issue of the social and political cleavages that tax reform caused to the nation. It shows how, despite several attempts to implement the new tax, regional politicians blocked its approval at the Senate because they feared that the income tax would mean the strengthening of the central government versus provincial ones.

Chapter two analyzes tax policies between 1930 and 1945. The 1930s' crisis opened a window of opportunity for tax reform, and the conservative governments of the decade finally managed to implement the income tax. Moreover, and against all odds, the income tax was a success by becoming the main source of tax revenue for the state in the early 1940s. This was due, to some extent, the cooperation of economic elites with what they perceived as sympathetic national governments. In Argentina, as elsewhere, in its early stages, the income tax was addressed mostly to upper-income holders. Nonetheless, this success had a less bright side. The income tax was associated with a political regime that was deemed to be illegitimate, because it was the inheritor of a coup d'état and was able to preserve power in the 1930s, thanks to electoral rigging. This was a sort of original stain for Argentina's progressive taxation.

Chapter three focuses on Perón's rule between 1946 and 1955. Perón's regime committed itself—at least during its first years—to the distribution of wealth from the countryside to the city and from capital to labor. Yet, progressive taxation was not a significant weapon in the process of distribution. In fact, this chapter argues that Peronism attempted to depoliticize tax issues. Its big achievement, as far as tax matters were concerned, was to suppress tax discussion from the agenda of trade unions and labor. This was a lasting legacy of the regime to the politics of taxation in the country. Notwithstanding the attempt to avoid political conflict surrounding tax matters, the bitter social and political conflict that started during Perón's rule meant that taxes were increasingly challenged from several sectors of the civil society as originating in a state in which trust was not possible.

Since 1952, tax evasion skyrocketed in Argentina. Chapter four explores the reasons for this behavior and links it not only to inflation but also to the political stalemate that the expulsion of Peronism from the political arena produced. The title of the chapter, "Into the Labyrinth," refers to the impossibility of reforming the tax system in a period in which rising prices and a challenging civil society were besieging an increasingly needed Treasury. This period showed a slow but almost inexorable decline of the progressive tax regime that had begun in the early 1930s. This is also a period in which some social identities related to tax issues, such as the middle-class, acquired greater salience. In fact, middle-class grievances were widely used as justification for noncompliance. The main permanent feature of this period was the end of Argentine society's trust in the state.

Chapter five explores the most important tax reform introduced by the national governments since the 1930s, the Value-Added Tax (VAT) in 1974. This new tax was implemented with relative success in a tumultuous political and economic time. Unlike other reforms, it had the backing of important private actors and it meant to implicitly recognize that progressive taxation might not be the path to the future.

Two final caveats are needed. This book is researched mainly from official records, although whenever possible, sources originating from civil society, such as newspapers, business associations' publications, pamphlets, etcetera, were used. Argentine tax bureaucracy was successfully "modernized" in the 1930s, and the tax agency produced an impressive quantity of reports and statistics. The accuracy of these records might be challenged, particularly after the state capacity to tax its citizens began to crumble. Still, these sources are indispensable, since it would be difficult to find alternatives. Most "alternative" accounts of Argentine tax policies are based upon public records. Most important, this book is about perceptions—rulers' perceptions about taxpayers' behavior; taxpayers' perceptions about the fairness of the system—and about how both the state and the civil society tried to shape each other's behavior as far as taxes were concerned. In this sense, public records are invaluable sources.

Lastly, Argentina is a federal country and therefore provinces (states) played a significant role in the shaping of the tax system. However, due to the usual space limits, this book focuses on national taxes. I am currently working on a volume on the history of fiscal federalism in Argentina in the twentieth century.

Chapter 1

Discussing the Income Tax (1914–1930)

In 1932, the Argentine Congress passed the first income tax law in the nation's history. However, Argentine politicians and intellectuals had been toying with the idea of the income tax for a long time. During the nineteenth century, the Argentine national Treasury was based upon customs duties (mostly taxes on imports, although there were also some levies on exports), which totaled to 75 percent of the total national income.[1] In 1890, a severe economic slump challenged this fiscal regime, and for the first time, following the British example, the possibility of introducing an income tax was considered. Besides this, in order to face the economic downturn, the national government levied a pack of excises—the so-called "internal taxes"—that diminished the Treasury's dependency on foreign commerce.[2] The debate about fiscal reform did not arise only out of the dilemmas posed by the crisis. Social and political changes influenced the public debate on taxation as well. The Socialist Party, created at the end of the century, found in the criticism of protectionism and the defense of cheap imports for the working class one of its main banners. As an alternative to import taxes, the Socialists proposed progressive direct taxation, particularly on landowners. They were not alone in their concern for tax reform. Since the end of the nineteenth century, social reformists concerned about the so-called "social question" asked for increased participation of the state to solve social problems. This demanded greater revenue, to which the income tax or other type of progressive duties might contribute.

Financial vulnerability was more apparent during World War I, when the breaking of the international trade deeply depressed state's revenues and caused major deficits.[3] The financial problems coincided with the culmination of the process of political reform of the

Conservative regimen initiated in the previous years. In 1916, the leader of the main opposition party, the Radical Civic Union (UCR), achieved the presidency of the republic in the first truly democratic national election in the country.[4] The links between democratization and tax reform were evident elsewhere, as greater popular participation in politics meant a stronger pressure on the government to shift the nation's tax base. In Argentina, even though the pressure from below was less intense, the Radical Party, encouraged by the necessity of funds or by its commitment to democratization, attempted—since the very beginning—to introduce the income tax in the nation.[5] Along with the tax reform, the UCR demonstrated a greater sympathy than had been demonstrated by the previous Conservative administration toward labor grievances, particularly those protecting workers' wages.[6] Nonetheless, in the field of labor legislation, the progress was slow. Similarly, the government tried to implement a more flexible monetary policy through the creation of a central bank. That policy was carried out in an improvised manner by the government, and the project of a central bank ultimately faltered. In the second Radical administration of the 1920s that had been lead by Marcelo de Alvear, the government attempted to implement an almost universal system of pensions and faced the opposition of both workers and employers. Finally, the reform stalled. In truth, the Radical Party's commitment to economic and social reform was mild, and most of their achievements were based on ad hoc practices rather than on fully developed plans. To some extent, this was related to internal divisions within the UCR and to the conflicts in the Congress. But also, as Pablo Gerchunoff and Horacio Aguirre assert, the Radical administrations of the 1920s lacked firm economic ideas, and they were "navigating between two worlds—the gold standard and the Argentina of the export boom, and the industrial take off" without being fully aware of the implications of this transition.[7]

The economic crisis opened windows of opportunities for tax reform. As in 1890, World War I cast doubt on the future of a fiscal regime based on the tariffs. Yet, as the 1920s passed by and the Argentine export economy recovered its former vigor, the introduction of new taxes became less pressing, and the reform lost momentum. Nonetheless, economic circumstances alone do not provide the whole picture of the decade. The income tax did not fall into complete oblivion. In 1924, the Chamber of Deputies passed the proposal of Víctor Molina, who was the finance minister in Marcelo de Alvear's administration. Only the opposition of the Senate prevented the income tax from being implemented in Argentina for the first time. This chapter explores in detail this attempted reform, which was not the first in the decade, but was the most consistently pursued.[8] The possibility of a new tax produced varied reactions from different social groups. This chapter focuses on those actors who were most able to influence the final outcome of the process: the rural entrepreneurs, the manufacturers, and the political elites of the interior. Argentine entrepreneurs maintained an ambiguous—and to some extent acquiescent—position toward the new tax and were disposed to tolerate it in exchange for more favorable economic policies. Although landowners or industrialists, through their corporate representations, were not supportive of the measure, neither were they the main obstacle to its implementation.

The fiscal reform was defeated in the Senate thanks to the active opposition of the majority of representatives of the provinces of the Argentine interior. To introduce the income tax implied the elimination of certain taxes and the unification of the fiscal system, both of which processes were perceived by the oligarchies from the less developed provinces as a threat to their precarious economic life. This opposition is the key to understanding the failures of the reform before 1932.

In the Aftermath of the War...the Need for Tax Reform

World War I significantly affected both the economic management of European states as well as their tax policies. Latin American nations, although far away from the battlefields, could not help being touched by the consequences of the war.[9] One of the most evident consequences of the war was the disruption in foreign trade, mainly the fall of imports, which depressed customs revenues. In Argentina, falling revenues combined with increased state's expenditure pushed deficit up. In 1900, the deficit was more than 9 million pesos *moneda nacional* (national currency), whereas it was over 150 million during the World War I.[10] In 1900, taxes on international commerce (mainly the import tax, but also an export tax and some fees charged to foreign goods at the port of Buenos Aires) amounted to 52 percent of total income. The situation had not changed in the 1920s: import taxes plus the other taxes on international trade still comprised around the 60 percent of the Argentine budget.[11]

Before the war, that dependency was not considered an urgent problem because of the general belief in both the continuation of prosperity and the limitless expansion of international trade. However, the war taught a hard lesson. Import tax collections fell to almost half the previous amount during the period, demonstrating the vulnerability of the revenue system. Between 1914 and 1919, the revenues of the national Treasury fell by 10 percent, and the national government deficit reached 50 percent of total collections at a time when obtaining foreign loans was a complicated matter due to the war.[12] This fiscal situation stirred a debate on the necessity of introducing new taxes.

Fiscal imbalance was accompanied by an economic recession—largely caused by war—whose lowest point was reached in 1917.[13] This critical juncture was faced by Radical Hipólito Yrigoyen, the new—and first democratically elected—president of the nation. Yrigoyen's finance minister, Domingo Salaberry, submitted to Congress an income tax project in 1918, with the objective of eliminating a foreseen deficit of 30 million pesos in the 1919 budget. The proposal was a mild one. It established a flat rate of 2 percent for every taxpayer and not very steep graduated rates from 0.5 percent to 7 percent for the highest bracket (over 100,000 pesos). Nonetheless, those with incomes ranging from 1,500 to 20,000 pesos enjoyed some family allowances. More important, corporations were subjected to a graduated income tax, ranging from 0.5 percent to 20 percent for those firms making more than a 4 percent profit annually. The commission of budget of the Chamber of Deputies, led by the Radical deputy Víctor Molina, reformed it. The new project augmented the duty paid by those with higher levels of income (up to 10 percent) and exempted the lower income groups (those with an income of under 2,500 pesos annually), although it lowered the tax on corporations' profits and dividends down to a flat 2 percent rate.[14] Salaberry's original draft, and Molina's version as well, attempted to moderately tap wealthy people. In Molina's version, the personal income tax was more progressive, whereas corporations obtained favorable treatment. Nonetheless, it is possible to assume that incorporated capital was not yet very significant within Argentine economy (perhaps the measure was addressed to foreign investors). On the other hand, incomes of under 2,500 pesos in Argentina after World War I were a sizable proportion of the population, and they were largely exempted from taxation.[15] As in other aspects of the Radical policies, such as salaries, rents, or prices of basic consumption items, in its design of the fiscal reform, the government tried to protect the popular classes' purchasing power.[16]

The Chamber passed Salaberry's bill in general in 1920, but their articles were never discussed *en particular* (separately) and therefore it was neither submitted to the Senate nor was it implemented. In the

Chamber's Budget Committee, the changes in the customs tariffs included in the "tax pack" by the executive branch aroused a major controversy that halted the discussion on the new tax.[17] The conflicts between the legislative and the executive branches were constant during that period. Yrigoyen faced a hostile Senate and did not obtain a majority in the Chamber until 1920, and most of his legislative proposals, including the income tax reform, were blocked by either senators or deputies.[18]

Before stalling in Congress, however, the income tax project stirred public debate in the Buenos Aires press and among economists, politicians, and businessmen. One of the most striking features of the debate was a consensus on the fact that the income tax, at least "in theory," was the most perfect fiscal instrument. In 1917, when rumors spread that the executive was considering the possibility of introducing the income tax in Argentine, the conservative newspaper *La Prensa* devoted a series of articles to the new fiscal instrument. One of its main conclusions was that the income tax was the most advanced mechanism designed by modern financial science. The scientific character of the tax was related precisely to the fact that it affected "incomes" and not capital or production, which were key for the economic development of a nation.[19] If not perfect, the income tax was better than the Argentine tax system at the end of the war. For *La Prensa,* the Argentine tax regime was "anachronistic, false, unbearable and it urgently needs substantial reform."[20] Even the majority of those who ultimately opposed the income tax agreed on its "scientific" superiority.[21] Only the economist Roberto A. Ramm Doman seemed to differ radically from this position.[22]

The income tax was not only the best scientific solution to public finances but was also the most equitable one. The salience of this issue was, to some extent, related to the social consequences of World War I. As elsewhere, the end of the war in Argentina was accompanied by an intense wave of mobilization and strikes, which culminated in an episode of violence and repression in the city of Buenos Aires at the beginning of 1919, known as the *Semana Trágica* (Tragic Week).[23] The UCR's governments demonstrated a greater sympathy for working-class demands that its predecessors had done and promulgated important pieces of social legislation.[24] Still, here, as in many other issues, World War I caused an intensification of former trends rather than a rupture. Although accelerated by the war, the idea that the state should act in order to solve social malaise had gained increased—although far from universal—support since the end of the nineteenth century. The "social question" occupied a significant place in the reflections of members of the elite who were facing the consequences of the process of "modernization" (urbanization, mass migration, and the beginnings of working-class activism).[25] Looking through these lenses, the income tax was an instrument of social justice and an antidote to revolution, and as such was presented by its defenders even before World War I. Thus, the income tax was not only a fiscal instrument but also a sort of social intervention of the state. The Conservative Oliver, although he did not support the income tax, recognized that the Argentine fiscal system was far from being equitable.[26] Guillermo Pintos, a liberal economist, believed that the income tax was one of the "fairest and most equitable" of taxes (and yet he opposed it).[27] Of course, equity and fairness were—and still are—contentious and ambiguous terms. In a broad sense, the idea was to ameliorate the lives of workers and popular classes by introducing the principle of capacity of payment in the tax philosophy of the nation: "[the tax system must] lay on the basic principle that incomes must pay according to their potentialities."[28] But beyond this—and some times around this—the consensus vanished. Hence, for *La Prensa,* the income tax was equitable if the rates were low and the tax burden was widely shared by many taxpayers. The newspaper seemed not to observe any contradiction between the idea that those who were better off should pay more and the idea that the higher the number of taxpayers the better. For Juan B. Justo, the Socialist leader, the situation was quite the opposite. The Socialist Party opposed the idea of a global tax that tapped every type of income. They proposed to create a progressive tax on land in order to tap what they considered to be the real source of privilege in the nation: the underserved wealth of Argentine *estancieros* (landowners).[29]

Nevertheless, there were few who challenged the income tax as a progressive device and hardly anyone who opposed the idea of making the tax system fairer by introducing the concept of the ability to pay. As Ernesto Hueyo (a Conservative economist) stated, the income tax had already gained the sympathy of Argentine public opinion.[30] If the public opinion was convinced and the income tax was both fair and financially efficient, what were the arguments displayed by its enemies? First, they noticed the technical difficulties in applying, for the first time, a sophisticated device such as the income tax. Thus, it was said that the government proposal was badly designed or that the administration did not have a well-prepared bureaucracy and that obtaining the cooperation of taxpayers was a challenging if not illusory task.[31] The Argentine Confederation of Commerce, Industry and Production (CACIP, after its Spanish name) a business association that brought together some of the most important associations of entrepreneurs of the country, published a note against the income tax that underlined the government's improvisation and haste in the drafting of the proposal.[32] Second, the income tax might not be adequate for an agrarian country like Argentine due to the instability of incomes in the rural sector and the necessity of attracting foreign investment and immigrants.[33] Third, there was a constitutional problem, since direct taxes were accorded to the provinces (states) in the Argentine supreme law.

Last, but not least, the nation was already suffering from an unbearable tax burden and could not tolerate any new tax.[34] This was, by large, the most frequent argument. The excessive taxation was linked to the excess in public expenditure.[35] For Carlos Ibarguren, a political enemy of President Yrogoyen, the "Executive branch has blindly resorted to this new tax with fiscal avidity, with a truly extortive goal, in order to cover the deficit in a bureaucratic budget with an excess of expenditures, which does not at all alleviate the burdens that lay on the proletariat."[36]

The idea of a spendthrift government associated with the Radical administrations became a litany in the 1920s and to some extent in the historiography. The building of a patronage network through the massive appointment of bureaucrats was allegedly the distinctive characteristic of the Radical governments, particularly under Yrigoyen. According to David Rock, patronage was the main connection between the party and its constituency, the middle classes, at least between 1919 and 1922.[37] Yet, this interpretation might oversimplify the budgetary performance of the Radicals administration. It is far from clear that the Radicals were different in this behavior from their Conservative predecessors.[38] Moreover, it is not a reasonable guide in order to understand the urge for a fiscal reform at the end of World War I or the persistence of the debate on the income tax during that decade. The deficits of the period 1914–1918 were caused not by growing public expenses but by the dramatic fall in revenues. In fact, public expenditures were cut during the war, although not as much as revenues.[39] The main purpose of the reform was to close the fiscal gap. Unable to have the income tax passed, the executive concentrated on the critical situation and approved some emergency policies. The most important one was a tax on the exports of some goods, if their prices rose over a certain level. This tax had been eliminated from the Argentine fiscal system in 1906, when the country was passing through an export boom, and it was no longer deemed necessary to sustain public income thanks to increase of import tax collections. In 1905, the export tax amounted to 5 million pesos, while the import tax collection was almost 100 million pesos. In contrast, in 1918, the export taxes crossed 50 million pesos, while import taxes were more than 88 million pesos.[40] During the 1920s, import taxes regained their former importance, but the export tax, created as an emergency measure, was maintained in spite of the opposition of all the political parties, exporters, and landowners and even the government's admission of its negative effects.

In 1919, the deficit was cut to 17 million pesos, and in 1920, the national Treasury obtained a positive balance of 72 million pesos.[41] These results helped the government to call off the issue of tax reform. This strategy of "wait and see" had been suggested by business representatives. For the CACIP, "The end of the war... guarantees for the next budget customs revenues that will be much higher than the estimated revenue of the new tax."[42] The Argentine Industrial Union (UIA), the main association of manufacturers in the country, although praising the income tax as a solution to the deficit, recommended postponing it since "The end of the big conflict changes the perspectives... for the next year."[43] But the Argentine economy and fiscal structure faced important challenges—beyond estate patronage—that would keep the debate on the income tax alive during most of the 1920s. The surplus of 1920 was misleading. One of the observers who noticed the less bright side of the situation was the British Commercial Secretary in Buenos Aires: "The financial results of 1920 were certainly the most satisfactory... but these resulted from exceptionally large receipts from import and export duties."[44] Since the end of 1920, public revenues decreased anew and expenditures increased.[45] Between 1920 and 1928, the Treasury registered a permanent imbalance, despite a 30 percent growth in collection, and the government resorted to debt to solve its fiscal problems.[46] The prosperity of the Argentine export sector in the years preceding the war had allowed the national government to finance its deficit through loans arranged in Europe and the United States.

But the structure and composition of Argentine debt changed in the aftermath of World War I. The tightness in the international market of credits made it difficult to obtain foreign loans. Between 1914 and 1924, the government financed its deficit through the so-called "floating debt," that is, short-term loans in lieu of long-term credit, which was less threatening to the financial stability of the state. Hence, the national government had a clear interest in finding alternatives sources of financing. In fact, the domestic market replaced, to some extent, foreign credit in these years. Nonetheless, this does not mean that the

Conservative administrations of the prewar period did not resort to debt. Actually, in 1900, the floating debt meant as serious a problem for the government of Julio A. Roca as it had meant for Yrigoyen in 1920; the difference is that in the first decade of the twentieth century, Argentina found available credit markets abroad and was able to "consolidate" her public debt.[47] Fortunately for the Radical governments, since 1924, the situation in the international and domestic financial markets improved, and the national government was able to finance most of its needs through long-term debt.

The necessity of both the Conservatives and the Radicals resorting to debt highlights another feature of the fiscal system based on import and export taxes: its procyclical tendency, that is, when the economic context was favorable, Argentine exports and imports boomed and so did revenue. When the boost cycle began, tax collections dropped, as the effects of World War I had clearly demonstrated. Contemporaries, even before the Keynesian ideas about countercyclical policies became commonplace knowledge, were well aware of this. Thus, politicians, businessmen, and some intellectuals developed a gloomier view of the soundness of the taxes based on international trade. The concept of elasticity became widespread to explain the advantages of the income tax, which was viewed as a scientific taxation system. In the above-mentioned articles published by *La Prensa* in 1917, the income tax was praised for bringing "greater flexibility" to the Argentine fiscal system.[48] In 1923, the participants in the first Congress of the University of La Plata (the capital city of the province of Buenos Aires) discussed the problems of public finances and reached the following conclusions:

> Although it could be admitted that the current revenue of the nation will increase in the future, this increase will scarcely match the necessities, also growing, of the national administration...It is unavoidable, therefore, to carry out the implementation of a more flexible and abundant system of resources...The Public Finances science and the practice have demonstrated that no other fiscal resource is ahead of the income tax as far as yield and elasticity are concerned. In Great Britain, the *income tax* has been the financial base of the war since its creation...The war of 1914 has demonstrated...that the customs revenues are the most uncertain ones as soon as a war breaks out even in neutral countries. [The income tax is] an indispensable solution in order to reach a greater fiscal equity.[49]

These ideas enjoyed a wide consensus and the above statement was signed by personalities of different ideologies, from Socialists to Conservatives.

If the issues of public debt and tax flexibility became powerful stimuli for the government to pursue fiscal reform after overcoming the critical conjuncture of 1918, this was due to a basic precondition: the national government was disposed to increase public expenditure. Thus, during the 1920s, public expenses grew faster than did the gross domestic product.[50] Despite criticism for increasing public expenses to build patron-client relationships within civil society, by pursuing the road to bigger outlays, the Radical administrations were not breaking with any national tradition of minimum state intervention and austerity. In fact, they were following the trend toward increased public expenses that had been initiated by the Conservative governments once the recovery of the 1890's crisis had become a reality. It is true that between 1916 and 1922, civil servants' salaries and pensions consumed 59 percent of the budget. But the platform was already a high one: the previous Conservative administrations devoted as much as 50 percent of public monies to the same goal.[51]

As mentioned above, World War I forced the government to cut outlays. Yet, it was apparent to many observers that the level of expenditures was not adequate for a complex state and society such as Argentina. The British Commercial Secretary noticed: "On the other hand, the expenditure of the country is not appreciably higher than that of pre-war years, which means that taxation per head has not increased and that the cost of government is not much heavier that before the war... It is not to be assumed that these developments are entirely beneficial or even meritorious."[52] The increased intervention of the state in economy, which took the form of providing basic services such as transport or sewage—or even a limited social protection—was not a creation of World War I, but it had begun in the second half of the nineteenth century in some western countries and in Argentina at the end of that century. This was the result of the complex problems that "modernity" posed to the working of society and economy. Thus, the investments in public works—particularly railways and water works—had accelerated at the beginning of the century under Conservative administrations; it came to a halt with the war and it resumed during the 1920s under Radical governments. Yet, UCR's expenditures in this field did not match the Conservative outlays in proportion to the budget.[53]

But the increase in public expenditure was not only the result of the executive willingness. In the case of the expanded budget for the army, the pressure of the officers and the political maneuvering in Congress of the minister of war, General Agustín Justo, explain to a large extent this outcome.[54] It is thus important to underline that as far as budgetary and fiscal policies were concerned, the authority in Argentina was fragmented (both within government branches and federal instances).[55] The participation of the legislative was crucial at shaping the amount and features of public outlays.

According to the Argentine Constitution, the budget law for every year, which included the tax laws as well, had to be presented by the president to the Chamber on May first of the year before, but during the 1920s this was never accomplished. Furthermore, Argentine public finances were based on the budget of 1923, with slight modifications until 1931. Contemporaries blamed the failure of fiscal reform and to some extent of the rising public expenditure of the decade on the deputies' inability to produce a new budget. The opposition blamed on the government for that.[56]

Outside Congress, intellectuals and members of the upper classes blamed the Congress for the situation of public finances, but at the same time linked this fact to the results of the electoral democracy. In 1924, the Radical Party split in two factions, one supporting former President Yrigoyen, the so-called *yrigoyenistas* or *personalistas* and the other opposed the pre-eminence of this leader, the *anti-personalistas*. The conservative newspaper *La Nación*, gladly welcomed the government of Marcelo Alvear, the second Radical president, and supported its financial program, but showed its concern regarding the failure of the fiscal reform and accused the *yrigoyenista* majority in the Congress for it: "The disastrous policy developed regarding this point [the fiscal reform] by the electoral elements who control the Parliament ruined the executive's plans...The groups that are under the influence of the former administration could not stand the fact of the second Radical presidency introducing order and legality where the first had founded its electoral strength with disorder and lavishness."[57]

The government found ways to expand public expenditure without legislative control. As the budget law used to reproduce the previousyear's accounts, the executive resorted to extra-budgetary outlays sanctioned by special laws or by executive or presidential decrees.[58] Besides the short-term loans, the government had two tools for make extra-budgetary expenditures: *acuerdos de gobierno* (government's agreements) and *leyes especiales* (special laws). The former amounted to more than 1 million pesos in 1923 and reached over 78 million pesos in 1922. The latter came out with the impressive figure of 259 million pesos in 1927 (the actual budgetary expenditure for that year was 614 million pesos), according to a survey of the Argentine Congress in 1930.[59]

Yet, to believe, as most critics did, that the government abused its power in order to expand expenses in a wasteful way is an oversimplification.[60] Public expenditures depended on many factors, among them a more complex state structure and society; and it is far from clear that a Conservative government would have adopted a different policy. The government itself attributed the difficulties of sending a timely budget draft to growing executive functions and increasing expenditures. It also denounced the reluctance of Congress to pass an income tax law, which would have solved some budgetary problems, as President Alvear's second finance minister, Víctor Molina repeatedly complained.[61]

The debate on the income tax survived in the 1920s, fed not only by the state's financial needs but also by an original intellectual inquiry into the economic future of the nation. As already mentioned, some of the participants in the controversy of 1918 believed that the implementation of the income tax could be postponed because a return to "normalcy" was guaranteed with the end of the war. What was the meaning of "normalcy" for most Argentineans in 1920? The probable answer to this question would be an international market characterized by free trade and a permanent and even growing demand of Argentine agricultural exports in the world market. The good performance of the Argentine exports was key for obtaining the resources that paid for the imports and ultimately for governmental revenues. Besides, a buoyant export economy eased the negotiation of essential foreign loans. This pattern had guaranteed an enormous economic success to Argentina before the war, and its restoration would allow the nation to shirk the much-needed fiscal reform after the conflict. This economy, which was based on agrarian exports, had required abundant foreign capital and labor. Some of the critics to the income tax emphasized that the new burden would be a powerful barrier to these foreign blessings. One of the participants in the 1918 controversy, Alberto E. Castex, stated in a Buenos Aires newspaper: "The tax on revenue, like other financial and economic instrument, is it not the match of a [certain] financial and economic stage, the industrial stage, [in which there are] plenty of capitals, stability in values, and profitability of business, a stage we have not reached yet?"[62]

This comment is easily interpreted as another justification of those who opposed the income tax. Nevertheless, the idea that the industrial stage had not yet been reached implied that that might be the (inevitable?) path to the future. In fact, Castex portrayed the industrial period in positive colors: "plenty of capital and stable." Some authors believed that the industrial option was the only one for Argentina.

World War I had demonstrated the risk of agrarian specialization.[63] Moreover, the recovery to "normalcy" could be an illusion. Although exports kept increasing during the 1920s, they did so in an unstable way and the net terms of trade deteriorated after 1917 and did not recover the prewar level until 1928.[64] One of the main defenders of the change of economic pattern for Argentina was Alejandro Bunge. In 1918, Bunge founded the *Revista de Economía Argentina,* which became his platform in the defense of a program of industrialization for the country.[65] In the *Revista de Economía Argentina* and in other public venues, Bunge defended the income tax as an inevitable solution to the nation's fiscal challenges. His participation was an active one. Salaberry's draft of 1918 followed Bunge's advice and thoughts on the subject.[66]

The link between industrialization and the income tax was protectionism. In the pamphlet published by the CACIP in 1918 against the income tax, the opinion of the UIA appeared separately. Whereas the main body of the text was signed by a large group of business associations, the manufacturers' representatives preferred to express their own opinion.[67] As it was said, industrialists complained about the improvised features of the proposed income tax and took a call to wait for the end of the war. Yet, they also showed a more enthusiast stance toward the new tax than did other businessmen: "On the other hand, [we] industrialists will see with great pleasure that the income tax will become the main source of revenue for the state."[68] That is, if the national government decreased its dependency on customs duties, these could be raised to such a level that they could become instruments of industrial promotion and not mere fiscal devices. Bunge made this connection more apparent in an essay of 1921 with the revealing title "New Orientation of the Argentine Economic Policy. Introduction to the Study of the National Industry." In that work, the author emphasized the risk of what future studies would refer to as "dependency": "But a country in the process of development, like our, has to periodically renovate its patterns; otherwise it may be in jeopardy of becoming stagnant in a primary period and becoming an instrument of more advanced nations."[69] One of the means to achieve the economic industrialization, and therefore economic independence, was the much-needed tax reform. This policy was a feasible one: "A well designed income tax—a long time awaited—and a customs regime adjusted to the necessities of the national production and industry, will not be difficult to carry out in the next years."[70] One of the paradoxes of this position is that it brought together uneasily those who favored an increase in customs duties and those who sought to liberalize Argentine foreign trade. For Bunge and the "protectionists," the income tax, by minimizing governmental dependency on import tax, would permit a major rise in duties; for the Socialists, or for free-trade supporters, the government's decreased dependency on the customs brought about by the income tax should mean a reduction of the duties. None would see their expectations fulfilled in the 1920s.

The Corporatist Experiment

In 1922, Marcelo T. de Alvear was elected president of the Republic. His government has been seen as a more conservative version of the Radical Party. In fact, the conservative press and many representatives of the former oligarchy welcomed the new attitudes embodied in the patrician figure of Alvear. Nonetheless, the reasons that encouraged governments to seek a fiscal reform did not vanish, and Alvear attempted on two occasions to introduce the income tax. Despite the economic recovery, the financial needs of the state did not decrease during the decade, and the desire to increase public investments made permanent the anxiety about the anachronistic structure of Argentine taxation. Furthermore, economic recovery since 1921 revealed some new problems. The reemergence of international markets meant that Argentina was able to import again. But it also meant a greater competition for domestic manufacturers. In the early 1920s, a public campaign arose in favor of revising Argentine tariff and protecting national industry.[71] Since a truly protectionists barrier would affect state revenues, the question of the income tax resurged. The CACIP debated the issues in several reports sent to Congress. In the first one the business association noted that in Argentina, there was no "excessive taxation," but rather a weak organization of the tax structure. It therefore demanded a more active protectionist policy.[72] Yet, the income tax was not advisable as a solution "for the time being, although it must be recognized that this tax, due to its features of fairness, has the qualities that will make it succeed once the nation has reached a greater political consolidation."[73] Nonetheless, as far as its position toward the income tax was concerned, the CACIP showed a relative inconsistency in the 1920s and few weeks later suggested to Congress the revision of the tariff and the introduction of the income tax with a 2 percent flat rate.[74] In effect, the entrepreneurs offered their support for a mild income tax in exchange for a major overhaul of the customs scheme in the nation.

The question of the income tax gained public notoriety among politicians and experts thanks to the visit of the French scholar Gaston Jèze to the University of Buenos Aires for three months in 1923. The foreign visitor criticized Argentine lack of organized budget and supported a technocratic approach to the solution of the fiscal problems: professional economists, and not politicians, should be in charge of complex financial matters such as the income tax. According to Jèze, a more powerful and autonomous finance minister would have had enough leverage to introduce the much-needed fiscal reform in Argentina.[75] For the French expert, the introduction of the income tax in Argentina was inescapable, not as a way to address social problems, but as the only means to deal with the tendency toward bigger public expenditures.[76] Jèze followed Adolph Wagner's idea that the state's expenses would grow faster than production as a result of the pressures of modernization and industrialization on its services and activities. Wagner's and Jèze's ideas were a blend of conservative—and even authoritarian—formulae with reformist approaches to the challenge of modernization and democratization.[77] In fact, Jèze's defense of the income tax was due to his orthodox position and his desire to keep public accounts in balance.[78] Beyond his ideology, the presence of a prestigious European professor in Buenos Aires, although it helped to legitimize a wide gamut of positions, ultimately reinforced those among the political and academic elites who defended the introduction the income tax. His conferences were published in the *REA* and were read and quoted by different sorts of politicians and economists, from Conservatives to Socialists.[79] Overall, Jèze's conferences contributed to keeping the income tax visible in the Argentine public disputes of the decade.

Rafael Herrera Vegas, Alvear's first finance minister, attempted in 1923 to institute a tax reform that would include the income tax. Herrera Vegas's fiscal policy aimed to modify customs duties and to introduce the income tax and a tax on inheritance among other important changes. Herrera Vegas's proposal was inspired by Alejandro Bunge, the then chairman of the Bureau of National Statistics. It envisioned a global flat rate of 2 percent for every taxpayer and a progressive surtax going up to 12 percent for those incomes over 300,000 pesos. The tax on corporations was set at a flat rate of 2 percent, allowing individual taxpayers to deduct this tax from their personal income tax.

As business representatives demanded, the project offered low tax rates, and ranching and farming were not particularly affected by the new tax, because both activities were supposed to have "small tax capacity."[80] To what extent was the government willing to heed the entrepreneurs' demands? There is no simple answer for this. On the one hand, and following Bunge's technocratic and corporatist views, one of the originalities of this new attempt at tax reform was the calling to private actors to cooperate in the design of the new laws. Moreover, the minister, aware of the difficulties of his plan, did not want to present it as an imposition and aspired to gather wide societal support for the measure. The government created several advisory commissions presided over by Bunge himself and composed of Guillermo Padilla, Víctor Valdani, Mariano de Ezcurra, D. E. Rubbens, and Antonio L. Lanusse, who respectively represented the Buenos Aires Stock Market, the Argentine Rural Society (SRA), the UIA, and the CACIP.[81] The introduction of the income tax for Bunge was part of a broader industrial ideology. In this ideology, the participation of the producers' representatives in the shaping of economic policy within a sort of technocratic-corporatist government played a significant part.[82]

On the other hand, the composition of the advisory commissions and its workings reflected Bunge's and the minister's ideas about corporatist government in Argentina. First, the most powerful economic elites associations were chosen—the SRA, the UIA, and the CACIP—whereas many other trade and producer associations were excluded, including labor unions.[83] Second, despite seeking the cooperation of the economic elites, the government did not renounce its desire of controlling the process of policy making. The Socialist Party satirized the commission and nicknamed it the *Areópago* (Areopagus), warning about its antidemocratic character because it implied a shift of power from Congress to the capitalist.[84] Yet, it was far from clear that this was the result. From the very beginning, representatives of the government opened every meeting by presenting their proposals and obtaining the approval of the business representatives. Bunge presided over the commission on tax matters, where he presented his own drafts for complex laws such as a tax on inheritances, the income tax, or the distribution of income between the national government and the provinces.[85] Due to the short time that had elapsed between their meetings in August and the discussion in Congress in August-September 1923, the role expected from the advisory councils was merely as endorsers to the executive's proposals.

The economic elites' participation in the councils speaks of their interests and their capacity to shape tax policy. The UIA, for instance, accepted without modification Bunge's proposal on the income tax "due to the fact that the tax [is implemented] as a trial." Moreover, though the manufacturers' association had serious doubts about the tax "if the executive branch, by proposing this bill, is following imperative reasons that makes it indispensable, the Argentine Industrial Union . . . would accept . . . with the confidence that the national government will have enough wisdom and the required prudence in order to apply this new tax."[86] Bunge's leadership in the commission became a source of trust for industrial entrepreneurs. However, this trust signified their handing over of the tax's technical shaping to the state's bureaucrats.

In fact, as far as the income tax was concerned, and once low rates were guaranteed, the business associations' main goal was to present themselves as part of the national work. In the above mentioned CACIP's manifesto in which the association advocated for an income tax, this position was regarded as a solution to find revenue in sources other than the "*trabajo nacional*."[87] Of course, by *trabajo nacional* (national work), the CACIP meant the domestic producers, but the choice of words reveals the discursive atmosphere of the times. The UIA, in particular, used the ambiguity of the work *trabajo* in Spanish to forge its own tax rhetoric in which social justice and defense of the national industry were cleverly wed: "The UIA understands that . . . it is not convenient to heavily tax the less affluent classes, that is, the working classes, considering the fact that the present taxes lay proportionally more on labor than on capital." And yet, the UIA was far from being the conspicuous representative of capital: "Last, the UIA believes it is necessary for the public authorities to become seriously preoccupied with the establishment of a distinction between the income produced by capital and the income produced by labor. It is not possible to defend the stand that the earnings of merchant or industrial bodies can be compared to those derived from bank deposit, bonds, mortgages, etc."[88] This meant that the income tax was accepted as part of the "social progress" of the times, and the UIA hoped to obtain the most favorable conditions in exchange of its acceptance. Thus, business and manufacturers' representatives in the commissions, who had been appointed by the finance minister, adopted a reactive or consensual stance, but rarely promoted their own agenda.

Bunge's activism was essential for the continued working of the commissions.[89] However, it is likely that due to the autonomous procedures of the government, business representatives came to understand that their efforts were purposeless, and their enthusiasm waned. Ultimately, the *Areópago* rested on fragile bases. Its continuity depended largely on the willingness of the government. When Víctor

Molina replaced Herrera Vegas as minister of finance, one of his first measures was to suppress the advisory councils.[90] Molina's decision to dispense with the participation of the economic elites, along with his plan to reduce the level of protectionism, aroused widespread criticism. The UIA stated that suppression of the commission was a "step backward," and *La Nación* widely echoed the discontent of the entrepreneurs.[91]

Business reaction arose out of the feeling of being neglected by public authorities, but the idea that the cooperation between economic interests and the government was yielding results was not completely accurate.[92] The main interests of the business representatives participating in the *Areópago* was not the income tax but customs duties. Since the end of the nineteenth century, Argentine manufacturers and other interest groups had demanded the creation of a *Junta Permanente de Aforos* (Permanent Valuation Commission) made up of the various business associations, which would design a favorable and stable import duties regime. However, this demand repeatedly failed, and Argentine entrepreneurs focused on lobbying at the national Congress, where the final decision on the tariff was taken. Both rural and industrial entrepreneurs had influence over the legislators, but the final outcome was as much the result of the fiscal needs of the state as of the pressure from business. Finally, in 1922, the government created the *Junta Permanente de Aforos,* but its constitution was never approved by Congress. This does not mean that business claims were not heeded. In 1923, amidst the governmental campaign for the approval of the income tax, the *avalúos* or *aforos,* the official valuations on which the Argentine ad valorem tariffs were based, were raised by 60 percent by the national Congress. This increase satisfied both the traditionally proprotectionist stance of the UIA and the *Sociedad Rural*, which, due to a difficult economic situation, had recently adopted a more favorable view on protectionism.[93] There was therefore a wide consensus on the need to reform the tariff. In 1923, only the Socialists seemed to oppose the increase of duties.[94] The 60 percent increase of the *avalúos* was the result of political bargaining within the Chamber and the Senate, but it was also enabled by economic circumstances. The recovery of the world markets and of Argentine exports made the government believe that an increase in the import duties would not be offset by a dramatic decline in imports.

For the UIA, the suppression of the commissions carried out by Molina at the end of 1923 originated in the new minister's free-trade ideology.[95]The manufacturers' publication referred to the minister's policy as a "reactionary" one.[96] However, the UIA's fears were exaggerated. In 1924, when Minister Molina tried to undo the 1922 tariff policy, the Senate rejected his proposal, and the government was unable to gather enough support in the Chamber of Deputies to override the Senate's vote.[97] Hence, even if those with business interests might prefer to be called to discuss economic policy, Herrera Vegas's councils were unnecessary as long as Congress remained open to the lobbying of private interests.[98] In addition to appease some business interests, the tariff reform of 1923 seemed to have eased the state's fiscal needs, and therefore made it possible to postpone the introduction of the income tax once again.

Still, it needs to be underlined that the Herrera Vegas's income tax proposal stalled in Congress and not in the advisory commissions. The government acted with caution. Herrera Vegas only submitted to the Congress partial measures such as different progressive stamp tax, licensing tax, real state tax, or land tax. The government found a justification for its timidity in the difficulties that were entailed in organizing the required bureaucracy for such a complicated system and in the slow parliamentary process.[99] These were real problems but, also, Herrera Vegas was afraid of the possible reactions. In June 1923, the government introduced a progressive real-estate tax, which was peculiar in that it was only applicable to the Federal Capital (Buenos Aires city) and the National Territories, while the interior provinces were exempted. The Socialist representatives complained about it and criticized Herrera Vegas's lack of commitment: "But now it seems that both the interests of the true supporters of the tax and of those who accept it as a lesser evil (as the finance minister, who privately, I know, is against the income tax, but who as a politician accepts it because he expects to balance the budget) have come together."[100] But the regional dimension of the conflict was fundamental. When the Socialist representatives responded to Herrera Vegas's initiative by stating that such a system promoted special privileges, a Radical representative from Tucumán responded: "How are we not going to protest from these seats when extraordinary ideas appear in the Parliament, when it is attempted to establish national direct taxes on the provinces under the form of land taxes, something perfectly and definitely established as a source of revenue for the states?"[101]

Beyond the minister's lack of commitment, the decision to present a partial income tax and to exempt the provinces from it demonstrates that the executive realized that the support of the proprietor classes was not enough in order to get the reform passed. Regional cleavages and their reflection in Congress were at least as important. Finally,

Herrera Vegas became exasperated with the process of parliamentary bargaining. The Senate reduced the executive budget by 15 percent, and the updating of the *aforos* was lower than the 80 percent proposed by the minister. Herrera Vegas's resignation called off further discussion on the income tax.[102]

Minister Molina's Income Tax Law Proposal and the Reaction of Economic Elites[103]

Víctor Molina replaced Herrera Vegas. Molina's proposal of tax reform was the most consistent and radical of the decade and aroused a major debate. One of the differences between the new minister and his predecessors was his clear commitment to the project. In 1920, during the parliamentary debate on the revision of Salaberry's draft, Molina stated: "It is a project which I love; it is almost my son in this chamber...because my purpose in occupying this seat is to modify the national taxation regime."[104] That year, the government increased some customs tariffs, and Molina, a defender of a freer trade policy, accused Salaberry—who, like himself, was a member of the still united Radical Party—of maintaining an archaic fiscal system and of having changed his mind concerning the income tax issue.[105]

The income tax project of 1924 tried to thoroughly reform the Argentine fiscal system. The new tax proposed the elimination of other taxes, such as the export tax, the *patentes* (licensing taxes) and the *contribución territorial* (tax on real estate) and a minor reform of the customs tariffs.[106] Moreover, the income tax was accompanied by a proposal to eradicate the internal taxes (provincial levies on production or on trade) in order to achieve the complete unification of the domestic market.[107]

The plan established five different types of incomes that would be subjected to payment, following a system of schedules on real estate, assets, incomes derived from trade and industry, those from farming and cattle ranching, and wages. The tax was graduated with a different scale for each schedule. Thus, profits from assets (and bank interest received, etcetera) would start paying 0.5 percent for incomes ranging from 1,001 pesos to 5,000 pesos and were charged with 11 percent for incomes over 300,000 pesos. Industry and trade incomes would pay 1 percent, and the highest rate chargeable was 12 percent. The rural sector producers had to contribute 0.5 percent of their incomes if their annual profits were lower than 10,000 pesos. The maximum they would pay would be 10 percent of their net incomes. Finally, salaried individuals received the mildest treatment.

They would only pay if their incomes were higher than 3,000 pesos, and the maximum rate applied was 7 percent. To these taxes on schedules, another nongraduated global tax of 2 percent would be added for all incomes, except those of workers.[108]

Molina's progressive proposal was relatively mild compared to its European models. Like its British counterpart, the Argentine income tax was split into two types: a progressive surtax and a proportional global tax. However, unlike in Britain, in Argentina, the progressive surtax was applied to the schedules and not to the global income. The rates were also different. Compared to the 12 percent maximum in the Argentine project, in the United Kingdom, the standard rate in 1920 was 30 percent.[109] France's income tax rates were similar to those incorporated into Molina's draft. In France, there was also a proportional tax, but this was in turn divided into two groups of payments: a flat tax of 7.2 percent on wages and salaries, and a tax of 12 percent on dividends and interests. Yet, the French tax system combined the income tax with indirect taxation, which focused on luxury and upper-class consumption items, while the Argentine system, even if reformed, was based on regressive indirect excise taxes.[110] Nonetheless, compared to both Salaberry's and Herrera Vegas's drafts, Molina's was a more ambitious—and to some extent—more progressive enterprise.

Economic elites did not show a complete reluctance to the income tax, and it was not even an important concern for them during the second half of the 1920s. Both the SRA and the UIA indicated their preference for the earlier scheme that had been attempted by Herrera Vegas. One reason for that could have been the feeling of having been disregarded. As a matter of fact, during the 1920s, the self-styled *fuerzas vivas* (literally, living forces) increasingly complained about being neglected by the government.[111] Besides, as has been shown, the major economic interests had participated in the elaboration of the Herrera Vegas project.

There were, however, other reasons for the upper classes' criticism of Molina's project. The rural producers fretted about the instability of their incomes during the decade and, therefore, they subtly introduced some demands in exchange for their support:

> In order to justify the opposition of this Society [Sociedad Rural] to the proposed income tax, it is enough to point out that owing to the unstable values of our country, the inconvenience of an income tax is apparent...The income will be arbitrarily measured and on many occasions the tax will have to be paid, not by means of the income derived from the capital but with the capital itself. [This] would have

> happened for instance if the income tax for 1920, when the *haciendas* had a remunerative value, had had to be paid in 1921, when the price crisis had absorbed a great amount of the cattle capital... Lastly, it should be borne in mind [that we lack] a regime for the permanent defense [of values].[112]

The SRA linked the "inconvenience" of an income tax to the absence of a permanent scheme to defend the values. By "values," the cattle ranchers meant the price of meat. During the 1920s, the international—mainly British—market for the Argentine meat plummeted, and the Argentine *frigoríficos* (meatpackers), in British and American hands, managed to transfer the cost of the fall in the prices to the *estancieros*. Argentine major commodities lost 60 percent of their value between 1919 and 1923. The decline was particularly extreme for beef prices, which between 1920 and 1922 dropped by more than half. In fact, beef prices did not reach 1919 levels again at any time during the 1920s.[113]

In 1923, the Congress passed a law stipulating a minimum price for Argentine meat in order to benefit rural producers. However, meat companies boycotted the legislation by refusing to purchase the produce. Big landowners and fatteners (those specializing in the high-quality product), who could not survive without the business offered by the packers, felt that the scale of their operations allowed them to weather the storm. Thus, they pressed for the suspension of the law, which in fact occurred at the end of that year.[114] The situation was harder for medium or small owners, the ranchers, and for cattle breeders, who were disappointed by the withdrawal of the minimum price measure. At that moment, the president of the SRA, Pedro Pagés, a medium owner himself, tried unsuccessfully to restore the former legislation.

Still, the lack of support of the Rural Society for the tax reform should not be overstated. In 1925, when the SRA made the above-quoted declaration, the market had regained momentum, and the minimum price enforcement was no longer an emergency.[115] Besides, the income tax was a secondary issue for the rural producers during that decade. In fact, the above quotation was one of the few references to the matter made by the SRA during that period. Probably, landowners, along with the remaining economic elite, were conscious of the difficulties surrounding income tax proposals and of the Radicals' low level of commitment to tax-structure reform.

To some extent, landowners were disposed to tolerate an income tax. The reform of the tax structure could have been a solution both to the government's fiscal problems and to threats to the landowners' wealth. This situation was obvious in the province of Buenos Aires. Provincial expenditures had rocketed since 1920, and the provincial government had attempted to increase the revenue by revaluing tax-paying land properties.[116] This situation recurred in 1927, when the governor of the province, the Radical Valentín Vergara, facing an enormous deficit, proposed the first new assessment of landed property since 1912, which was met by anger from the proprietors.[117] In both cases, the Conservative representatives at the Buenos Aires legislature became the landowners' best allies; one of the former's proposals was to establish an income tax to organize public finances. In 1932, when the National Congress finally introduced the income tax, a Conservative deputy from Buenos Aires, Manuel Fresco, while emphasizing the paradox of a Conservative legislature approving the quintessential progressive law, recalled their support for the income tax in the Buenos Aires legislature and their fight against the revaluation measure:

> The Honorable Chamber discusses and will pass, with the votes of the parties called reactionaries, one of the greatest social achievements of the taxation regime . . . the income tax. The deputy Vicente Solano Lima recalled that in the Buenos Aires Legislature, when the law of revaluation was being discussed, our voices rose from the seats that we represented, reiterating the need for the progressive tax.[118]

Thus, in the 1920s, the income tax was responsible for only a small place in the *estancieros* representatives' worries compared to the problem of international market conditions or the concern about the rising public expenditure. However, seen as a solution to the latter, and combined with other favorable measures, the landowners were not completely against the tax reform.

A similar story could be told about the industrialist's position. Like the SRA, the UIA preferred the Herrera Vegas version of the tax. However, the association representing the industrial entrepreneurs had additional reasons for criticizing Molina's proposal. They felt that their sector was being heavily taxed, and comparatively, they were right. The net profits coming from trade or industrial business started being taxed as low as 1.000 pesos at rates of 1 percent, while rural business incomes started to pay 0.5 percent at 2.000 pesos. The maximum taxation was 12 percent for the industrialists compared to 10 percent for the rural producers.[119] Manufacturers also disagreed on the pattern of taxation chosen. They asked for the flat tax to be charged on each schedule and for the progressive tax on the global income, as had been the case in the proposals of 1918 and 1923. Their objective was to eliminate or to minimize the graduations within the scale, and therefore reduce the burden of taxation for the upper echelon. Another concern for the manufacturers was how to define profit. According to article 60 of the law, net profits included that part of the income devoted to the increase in the capital of a company. Entrepreneurs asked for tax exemption on these profits because if "they are originally profit, in truth they do not have the same goal, because they are used for the further development of the commerce or industry, which in addition to being beneficial for the country, is the origin of further profits, ultimately incomes, for the future."[120] Moreover, the industrialists wanted the graduate rates on the shares, bonds, debentures, and other kinds of assets of the corporations to be replaced by a flat tax of 2 percent and its discount at the final payment, as was drafted in the Herrera Vegas proposal.[121] This complaint mainly concerned the interests of the large entrepreneurs, who were acquiring a strong position within the UIA's management. They were worried that heavy taxation would discourage potential shareholders. Corporations, although not fully developed in Argentina, were of particular significance for the industrial sector. In 1927, 50.1 percent of the total incorporate capital belonged to industrial companies, whereas trade and rural companies accounted for 24.5 percent and 16 percent respectively.[122]

Nonetheless, in the 1920s, the income tax reform was not very important to the manufacturers compared to other issues such as protectionism and social policies. Indeed, the possibility of a reduction in the customs tariff was seen as more dangerous than the income tax. This had been the case in 1922. Before Herrera Vegas called business interests to discuss fiscal policy, industrialists accepted the idea of the income tax but fretted about its possible impact on the tariff.[123]

With Molina in office, the danger of an unfavorable—from the UIA's point of view—tariff reform seemed more apparent. Molina's proposals included a reform of customs duties. It would eliminate the so-called *adicionales* (additional taxes) of 2 percent and 7 percent added to all goods entering the country. Some specific duties were reduced, such as those on the *yerba mate* (Paraguayan tea), olives, or cheese. And finally, some articles, such as iron, steel, zinc bars, or building materials were exempted from import taxes.[124] These reductions were part of a larger plan announced by the minister to Congress and to some newspapers in the capital, which stated that the introduction of the income tax presaged the slow decline of import duties as the main source of governmental revenue.[125] As soon as Molina made his statement, the UIA addressed him: "*Excmo.* Minister: The declarations published in some newspapers of the capital, attributed to you, about the possible changes in our economic policy, have seriously worried the E.C. [Executive Committee] of the Argentine Industrial Union... We understand that it is convenient for the country to firmly maintain the protectionist thesis."[126]

Still, the threat of removing customs tariffs was a remote one. The first years of income tax implementation were always difficult, and the Argentine government could not afford to shut down the customs. Even the confident Molina recognized "that now the customs revenue is the most important state resource; and the government cannot accomplish the program of improvement of the taxation system by reducing abruptly or by eliminating this indirect tax, because it would risk provoking incurable imbalances."[127]

Like the rural producers, the UIA understood that the approval of the income tax was a difficult task for the government, and therefore they did not devote much energy to attacking it.[128] On the other hand, some behavior suggested that industrialists, like rural producers, were ready to accept the new tax. First of all, their criticism focused on the technical aspects of the reform without challenging the philosophy behind it or even asserting a positive judgment: "The Argentine Industrial Union recognizes... that the current taxation system is old-fashioned and hardly equitable... it does not distribute the public burden in the rightful proportions, according to the economic capacity of the taxpayer."[129] Of course, this could be a rhetorical device. But even as a rhetorical device, it set a limit on the entrepreneurs' criticism.

Moreover, industrial entrepreneurs also had some interests in fiscal reform. The financial turmoil of the 1890s had provoked a lack of confidence in the financial condition of the interior provinces, and their governments found it increasingly difficult to borrow money from abroad. To counteract this constraint, many provinces introduced new taxes on production and consumption. Some of these were disguised duties on the inter-provincial trade, something that was forbidden by the Constitution.[130] The heterodox fiscal "solutions" established by the provinces became a regular feature of turn-of-the-century Argentina as the economic gap between the burgeoning littoral (Buenos Aires and the other provinces located on the Atlantic coast) and the less developed interior grew faster. The situation had not changed in the 1920s, and this hindered the development of a unified national market. The industrialists, whose production, unlike that of rural commodities, was entirely devoted to the domestic market, saw this situation as an obstacle that had to be removed.[131] Luis Colombo, the president of the UIA, made a direct criticism of the fiscal policies adopted by some provinces in a conference of governors celebrated in the province of La Rioja in 1927. While Colombo's speech blamed the national government for some obstacles to the economic development, it also blamed local administrators for their reliance on import taxes and their role in the overlapping of taxes:

> Not only is the customs a protection device...Taxation and budget laws are in fact basic elements to guide and guarantee the progress of industries...And as a matter of fact we have reached the taxation excess all over the country...On the other hand, and I must refer to some provinces represented here, the creation of some customs barriers hidden behind the 'consumption tax' cannot be referred to as industrial protection.[132]

The industrialists' representatives understood that the provincial taxes were connected to interior budgetary disarray and, therefore, that the transformation of the national tax structure could have brought a definitive solution.

The only proprietors' association openly opposed to the income tax was the CACIP and, as has already been noted, its position was rather inconsistent during the decade. The CACIP had been formed in 1916 with the aim of putting together the different interests of the proprietor groups in order to face the new political scenario (namely, the process of democratization and the arrival of the Radical Party to the government).[133] The CACIP developed a strong economic nationalism through its activities and tried to strengthen the links between the entrepreneurs of the littoral and those from the interior. The president of the CACIP, Méndez Casariego, deputy for the province of Entre Ríos in 1920, stated: "Without being a constitutionalist, I think I can assert that this is a tax that belongs to the states."[134] The CACIP's position was increasingly radical throughout the decade. In 1928, at the third National Economic Conference, a meeting of all the national producers, the directors of the CACIP announced prior to the reunion: "Of course, the income tax project has an unfavorable welcome. Our institution has expressed its categorical opinion against this system and has explained...the constitutional and practical reasons to oppose its implementation in Argentina."[135]

Nonetheless, this has not always been the CACIP's point of view. In August 1923, the CACIP had submitted a document to the Senate complaining about the proposals of new taxation passed in the Congress. The American chargé d'affaires in Buenos Aires, reported this about the CACIP statement: "Of the impost on movable values, it says that economic conflicts must result, since it is inflicted in addition to provincial charges; further that it is an unjust and partial tax as it falls on some kind of income and not upon others and can show no reason for discrimination. A tax on general income, it is considered, would be preferable."[136] Therefore, the CACIP position had shifted during the 1920s. It was probably its concern for the less affluent provinces that motivated the CACIP to oppose the income tax. Nonetheless, even the CACIP was aware that the permanent provincial and national deficit and the pernicious effects of overlapping duties, even for the producers of the interior, meant that an income tax could not be absent from Argentina for much longer.

On the whole, Argentine economic elites showed a remarkable consensus on the income tax issue. For both rural producers and industrial entrepreneurs, the income tax was not a major concern during the decade, and although they disagreed on the governmental proposal of 1924, they received the pro income tax atmosphere with mixed feelings. The prospect of heavier taxation was a gloomy one, but the final arrangement of the public finance deserved its support. As Alejandro Bunge put it, "The worsening of all these problems will lead us to revise our fiscal system. It is not only an anachronism, but also insufficient to match the necessities of the Nation. The income tax, in spite of all the criticism, will be finally accepted."[137]

The Reaction of the Interior's Oligarchies: The Debate on the 1926 Budget

Fiscal reform would probably have been achieved had the interior's representatives in the Chamber of Deputies and the Senate not impeded it. Molina's project was stuck in the Treasury Committee of Congress during Alvear's administration. The main opposition arose in the Senate; the issues at stake corresponded to the interests of the interior provinces. For those against the reform, one of the main problems was article 67 of the Constitution, which stated that direct taxation belonged to the provinces and that the federal government could only establish this kind of taxation as a temporary resource.[138]

Most important, the income tax act would be accompanied by a centralization of the entire tax structure. In June 1924, Minister

Molina launched a proposal to unify taxes, which seriously eroded the financial autonomy of the provinces. It established that the national executive power had the exclusive right to collect domestic taxes. It also included some measures of punishment for provinces that disobeyed the law, which had not been contemplated in previous proposals of unification.

The taxes on consumption and trade were essential for some provinces. Mendoza, in the Argentine far west, obtained 89.13 percent of its public revenue through it. Tucumán, in the northwest collected 38.92 percent of its income in this way. The reactions to the government proposals came not only from the would-be losers. The chairman of the Domestic Taxes Bureau warned the minister: "It is not possible then in the current situation, which is the result, to a great extent, of the inertia of the public authorities...to drastically withdraw from the provinces these resources of revenue which, to a different extent, all provinces have established."[139] Facing a major threat to their economies, the provinces reacted vigorously. In September 1924, the deputy of the province of San Juan, Belisario Albarracín, proposed in Congress a meeting of the representatives of the provinces to organize a new national fiscal system more suited to the interior's needs. Albarracín observed that the application of domestic taxes by the federal government since 1890 had been the first attack on the provincial rights and Molina's fiscal reform the latest one: it represented "the exaggeration of the centralist spirit."[140]

Between 1924 and 1928, the political mobilization of the interior elites was at its peak. In June 1926, the first governors' conference was held in the city of Salta, in the northwest of the country near the Bolivian border.[141] The governors of Salta, Jujuy, Santiago del Estero, and Tucumán, and representatives of Catamarca and La Rioja attended the event. One of the conference's conclusions was to pressure the Congress to approve an ambitious plan of public works for the interior.[142] The active governor of Jujuy, Benjamín Villafañe, immediately became the main speaker of the group. In a letter addressed to the governor of Mendoza, Alejandro Orfila, Villafañe wrote:

> I think, Governor, that due to the domestic taxes issue, our federalism and the future and life of our nation are at the stake...To this threat, the threat of the income tax should be added. If such an attack succeeded, the provinces would remain with no municipal revenues or direct duties...It is my deep conviction, sir that the provinces must fight for the *devolución* (return) of the domestic taxes.[143]

The governors' strategy was successful. In 1925, the income tax reform was paralyzed, and the national government eliminated this source of revenue from the budget of 1926. Molina complained about the legislators' attitude: "Even though the resources have been calculated on the basis of the current tax laws, the executive dares to require from Your Honorable Chamber the tax law reform—particularly the passing of the income tax."[144]

The interior provinces' reaction went beyond blocking the tax reform. Taking advantage of the weakness of the national government due to the split in the Radical Party, the representatives of the provinces pushed forward their project of a vast public works program. This was reflected in the modifications introduced by the Senate to the 1926 budget. The Senate altered the original proposal—a transposition of the last budget to the first eight months of 1926—and added extraordinary expenses on public works to the tune of 150 million pesos (the total ordinary expenses were 650 million). In addition, the upper chamber added a new item in the budget devoted to the building of railroad tracks in the interior provinces to the amount of 33 million pesos.[145]

A more detailed account of the modifications introduced by the Senate to the original proposal is quite revealing. The main victim of the reform was the Federal Capital (Buenos Aires city), which lost 8,410,000 pesos of the formerly proposed investments. An investment of 8,400,000 pesos in the new port facilities of the capital was eradicated, which meant a major shift in an expanding budget. The second loser was the province of Buenos Aires. Most of the suppressed earmarked programs had clear social goals. The main beneficiaries were the provinces of the west and the north of the country, and the main goal of the additional expenses was public works. Salta, Catamarca, Jujuy, Tucumán, Mendoza, San Juan, and San Luis were among the beneficiaries of railway investments that were aimed at linking the less affluent areas of the country with the neighboring nations, Bolivia and Chile. This responded to a long-standing desire of the interior elites, who felt far away and isolated from the port of Buenos Aires and who demanded better connections with other markets.[146]

The Senate-reformed budget for 1926 was one of the most controversial issues discussed in the Chamber that year and took up several days of debate and almost two volumes of written records in the *Diario de Sesiones* (congressional records). The interior governors launched an active campaign of support for the Senate's proposal. The governors of Mendoza, Salta, Catamarca, La Rioja, Jujuy, Santiago del Estero, and Tucumán addressed messages to the Chamber and to the deputies urging them to fight for the approval of the Senate's reform.[147]

The Senate's draft reached the lower chamber for appraisal in July 1926. The congressmen who opposed the budget pointed out the anomaly of the process. According to article 44 of the Constitution, the upper house had no right to levy taxes or to introduce new expenses into the budget. The Socialist deputies, in particular, complained about the over-representation of the interior provinces (in terms of population) in the Congress and accused the Senate of usurping the chamber's function: "I address the deputies from the littoral provinces, who can therefore lose their legitimate influence, not only in the Senate where they have already lost it because of the constitution itself, but... also in this Chamber if this new system of approving the budget is introduced."[148]

The Socialist representatives proposed the reform of the taxation system in the nation and in the provinces. In the latter, they encouraged a land tax as a means of reducing the provinces' dependence on the customs duties and as an attack on the perceived privileged proprietor classes of the interior. In the former, as customs duties would become less significant for the provinces, Socialists supported its substitution for the income tax. The interior elites opposed both solutions. They argued that the land in the interior, unlike that in the pampas, lacked value and could therefore not be taxed. The public works were needed to "add value" to the empty lands of the interior: "Those who want the nationalization of the domestic taxes and the abolition of the current tax overlapping also want the provinces to levy on the lands for survival. But, what is the value of the land in depopulated and unproductive areas?"[149]

The quest for the "return" of the domestic taxes—that is, the levies on some products imposed by the federal government after the 1890s crisis—was central to the interior demands. These levies were direct taxes and therefore they belonged to the provincial realm. In fact, public works expenses were seen as a part of this return: "What gifts, Mr. Deputy?... It is hardly the minimal refund for what the nation withdraws from the provinces."[150] The income tax was contemplated as another form of direct taxation; and the provinces felt it was their choice whether to implement it or not. From the point of view of the provinces, a national income tax was the culmination of the process of financial deprivation that was being carried out by the national government.

The Chamber rejected the Senate's budget and opted for maintaining the provisional system of using the last budget, which entailed passing expenditures and resources every month. The deputies' decision was again discussed in the Senate in July 1926. The majority of senators opposed the decision of the Chamber and defended their former project. Sixteen out of nineteen senators approved the budget and seventeen out of twenty approved, in particular, the public works annex.[151] This overwhelming majority is important for two reasons. First of all, in order to reject for a second time the Chamber of Deputies' proposal, the Senate needed a two-thirds majority of the votes. Second, it shows the provinces' commitment to a budgetary organization, no matter their political affiliation. The only three votes against the Senate's budget came from the two Socialist representatives of the Federal Capital, Juan B. Justo and Mario Bravo and from the Radical Delfor Del Valle, who represented the province of Buenos Aires. Conservatives and Radicals from both factions agreed to the proposal. As one of the Senators stated, "When the budget is discussed and approved, we, the representatives of the interior provinces, have the best opportunity to do something in favor of them."[152]

This Senate initiative was supported by the executive power, which, facing the division of its own party, encountered enormous obstacles in regularly passing a budget.[153] However, this was more the result of the political circumstances rather than a reflection of the commitment of Alvear's government to the fiscal paralysis promoted by the interior oligarchies. In fact, the president of the republic was still supporting Molina's ideas and in his speech to the Senate that same July reminded the representatives of their duties and responsibilities and begged for the approval of Molina's income tax bill.[154]

The results of the alliance with the interior representatives in the Senate were too meager for the government's attempts at fiscal reform, but fruitful for the interior elites. In August 1926, the Senate's proposal—slightly modified—was submitted to the deputies. The proposal had a large probability of being passed because according to article 71 of Argentina's Constitution, a bill revised a second time and approved by the upper chamber could only be rejected by the lower chamber with the support of two-thirds of the representatives.[155] The Senate-reformed budget for 1926 was passed. Out of ninety-five deputies, fifty-three voted against the Senate's project, but sixty-five were needed to reject it.[156]

The interior's opposition to the taxation reform in the 1920s was aided by the split within the Radical Party, which made the national government more vulnerable in both the Chamber of Deputies and the Senate. Second, as the Socialists repeatedly complained, the representative system favored less populous provinces, not only in the

Senate but in the Chamber as well. The economic situation itself helped the interests of those who opposed the income tax. Despite the fiscal deficit, between 1924 and 1928, exports and imports recovered their former strength and, what is more relevant as far as the fiscal system is concerned, the government weathered the debt storm. Alvear's administration converted the pressing floating debt into longer-term obligations and resorted to the buoyant international (mainly US) credit market to finance the deficits.[157]

Nonetheless, the postponement of important fiscal decisions and the inflated 1926 budget took its toll on the Argentine Treasury. In 1927, the fiscal deficit was the largest ever, more than 160 million gold pesos.[158] Alvear's government half-heartedly resubmitted Molina's proposal in 1928. However, the presidential elections to be held that year occupied the entire attention of Congress. A report by a commercial attaché of the British embassy in Buenos Aires mentioned the government resignation and still identified in the provinces the main obstacle to the tax reform:

> The most striking feature of Argentine fiscal practice is the absence of any income tax... The proposals of the Government, first presented to Congress in 1924... were re-submitted in 1928 without any real expectations of action being taken on them. It is recognised that the income tax must eventually take its place in a more scientific system... but it also recognised that it must be accompanied by a revision of the tariff system, land taxes, trading licences and internal revenue duties, all of which present formidable difficulties, especially the aspect of the division, by consent or legislation, between the central and provincial governments, of the proceeds of a solely federal system of internal revenue taxation.[159]

After a decade of struggling with the meanings and objectives of fiscal reform, Argentina had lost a precious opportunity to introduce the income tax under democratic rule. Of course, this is something contemporaries could not know.

Chapter 2

Economic Elites, Legitimacy, and Progressive Taxation (1930–1945)

The income tax law was passed by Argentine Congress in 1932. This chapter explores its working in the 1930s until the moment before the rise of Juan Domingo Perón to power. Around the mid-twentieth century, the income tax became the single largest source of revenue for the Treasury. In addition to the income tax, new taxes were created in the early 1940s, which made the Argentine tax system increasingly progressive. These taxes and the new economic capacities of the state allowed the national government to weather the economic storm and to successfully substitute the customs' falling revenues.

The cooperation of the civil society is essential in order to make a complex tax device, such as the income tax, work. The state has to be able to gain the citizens' trust in order to obtain this cooperation. Moreover, the cooperation of some citizens in particular is crucial. The income tax became a successful fiscal tool in the 1930s in Argentina thanks to the cooperation of the economic elites. Businessmen—owing to their position in the economic system and their bargaining power—represented an obvious target for Argentine policy makers.[1] Moreover, as in many other countries, the income tax in Argentina originally addressed upper incomes rather than aspired to universal taxation, making business cooperation even more important. In this chapter, the reasons for the cooperation of the economic elites with the tax system designed during the 1930s will be elucidated. Also, I will show the vicissitudes of that cooperation.

In the 1930s, Argentine governments were able to gain economic elites' cooperation for their tax projects, but were less successful in imposing an image of fairness among social classes. The income tax passed in 1932 had been originally drafted by the authoritarian government of General José Félix Uriburu, and therefore many in the opposition tainted the law with the stain of the dictatorship. Furthermore—and more significantly—the income tax was associated with the governments of the 1930s that resorted to electoral rigging. These administrations faced a permanent deficit of legitimacy, which-they bequeathed to the income tax.

The 1930's Coup

In September 1930, a coup d'état overthrew Hipólito Yrigoyen from power. The Congress closed during 1931, and parliamentary life did not begin again until March 1932, although even then the Radical Party was excluded. The so-called provisional government formed by General José Félix Uriburu in 1930, which was dealing with the effects of the Great Depression, arranged a broad project of fiscal reform, which included an income tax. The first consequence of the world economic slump was the fall of Argentine exports and, subsequently, a dramatic decline in imports.[2] As in World War I, the collapse of international trade played havoc with the state's revenues, which were based on import taxes.

Between 1929 and 1932, customs revenue fell by 30 percent in real terms.[3] The global financial meltdown made it harder than ever to get access to foreign !oans, and deflation meant that the cost of repaying the debt was rising.[4] State's deficit crossed 4 percent of the national gross product, and the debt service represented 18 percent and 29 percent of the budget in 1930 and 1932 respectively.[5]

In order to cope with the situation, the provisional government attempted to limit expenditures and to obtain larger revenues. Between 1930 and 1932, public outlays were cut by 22 percent.[6] At the same time, mail and telegraphic rates were raised, the import tariff increased by 10 percent, and new taxes on petrol and some business transactions were created.[7] The income tax was proposed by the finance minister in 1931 and implemented in February 1932, although immediately after, it was revised by Congress.

The 1930's coup, however, was not directly linked to the world depression but to the lack of satisfaction of growing numbers of political, military, and social groups toward Yrigoyen's government. Although most of those who opposed Yrygoyen still believed in the adequacy of liberal rules for guiding Argentine politics, some of them—including the leader of the coup, Uriburu—drew their ideology from the authoritarian right-wing political movements that had begun to emerge in Europe. Uriburu was an admirer of Mussolini and the Spanish dictator Miguel Primo de Rivera and believed that the liberal system of representation was doomed and that Argentine politics had therefore to be recast in a new corporatist mold.[8]

However, the fiscal policy designed by the provisional government did not arise out of corporatist pressures. The main factor pushing the economic-policy agenda was the critical situation of the Treasury. Uriburu did not demonstrate a particular interest in economic matters. In fact, the income tax and other fiscal reforms were originally proposed by the professional economists who staffed the national bureaucracy. Raúl Prebisch, the subsecretary of finance, who had been appointed by the provisional government and was a former official of the Banco de la Nación Argentina, where he had organized the *Oficina de Investigaciones Económicas* (Institute of Economic Research), claimed to have been the creator of the income tax in the nation. His claim was a plausible one. In the 1920s, Prebisch had read Henry George's theories on taxation and in 1923 had visited Australia, commissioned by Herrera Vegas, to study that country's income tax. According to Ernesto Malaccorto, who would become the first director of the income tax bureau, Prebisch and Malaccorto himself had drafted the tax reforms during their trips to El Tigre (a suburb of Buenos Aires) in 1930.[9] Of course, technocracy and corporatist representation might converge since both were based upon the notion that experts—economists, engineers, or entrepreneurs—were particularly entitled to manage economic affairs and that they should exclude politicians from this management.[10] Thus, Prebisch and his group of economists believed that Uriburu's dictatorship was a good opportunity to get the income tax enacted without political interference.[11] Yet, they were not willing to accept business intervention either. Probably, the lack of a fully developed industry in the nation flawed business claims to expertise in economic matters, and business representatives were unable to present a common technocratic front with economists and experts.

Besides, the governmental corporatist project was doomed to failure. Uriburu's plan lacked support among military and civilians alike and very soon began to unravel, forcing the dictator to call for elections and to give up power. Uriburu was well aware of his weakness. It is revealing that the government introduced an important number of emergency tax measures, but hesitated about the income tax. According to Prebisch, Uriburu fretted over the animosity of his allies within conservative groups and the oligarchy. In late 1931, the finance minister told Prebisch that the president was not going to accept the tax, especially since the passing of power was already scheduled to take place in three months. Yet, Prebisch boasted that in a conversation with Uriburu, he had persuaded the dictator of the need to implement the new tax.[12]

At the beginning of 1932, Uriburu signed a decree introducing the income tax in Argentina. The income tax was divided between a flat tax on schedules and a global progressive surtax for those incomes over 25,000 pesos. The graduated-progressive system was applied to the global tax and not to the schedules, as the entrepreneurs had demanded during the 1920s. The four categories of taxpayers subjected to the schedules tax were: rural incomes; capital assets; commercial and industrial incomes; and personal work (that is, wages and salaries). As in the British model, the different schedules were not only sources of incomes, but were also subjected to different rates, which made this income tax progressive, even if it was a non-graduated one. Thus, rural producers would pay 4 percent of their incomes if they worked their lands and 6 percent of their incomes if they were absentee landowners. If the tax value of the land was under 25,000 pesos, those incomes were exempted. The second category, those incomes coming from shares, bonds, etcetera, would pay 6 percent. The third category, the incomes derived from industrial or commercial activities would pay 6 percent save in the case of those firms or individuals selling less than 50,000 pesos annually, who would pay like fourth-category taxpayers. This meant a significant advantage for manufacturers or traders when compared to Molinas's project. In the latter, they were charged up to 12 percent according to the income (see chapter 1). Even more important from the point of view of the industrial entrepreneurs was that the introduction of the income tax did not mean the reform of the tariff system. (In 1931, the customs tax had been raised due to the world depression and the fiscal necessities of the state; the domestic market seemed to be guaranteed for national producers). The most complex regime was devised for fourth-category taxpayers (workers) whose rates were graduated, from 0.5 percent for those earning 175 pesos monthly to 4 percent for those earning more than 2,000 pesos monthly.[13] Finally, those whose incomes exceeded 25,000 pesos had to pay a surtax ranging from 2.5 percent to 7.77 percent.[14]

Although it heeded entrepreneurs' demands, this was a complex scheme and one that attempted to give some progressive features to the tax, not due to its rates (milder than those envisioned by Molina in 1924) but to the different treatment of every single schedule. Prebisch and Malaccorto, in their recollections at the end of their careers, asserted that they seriously took into consideration the issue of social justice when they drafted the income tax, but it is also probable that they were trying to present a rosy picture of their biographies since the main rationality behind the income tax design was the desperate need for revenue.[15] Moreover, the reason for the complex form adopted by this income tax proposal might be due to the influence on Prebisch of the Australian system, which was similar to the British one.[16]

This first draft still had a venturous future. The income tax would start to be collected in February 1932, shortly before the transfer of power. The capacity—and legitimacy—of a provisional and weak government to implement such a major reform of the Argentine fiscal system were dubious, and the provisional authorities recognized that it was for the Congress to shape the final form of the income tax and to implement it.[17]

The 1932 Reform: Between Acquiescence and Resistance

In February 1932, the first elected government after the 1930s coup took office. The new elected president, Agustín Pedro Justo, was one of Alvear's former ministers,. The administration of Justo was challenged from the very beginning by political and economic problems. Justo's electoral victory, which took place with the support of the *Concordancia*, (a motley coalition of: provincial conservatives; some former *antipersonalistas* Radicals; and a right-wing scission of the Socialist Party, the Independent Socialist Party, was based upon the banning of the Radical candidate, Alvear, to the presidency, and upon the abstention of the UCR. Hence, the Radical Party asserted that the new government was illegitimate. Economically, the new administration was as committed as the provisional government had been to fiscal orthodoxy amid the world depression. One of the government's main goals was to avoid default in order to maintain Argentine credit reputation in international markets. Therefore, the income tax and other reforms, such as the introduction of a sales tax that had been carried out by the national government in 1932, were the result of a stubborn commitment to fiscal balance and to honoring debts.[18]

Nonetheless, the new taxes meant a major transformation of the Argentine tax regime. Despite its fiscal goals, the symbolism of the new tax was clear. The income tax was associated with a fairer distribution of wealth. This was an important point for a government whose democratic credentials were at the least, dubious. Therefore, the government had an important incentive to present its tax policies as reformist, as far as social matters were concerned. A deputy from Santa Fe, participating in the parliamentary debate of 1932, emphasized social issues over others in his support for the tax: "The income tax…means a great conquest for its social and justice aims."[19] As the 1930s passed by and the government was unable to solve the problem of its legitimacy, the social meaning of taxes acquired greater salience.

The Congress discussed and passed the income tax law in April 1932, introducing minor modifications to Uriburu's bill. Income categories were the same and the rates of every schedule were almost identical. Real estate was divided into rural real estate and urban real estate. The rural producers would pay 6 percent of their income when they did not work their land directly. Those proprietors who worked their plot would pay a tax of 4 percent. Finally, the proprietors whose lands were valued at less than 25.000 pesos were exempted.[20] The military government's proposal included a provision that established a minimal taxable income of 1 percent of the value of the land for every rural unit (that is, all rural exploitations were supposed to obtain at least a minimum profit that was estimated at 1 percent of the value of the land). However the Congress eliminated it, arguing that it could become a tax on actual capital instead of one on income.[21] As shown in chapter 1, this was one of the main landowner complaints against Molinas's proposal.

Capital assets were levied at a 6 percent, while the benefits derived from industrial or commercial activities had to pay 5 percent. In order to prevent the lowest incomes from being damaged, the new law stated that those businesses returning less than 50,000 pesos annually would be levied as wage returns.[22] The incomes derived from wages were levied also on a flat-rate basis. However, the law established a certain gradation. The rate was 4 percent, but was charged to the total income only when it exceeded 24,000 pesos. Otherwise, the tax was applied to the 75 or the 50 percent of the total income, according to the level in the scale. Incomes lower than 300 pesos were exempted.[23] The new proposal benefited those who earned high salaries, which had been charged at up to 10 percent in the former draft. However, these were not numerous.

The passing of the law in April 1932 was a sort of emergency measure aimed at buttressing the policies implemented by the provisional government. It may be recalled that the income tax was collected from February, and its legality was dubious. Therefore, the Congress wished to rubberstamp the law in order to allow the regular working of the tax. In December 1932, however, the income tax suffered from further reforms. The most important of these was the suppression of the differences in rates paid by every schedule, with the exception of the fourth category, which made the existence of different taxpayer categories almost meaningless.[24] Thus, the first, second, and third categories of taxpayers would pay a flat rate of 5 percent, whereas workers would pay 3 percent. The Budget Committee of Congress justified this measure as a necessary simplification of the tax process: up to that moment, taxpayers had to fill in a different return for each type of income they received; from that moment on, they were subjected to a single global tax process. But there were also some conservative aspects involved in this decision: as the representative of the Budget Committee in the Chamber stated, the existence of different rates among schedules conspired against equality before the tax law.[25] That is, conservative deputies refused to consider the possibility that some sources of income deserved to bear a heavier fiscal burden than others due to the origin of those incomes. Still, the law was actually dividing the taxpayers into two categories—salaried and others—and implicitly recognizing that salaried taxpayers deserved special treatment from the tax authorities, although the difference in the rates applied to the fourth category and the the rates applied to other categories was minimal. Besides, in the search for greater revenue, the new law changed the global surtax and introduced the graduated tax from the income bracket 10,000 pesos onward.[26] Overall, the new law reduced the already tepid progressiveness of Uriburu's bill. From that moment on, the progressiveness of the income tax would depend on the steepness of the graduation within the global surtax.

How did Argentineans receive the new taxes? One of the problems of the tax reform was its origin in the dictatorship. The government, the opposition, and most citizens were well aware of this fact. The introduction of the new legislation at the end of the "provisional" government caused uneasiness about the legality and legitimacy of the measure. In February 1932—coinciding with the beginning of collections of the income tax from wages—criticism from the Buenos Aires press regarding the implementation of the new taxes mounted. The Socialists noted that the introduction of the new taxes under a nonconstitutional government was illegal.[27] Socialists and some trade unions that were linked to the Socialist Party challenged the income tax and the sales tax. The Socialists cried out against the inclusion of wages and incomes derived from labor into the categories of taxable incomes.[28] Furthermore, following their traditional complaints against landowners' privileges, the Socialist Party opposed the suppression of the minimal income for rural enterprises arguing that this was a "gift" to large Argentine landowners.[29] For the Socialists, the existence of a minimum rural income was beyond doubt, because in their view, even if the *estancia* (a large landed estate) was not profitable in the narrowest business sense, it did obtain the rents derived from possession of the fertile lands. Still, the campaign against the income tax did not appear to stir workers' mobilization.[30] The Socialist press collected the declaration of several trade unions, and of the umbrella organization, General Confederation of Labor (CGT) denouncing the income tax as a tax on labor.[31] In April 1932, the CGT sent a letter to Congress asking for the abolition of the income tax for the fourth category, arguing that workers were suffering the effects of the crisis and of the increase in consumption taxes. As was done by the Socialists, the trade unionists stated that wages were not truly "*rentas*," and that they therefore had to be exempted from the tax.[32] However, the unions' mobilization against tax reform did not have major significance. The economic downturn and the repression carried out by Uriburu's dictatorship had weakened the trade unions' activism and influence.[33] What the opinion of the workers on the income tax was is almost impossible to say. The unions' campaign against the income tax seemed to be exhausted very soon. Ultimately, actual acts of resistance were scarce.[34]

One of the paradoxes of the criticism of the lack of legitimacy of the new taxes is its presence even among some of those who supported the coup of 1930 or welcomed the fall of Yrigoyen as an unambiguous blessing. Thus, the Independent Socialist Party argued that "the decree is illegal, like all decrees on reforms, reduction, increase or creation of new taxes by the Provisional Government."[35] The conservative newspaper *La Prensa* resorted to the issue of legitimacy and legality as well in order to reject any intervention of the state in the economy, including new taxes. In March 1932, when the national government was trying to enforce the tax laws, *La Prensa* denounced the "threatening attitude adopted by the minister" and stated that "the question arises whether the country is financially still under the 'de facto' regimen, in view of the disregard paid to the whole system of the constitution."[36]

But the question of illegitimacy was a particularly dangerous weapon. For those who aspired to rule the country in the aftermath of the failure of Uriburu, distinguishing between the origin and the practice of power became paramount. Thus, Uriburu's administration was condemned only by its arbitrary and violent practice of power. The fact of it being a regime that originated in the overthrow of a democratic government had to be underplayed, since most rulers in the

1930s had participated in the coup against Yrigoyen. Thus, when the new elected government assumed power, it intensified the criticism against the past provisional rulers in order to underline the differences between both administrations. In February 1932, in an article significantly entitled "Tortures and Taxes," the Socialist newspaper *La Vanguardia* stated that the campaign of reprobation of Uriburu's government for its use of torture might divert the public attention from other important issues such as taxation: "The brand-new government of General Justo has not yet said a single word of repudiation against the thirty absolutely illegal taxes that it has inherited from [Justo's] companion of adventures, the General Uriburu."[37]

The government was aware of the difficulties that arose from the ongoing legislation between the de facto authorities and the elected ones, and the strategy of defaming the previous administration had clear limits. As its own origin was not completely without stain, the new government had, to some extent, to legitimize the dictatorship. Thus, the deputy of the Budget Committee in charge of defending the income tax in the Chamber stated: "It was necessary that a government like the provisional one, characterized as a reactionary one, came to establish [the income tax] at a critical financial moment and that a Congress, with a majority of non-Socialist parties, definitively passed it."[38] A Buenos Aires conservative representative went even further: "The Honorable Chamber discusses and will pass with the votes of the representatives of parties that have been accused in this Chamber of being reactionaries, one of the greatest social conquests...the income tax, a perfect fruit of the Revolution of September [the 1930s coup]."[39] That is, the provisional government and Justo's *Concordancia* shared the legitimacy derived from efficiency and a commitment to solving the economic problems. Moreover, even if deemed to be reactionaries, they were the ones who dared to reform the tax system in a truly social fashion.

In order to keep alive its economic policies, the national government was encouraged to legalize the acts of the dictatorship. Hence, in February 1932, in response to a lawsuit against the stamp tax inherited from the "provisional government" the State Attorney stated that:

> Although the power to impose or increase taxation was an essential right conferred on the legislative power, this right did not prevent, during the abnormal situations through which the country was passing, that power being vested in the Provisional Government, endowing it with the same attributes and prerogatives. To avoid dangers of

> every order which might threaten the country...This was recognized by the Supreme Court of Justice in its decree of September 10, 1930, and those were the reasons that moved it to recognize as valid the acts of the revolutionary government.[40]

The national government could not escape the fact that its legitimacy did not derive entirely from the November 1931 elections. Its association with the 1930's coup—conveniently baptized "revolution"—was inevitable. But of course, this "revolution" was an illegal act in itself. The Supreme Court's September 1930 sentence (referred to above) was, in fact, an attempt to give constitutional legitimacy to the overthrow of Yrigoyen. Thus, in his analysis of this sentence, Carlos Nino implies that the Supreme Court was committing an illegal act and was therefore contributing to the creation of juridical bases for the social legitimacy of illegal behavior among Argentineans.[41]

The main opposition to tax reform coalesced around the *impuesto a las transacciones* (tax on transactions) for its impact on some groups of taxpayers. The implementation of this sales tax caused intense unease among traders and petty merchants. In May 1932, the *almaceneros* (merchants) of the province of Buenos Aires were called to shut down their stores for a day in protest against the tax on transactions. Owners of hotels, restaurants, and coffeehouses supported them, and according to *La Vanguardia*, the merchants' strike was successful.[42] In September 1932, a committee representing the commercial interests of the Province of Buenos Aires called upon their constituencies to disobey both laws, the income tax and the sales tax, on the grounds of their unconstitutionality.[43] The UIA, although it did not join the movements against tax reform, warned the government of the public hostility toward the reform: "The passive resistance, the silent protect, the spirit of open repudiation, are the common features of every field of the *trabajo nacional*. We will fail to comply with an elementary duty of loyalty if with an erroneous notion of cooperation with public authorities we keep this fact silenced."[44] The public announcement of an increase in the rates of the tax on transactions from 3 to 5 per 1,000 sparked the protests.[45]

The movement was kept alive by the spontaneous decision of individual taxpayers to not pay the tax.[46] A "Popular Commission for the Repeal of the Tax on Transactions and the Income Tax on Commerce" was formed, which claimed to represent around 150,000 people from commerce, industry, and production, the so-called *"trabajo nacional."* But, as its name denoted, the Popular Commission represented mainly the merchant associations.[47]

In a Memorial sent to Congress, the Popular Commission expressed the main discrepancies of commerce with the governmental tax policy. The 1930's coup had brought the hope of a national renovation. Yet, the original expectations were quickly betrayed by a government that introduced new and excessive taxes. When the society reacted against these taxes, through public meetings, the de facto authorities responded with violence: "Under the intimation of police edicts which cut the right to reunion and petition, the tax on transactions was created."[48] The new taxes were rejected by the majority of the population and, still, the new elected government decided to continue the policy initiated by a repressive authority in lieu of heeding the popular voice. Therefore, it was not the origin of the provisional government but its practice of power that made the new taxes illegitimate. The new government could not continue this practice of maintaining taxes that were so unpopular. The *impuesto a las transacciones* was an unfair device since it was levied on the same good as many times as the good was sold (what is referred to in modern tax parlance as a cascading tax). It did not take into account real income (profits) but only the results of the sales and, last but not least, the tax on transactions allowed "public officers to revise the taxpayer's account books, his notes and personal documents."[49] That is, the government violated fundamental rights to privacy.

The Popular Commission understood that the income tax ought not to be applied to merchants. The main reason was that their taxable income was based on estimations and not on actual profits.[50] However, they did not mention that this measure helped traders to preserve privacy. Overall, its case against income tax was weaker than was its case against the *impuesto a las transacciones.*

In September 1933, the DGIR (the Income Tax Bureau) realizing the difficulties in collecting the new tax adopted a harsher stance toward taxpayers. In October, the National Congress of Commercial Institutions called a lockout of traders and small workshops and to resist payment of the tax for thirty days after the closing of business.[51] The movement of resistance lasted more than a year and it evolved in from a constitutional toward a more open economic demand. This led to a growing separation in the debates between the income tax and the *impuesto a las transacciones.* Both were "illegal," but from the point of view of the merchants' interests, the income tax was more acceptable than the tax on transactions. The latter was particularly harsh on their business: "The resistance to the sales tax... is believed to be mainly attributable to the fact that while income tax is only charged on profits, the tax on transaction affects all operations, irrespective of whether they are profitable or not."[52] Of course, small merchants did not mention the fact that the income tax was more difficult to monitor for professionals and for middlemen than it was for labor or big entrepreneurs. Therefore, the income tax was a less intrusive device than others that had been introduced by the 1930s governments. This evolution of the resistance to the tax on transactions coincided with an increase in the general acceptance of the income tax. Ultimately, the resistance to the *impuestos a las transacciones* was successful, and at the end of 1934, the government replaced it by a new *impuesto a las ventas* (sales tax) that was charged only once on exports and on some industrial goods. Commerce was exempted, and the DGIR conceded a sort of fiscal amnesty to merchants as far as the *impuesto a las transacciones* was concerned.[53]

The Rise of Income Tax and the Cooperation of the Economic Elites

Despite the initial difficulties and unlike the case of the *impuesto a las transacciones,* resistance was not the main characteristic of the first years of the income tax history in Argentina. The income tax steadily achieved a significant role within the Argentine fiscal system becoming the single largest source of revenue for the Treasury since 1942. Although we lack reliable data about evasion or fraud, the data about collection seem to prove that the tax became more efficient and progressive as the 1930s went by.

Since its implementation and up to August 1933, the national Treasury collected 120 million pesos from the income tax. One of the first reports issued by the DGIR showed its satisfaction with the working of the system.[54] In 1932, the income tax represented a 0.62 percent of the GDP; in 1943, it reached 2.56 percent.[55] Since an early date, the income tax (personal and corporate income tax) became the third largest source of tax revenue for the federal government, and since 1942, it became the largest single one. In 1932, the income tax accounted for 8.5 percent of the total tax revenue collected by the federal government, and it exceeded 34 percent in 1944 (see figure 2.1).

Of course, it is possible to consider this a relative success. Put together, the new sales tax and the old *impuestos internos* (excises) made a greater contribution than the income tax to the Treasury. It is also possible to argue that the success of the income tax was related to the weak performance of customs revenues (due to the impact of the depression and later to the trade restrictions caused by World War II). Nonetheless, the income tax grew faster than the sales tax

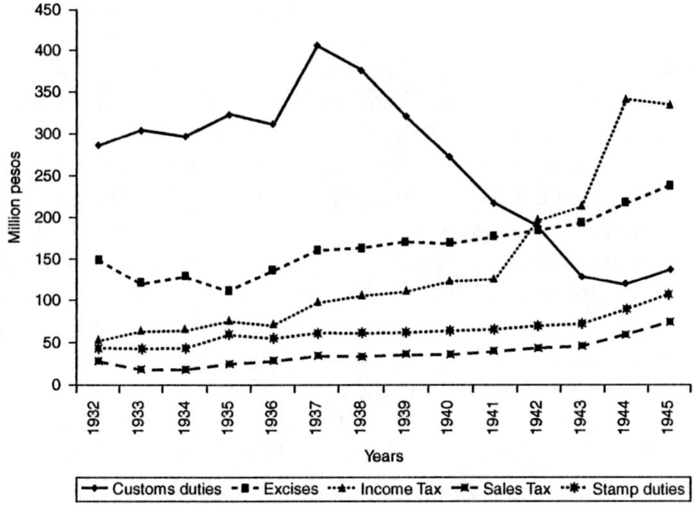

Figure 2.1 Argentine federal government tax revenues, 1932–1945
Source: Diección General del Impuesto a los Réditos, *Memorias*, (various years).

and the excises during the period, and the dramatic decline of customs revenues did not guarantee that taxpayers were willingly to pay the income tax. This was not an easy task because whereas customs duties were invisible taxes the income tax was a visible one.

Still, between 1930 and at least 1933, the severity of the economic depression made tax revenues insufficient to finance the Treasury, despite the commitment to austerity displayed by the "provisional government" and the succeeding conservative administration.[56] The national government found new and ingenious ways to collect money. As a reaction to Britain's decision to abandon the gold standard and in order to avoid the depreciation of the peso, the government decided to monopolize operations with foreign currencies. This would have momentous consequences in the degree and capacity of the state to intervene in economic matters. The first goal of this measure was to allow the national government to pay the foreign debt. The national government allocated the scarce foreign currency by following a hierarchy of priorities within which the payment of debt occupied a prominent position.[57] This caused, among other things, the government's refusal to provide foreign currency for imports that were qualified as "secondary" and the development of a black market for foreign currency.

In 1933, the peso was devaluated. This meant that the foreign debt became more onerous. In order to solve this and some of the above-mentioned problems, the government set a double market for foreign currency, an "official" and a free one; it also imposed the requisite rule of obtaining import authorization before making any purchase in the international market. The government purchased the currency it needed in the official market from the exporters and sold it in the free market to those who demanded foreign currency to pay for their imports. By doing this, the government obtained a profit, the *diferencial del cambio* (exchange differential rates).[58] This policy served to support the prices that Argentine producers obtained for their commodities, but it also reflected the limits of the tax reform. Not every cent could be obtained from taxes in the critical circumstances of the 1930s. The exchange differential rates became very important as a fiscal tool during the decade. In 1934, the Treasury obtained 90 million pesos out of the control of exchanges, whereas the income tax yielded 66 million. In 1940, the exchange differential rates provided the government with 200 million pesos, and the income tax provided it with only 125 million. Yet, the control of foreign currency depended ultimately on the working of the international trade. If imports or exports failed, this source of income was also vulnerable. Thus, in 1943, the fall of imports shrank the revenues that were coming from the sale of foreign currency in the free market to 43 million pesos, whereas the income tax showed a greater resilience, contributing with 215 million pesos to the national Treasury.[59] The income tax had become an indispensable source of revenue for the state.

As originally conceived, the income tax was mildly progressive, and the rates were moderate and stable during the 1930s. The lowest incomes never paid more than 5 percent, and those over 200,000 pesos annually never paid more than 12 percent of their revenue to the Treasury. In 1943, the rates increased for the highest incomes and decreased for the lowest ones. Thus, the wealthiest people in the country paid an average rate of 20 percent of their annual income in lieu of the former 12 percent. The lowest ranges of incomes benefited from a decline in their rates from 5 to 3 or 3.4 percent. In general, everyone earning more than 15,000 pesos annually saw an augmentation in the rates at the beginning of the 1940s. Nonetheless, the maximum rate of 20 percent was still mild for international standards.[60]

Does this stability of rates mean that the income tax did not encourage a greater progressiveness in the Argentine fiscal system? Not necessarily. At the beginning of the period (1934), the lowest bracket of incomes, those who earned less than 5,000 pesos per year, contributed 11 percent of the total income tax collections, whereas those who obtained more than 200,000 pesos annually paid 15 percent of the total collected. In 1937, without any alteration in the rates, 19 percent of the total amount collected came from the highest incomes, whereas the contribution of the less affluent taxpayers was lowered to around 7 percent. In 1943, after a reform that increased the rates for the wealthiest, their contribution skyrocketed to almost 38 percent of the total amount. It is worth noting, however, that this last jump was not only the result of an increase in the rates but also an increase in the actual number of taxpayers in the upper bracket. Another salient feature is the important contribution of a group of middle-class taxpayers (between 25,000 and 50,000 pesos) who paid a greater global amount of taxes than did some better-off brackets. Nonetheless, this situation ameliorated as the decade went by. (See table 2.1).

Therefore, the income tax, even without major alteration in the actual rates, provided a useful tool for making the Argentine fiscal system more progressive. Of course, the existence of excises, increasingly significant in the total revenue of the state, altered the possible benefits of the income tax as far as the progressiveness of the system was concerned. Nonetheless, it is noteworthy that the income tax became more progressive without altering its rates due to the increase in collections and efficiency.

In 1933, the Socialist deputies challenged the income tax as it had been devised by the national government. They asserted that the system was not going to achieve its objective of social justice. They considered that the actual wealth resided in the hands of a few privilege ones, the landlords, and to the Socialists' amazement, the rate applied to the incomes that had been derived from land had been lowered to a 5 percent from the original 6 percent of the 1932 project.[61] The Socialists also pinpointed the fact that the upper echelons of income

Table 2.1 Distribution of tax efforts among taxpayers (sample), 1934–1943

Ranges (in pesos)	1934		1937		1940		1943	
	No. of taxpayers %	Tax paid %	No. of taxpayers %	Tax paid %	No. of taxpayers %	Tax paid %	No. of taxpayers %	Tax paid %
Up to 4,999	66.9	11.4	57.7	6.9	58.8	7.2	47.3	1.4
25,000–49.999	3.7	15.2	5.5	15.7	5.3	15.4	8	12.3
Above 200,000	0.2	15.6	0.3	19.4	0.3	19.4	0.8	37.8

Source: Dirección General del Impuesto a los Réditos, *Memorias* (various years).

had more options of evading the payment.[62] The greater possibilities of evasion for the wealthiest taxpayers were apparent to everyone. The Ministry of Economy, in its annual *Memoria* of 1932, stated this fact by emphasizing the obstacles in the path of completing the collection of those nonsalaried incomes in contrast to "the tax on the wage-earners, that responded generously to the foreseen figures; it has been withheld without major difficulties since February."[63] A critic of the tax working stated that the "income tax in our country lay... almost exclusively on workers, due to the total evasion of the capital incomes."[64]

Yet, the critics missed important points. The most affluent classes had more opportunities to "cheat" because, unlike salaried people who saw their payments withheld, businessmen had to make a personal return on their incomes. In spite of this, the upper classes did pay. As the economics minister, Federico Pinedo reported to the Socialist deputies, "Obviously, the retention system... makes it extremely difficult to elude the payment of the tax for the incomes [derived] from personal work... But the supposition that the rest of the taxpayers are unwilling to fulfill the requirements of the law... is an unfounded one."[65] In fact, contribution from wages accounted for only a 14 percent of the total collected in the first year of the income tax existence, whereas other categories of taxpayers contributed with 86 percent of the revenue.[66] Some other figures show the Argentine taxpayers' willingness to cooperate. The taxpayers were required to register themselves in an income tax national registration list in order to pay their taxes. During the first half of the 1930s, the number of registered citizens rose. In 1933, there were 345,919 taxpayers registered, which included 270,891 new taxpayers registered in the last twelve months. In early 1937, there were 432,400 taxpayers already registered, and in 1938, there were 460,309.[67] Moreover, the very rich, the firms, and the corporations were subjected to monitoring.

The bureaucratic tool devised for the collection of the income tax accounts to some extent for its—at least relative—success in the 1930s. In order to implement the fiscal reform of 1932, the government created the Income Tax Bureau (DGIR), which became the main collector of revenue for the Treasury at the end of the decade. The success of the DGIR was based upon the improvement of its bureaucratic skills and upon its autonomy. One of the main goals of the DGIR was to form a body of inspectors to monitor the compliance of the citizens' fiscal duties. Their results were positive: in 1935, for instance, inspectors' activities produced 20 million pesos out of the 84 collected for income tax payments.[68] Their work was becoming more and more professional and specialized. During the first years of application of the new tax, they devoted most of their time to collecting taxes and to advising taxpayers, but they soon developed expertise in monitoring taxpayers' compliance. The DGIR was proud of their employees' skills: "50 percent of the inspectors have degrees on commercial studies; there are also some persons who, although they did not have a title, demonstrated through the tests their competence to carry out the necessary functions."[69]

Of course, this could have been a propaganda device of the institution, but some factors pinpoint the efficient of this bureaucratic body. Even the opposition acknowledged the DGIR's efficiency. The Socialist representatives, at the same time that they criticized the upper classes lack of solidarity, supported the DGIR practices: "I must acknowledge this, because I have attended on several occasions the mentioned bureau [DGIR] and I have checked that the [bureau] and all its employees show great enthusiasm for resolving the now famous doubts of the bad taxpayers."[70] In 1939, the DGIR monitored 29,000 tax returns out of a total of 144,923. Of course, if the taxpayer was not registered and did not fill in a return, he or she was not subject to the inspection.[71] Yet, as Facundo Alvaredo noticed, this meant an audit rate of 20 percent, which was higher than the percentage of inspections carried out today in countries such as Spain. Besides, since wage earners did not fill a return, most of the taxpayers audited came from the upper classes.[72]

The increase in the number of taxes collected by the DGIR shows the government's reliance on its efficiency. In the four first years of its existence, the DGIR collected the revenues coming from the income tax, the sales tax, *patentes*, and *sellos* (stamp duty). Since then, almost every new tax or duty created by the national government was collected by the DGIR. Thus, in addition to its original functions, the DGIR was in charge of duties on professional soccer tickets, oil, and mines as well as the inspections of corporations. In 1942, it assumed the collection of the surtax on fuel and coal sales. Moreover, as the administration office for the control of foreign currency exchange was suppressed, the DGIR took over its functions.[73] In 1943, as a result of an important tax reform, the DGIR started to collect revenues from two new taxes: the emergency duty on horseracing bets and the so- called transitory tax on extraordinary profits. The DGIR became the federal state's most important fiscal tool. Its growing importance and the larger revenue allowed it to reduce the rate of expenses incurred in the collection of taxes. Thus, the rates of expenditures for amounts collected were around 3 percent during most of the decade, but in 1942 the revenue was so high that the rate decreased to 2.6 percent.[74]

The federal government reinforced the Income Tax Bureau financially and bureaucratically. In 1943, the DGIR obtained two important measures from the national government: first, an increase in its budget in response not only to its own petitions but also to the necessities that arose from the implementation of the new taxes. Second, and equally important, the right to act in justice courts with its own representatives. This was a traditional DGIR demand, and it was perceived as key in order to obtain favorable results in the different judicial cases in which the nation and some taxpayers were involved. As the DGIR stated, "The fate of an entire fiscal policy could even depend on the interpretation that ultimately the Justice gives to the laws of whose execution this Office is in charge."[75]

The efficiency developed by the Income Tax Bureau depended on the consolidation of a group of economists within the state apparatus, who were willing to modernize Argentine tax regime and bureaucracy. The economic depression meant that the national government had a wide margin—and willingness—to elaborate major fiscal reforms. Congress approval gave legitimacy to—or at least minimized the illegitimacy of—the most unpopular policies, such as the expenses cut, which had been applied by the conservative governments during the height of the depression, but had, in many instances, been designed out of Congress.[76] In the economic policy making of the decade, a dynamic, young, and brilliant group of economists who had been educated in the Faculty of Economy of the University of Buenos Aires understood that their mission was to rule the economic future of the nation without the interference of politicians. The very complexity of the new economy, which had been derived from the depression, made these technocrats increasingly needed.[77] This process of professional autonomy crystallized around the figure of Raúl Prebisch in the 1930s. Prebisch, while at the Banco de la Nación, called a group of young economists from the University of Buenos Aires to contribute to the research tasks that he was carrying out at the bank. This group, known as the *trust de cerebros* (brain trust), was the origin of the economic technocracy of the 1930s.[78]

Prebisch's team was in charge not only of creating the new taxes but also of making the tax machinery work. As Jimena Caravaca remarks, the very success of the DGIR depended on the development of what she refers to as the "field of economists" since the beginning of the twentieth century.[79] In July 1932, Prebisch's friend and former student, Ernesto Malaccorto, was appointed director of the recently created DGIR. Malaccorto showed a remarkable commitment to efficiency, that is, to maximizing tax revenues for the Treasury. In a 1971 interview, Malaccorto recalled his conversation with President Justo when appointed Director of the DGIR:

> What do you need in order to reorganize *Réditos*? I answered: Mr. President...three things: first, administrative autonomy...second, that nobody be hired for the new bureau without passing an exam; and third, that politicians do not bother me...In the six years in which General Justo was President, he never pressed me: not even for the appointment of an office boy.[80]

Malaccorto gathered a group of four or five young economists who had been working with him at the Banco de la Nación and orientated bureaucratic efforts toward the collection of revenue. Although the law established the payment by schedules, the DGIR first focused on collecting the tax from fourth-category taxpayers due to the relative ease of this task. As Malaccorto recalled, they were guided by a "pragmatic criterion"; the main question was, "Where can we collect first?"[81] Only after beginning to collect some revenue, and after its implementation in Buenos Aires, the DGIR focused on extending the bureaucratic network to the rest of the country, reproducing the structure already created for the capital city.[82]

One of the most ingenious devices created by the tax bureaucracy was the system of payment to be applied to fourth-category taxpayers and others. Income tax was withdrawn from workers' wages by their employers every month, after deducting the minimum nontaxable income and the family allowances, that is, the system known as "pay as you go," or "pay as you earn." The same system of withdrawing at source was applied to other types of income. This system eased collection and allowed the national Treasury to obtain a permanent flux of resources. Moreover, by sidestepping the process of filling in a return, the system reduced the impact of tax evasion. This capacity to implement the "pay as you go" scheme reflected the sophistication of the Argentine tax bureaucracy as compared to that of other tax bureaus.[83]

Hence, Argentine income tax mixed voluntary tax returns and the withholding of taxes by the employers. This required an important degree of collaboration. Bureaucratic efficiency alone cannot provide the entire picture of the early success of the income tax system in Argentina. Another significant factor lies behind it: the semi-voluntary cooperation of the economic elites. The complexity of the new tax and the threats of resistance displayed in 1932 made the government aware of the necessity of finding the support of some social actors, in particular among the large taxpayers. The executive manifested its desire to obtain the cooperation of the economic elites. The creation of the DGIR was accompanied by the organization of an Honorary Committee of Taxpayers and a Tax Tribunal. The former was an advisory institution of the DGIR; the latter was made up of independent taxpayers in charge of revising claims against the tax administration.[84] Both bodies aimed to offer the image of neutrality of the state in the implementation of tax policy and the willingness to cooperate with certain taxpayers. Moreover, cooperation from businessmen was much needed, taking into account the sophisticated system of collection designed by Argentine bureaucrats.

Elites' willingness to cooperate did not arise out of their capacity to shape the income tax or other devices during the decade. After Uriburu's fall from power, the corporatist response to Argentine policy-making problems was progressively abandoned. Economic elites played some role in the shaping of economic policies through their participation in corporate boards. However, as far as the shaping of taxes was concerned, the proprietor classes' influence was minimal.

The fact that the income tax rates in its first years of existence were not very high and that the income tax was even better than other alternatives made it easier for the government to gain the support of the business class. Not only was the income tax more favorable to elites' interests than former projects, but it was also accompanied by a manifest commitment of the new governments (the provisional one ruled by Uriburu and the presidency of General Justo) to reduce public expenses. Therefore, it is not surprising that the *fuerzas vivas* contributed sympathetically to the "patriotic loan" solicited by the national government in May.[85]

Overall, business representatives had reasons to defend the income tax, in particular, and the government tax policies, in general. As already shown, Argentine manufacturers understood that the income tax was a legitimate and progressive tax and that it was preferable to other kinds of taxation. Within the business class, manufacturers were the most supportive of the income tax. In 1932, the UIA showed its sympathy to the new tax policy:

> Unfortunately, the dire gravity of the situation...demands urgent and severe measures...forces us to accept the mentioned taxes...There is no purpose—but to undermine the prestige of our institution—in

> opposing measures that even if drastic are unavoidable, unless without jeopardizing the stability of the trades we represent.[86]

In 1931–1932, the industrialists supported both the income tax and the tax on transactions. But their support for the latter was conditional: it had to be a transitional tax until the income tax was fully implemented.[87] Yet, even if conditional, the manufacturers demonstrated a greater compromise with governmental tax policies than did merchants or other groups.

In 1936, the UIA complained about the tax burden it bore. The sales tax and the income tax were mentioned as part of that burden. However, the main goal of the campaign was to suppress or to reform the system of *patentes*. The association stated that the licenses overlapped with the new sales tax and that the rates were set in an "archaic" fashion.[88] As in the case of the tax on transactions, the income tax was preferable to the licensing tax. This reflected not only the mildness of the income tax rates, but also the efficiency of the tax collector. Licenses were increasingly monitored and efficiently collected by the bureau in charge of this tax. In 1933 and 1934, the Treasury collected around 15.5 million pesos from this tax. In 1935, it got 16.5 million, and in 1936, when the UIA complained about the tax, it reached 18.4 million. The tax was substantially reformed, and in 1937, the national government only obtained 2.5 million pesos from this source. However, this loss was made up through revenues coming from the stamp duty (from 55 to 63 million), from the sales tax (28 to 34 million) and a significant increase in the collection of the income tax (from 71 to 99 million).[89] Therefore, manufacturers achieved some of their goals without cutting the income tax.

The rural sector also had its reasons for feeling at ease with the new tax. Apart from a mild rate, the rural sector obtained some advantages in an early reform of the income tax law at the beginning of 1933. In the 1932 original law, those landowners who did not work the land by themselves paid a basic rate of 6 percent, whereas those who worked their plots contributed with 5 percent of their incomes. In addition, small landowners, whose properties were worth less than 25,000 pesos, had to pay the 4 percent, which introduced a degree of progressiveness. Finally, the 1932 tax had established a minimum land taxable profit of 5 percent of the value of the land, which was based upon the idea of a differential rent of the land in Argentina. The new law of 1933 eliminated the differences among categories of landowners by establishing a uniform basic rate of 5 percent for all rural producers. It also caused the disappearance of the minimum income on the grounds that due to the difficult economic situation, the income tax was levied on "non existent incomes, that is...it is not a tax on income, but in reality, one on patrimony or capital."[90] Moreover, the rural sector enjoyed some other advantages compared to those enjoyed by the manufacturers in the taxation system. When the sales tax replaced the *impuesto a las transacciones* in 1935, the rates were 1.25 percent for sales in the domestic market and imports (the majority of them made by industrial producers) and 3 per 1000 for the exporters, many of them rural producers.

In fact, the income tax had a greater effect on urban than on rural activities (table 2.2). Since the very beginning, commercial and industrial activities represented a larger portion of the total taxable income than did the rural activities within the income tax regime. In 1934, trade and industry filed returns for 27 percent of the total taxable incomes. In 1942, the importance of the commercial and mainly industrial activities, as far as the income tax was concerned, was even greater, almost half of all the taxable profits. Rural incomes, on the contrary, represented on many occasions a contribution that was inferior to wages. This pattern reflected to some extent the transformation of Argentine economic structure. As the decade went by, industry gained importance at the expense of agriculture and ranching.[91] However, even with the addition of trade activities, it is not probable that manufactures represented 45 percent of the national

Table 2.2 Taxable income by activity (percentages) 1934–1942

Type of activity	1934	1935	1936	1937	1938	1939	1940	1941	1942
Urban real estate	19.27	18.31	16.15	14.37	16.0	16.36	13.44	11.79	9.55
Rural estates	14.74	14.71	23.41	22.14	18.83	19.86	16.02	16.75	12.74
Bonds, financial assets	13.73	13.53	10.51	9.48	9.45	10.62	10.61	10.94	13.53
Trade and industry	27.1	29.58	29.24	34.37	34.4	29.13	37.67	39.1	45.04
Salaries of professionals	5.2	4.83	5.14	5.25	6.03	6.57	6.16	5.65	5.29
Employees' wages	19.9	18.99	15.52	14.35	15.26	17.43	16.06	15.74	13.82

Source: Dirección General del Impuesto a los Réditos, *Memoria*, (various years).

income in 1940, or that the rural production accounted for only 13 percent of the national income.[92]

Once the new taxation system was enforced, rural entrepreneurs understood that it was preferable to other forms of taxation, such as the taxes on property applied in the province of Buenos Aires. Thus, in 1937, the conservative governor of Buenos Aires imposed an additional tax of 0.25 to 1 per 1000 on the land tax paid by big proprietors with the aim of building "cheap houses" in the province. The governor was trying to woo the support of the growing urban popular classes of the province, but his policy caused a reaction from the Rural Society. The *estancieros* demanded that the landed estates be levied only by the income tax.[93] This became a regular feature of rural businessmen in the following decades.

Two reasons explain the benefits that the rural producer obtained from the national taxation system. First, the sophisticated accountant system required by the income tax allowed the landowners to claim that they were not ready to face the same demands as other producers. The rural entrepreneurs argued that their situation was more vulnerable than that of the other sectors of the economy, as far as the income tax was concerned: "The farmers and cattle ranchers are, without a doubt, one of the sectors more affected by these questions...the difficulty in making inventories, the annual expenses, the deductions on investments."[94] The government accepted these arguments and in 1938 implemented a specific system of returns for the rural producers that avoided the monitoring of the account balances.[95]

The other advantage for rural produces lay in their reluctance to incorporate their enterprises. It was easier for the authorities to inspect the accounts of a corporation and subsequently to collect the tax from it. Corporations, like individuals, had to register themselves in the DGIR for payment of the income tax. In 1935, only nine agricultural corporations were registered in the income tax administration, contributing 2 percent of the total amount paid by corporations. That year, the 621 industrial corporations contributed 44.9 percent of the total tax amount.[96] In 1940, there were already 349 rural companies registered in the income tax administration, which represented 8 percent of the net taxable income. There were also 1,877 commercial and 907 industrial corporations. But commercial enterprises represented 32 percent and industrial companies 40 percent of the total net taxable income.[97] Therefore, the growth of income tax collection in the 1930s was based upon the rise of industry: "The net income of commerce and industry is the one that receives more intensively the incidence of the measure adopted in order to maintain the collective capacity of payment."[98] This was not only the result of the economic transformation of the nation, but also a deliberate state policy. Thus, the bases for the promotion of industrial activity were established because to some extent the state increased its revenues, thanks to the development of manufacturing enterprises.

Overall, business in general obtained favorable treatment. For instance, shareholders could deduct for their tax returns the taxes on profits already paid by corporations. That system was inspired by the British income tax. However, this was not an extended practice, and most countries applied both the income tax on dividends and the tax on corporation profits without allowing further deductions.[99] Other loopholes in the legislation guaranteed further benefits to the corporations. The Argentine law authorized the existence of anonymous shareholders, who easily evaded tax payment on the income derived from those assets. This encouraged the formation of corporations as a way to evade taxation.[100] To sum up, corporations, rather than individuals, were benefiting from the income tax legislation. This could have meant a regressive effect in the distribution of wealth.

Argentina's entrepreneurs found a more amicable government than ever in the conservative coalition that ruled the country during the 1930s. For the economic elites and the government, these years were, to some extent, a honeymoon after the precedent troublesome Radical period and before the no less conflictive Peronist one. One good example of this is the favorable attitude of the business class toward the growing state intervention in the economy, despite this being a radical departure from the traditional liberal ideology espoused by entrepreneurs. Although to some extent bewildered by the growing complexity of the economic decisions, the upper classes could not avoid perceiving the government's sympathetic attitudes toward their requirements. Business representatives joined in the different agencies created to deal with economic policies, prices and so on, such as commodities boards on wine, Paraguayan tea, or meat, and they participated in the Central Bank and the corporation in charge of the transport system in the city of Buenos Aires, which reinforced the convergence between the government and the economic elites.[101]

This vision could be easily found in the publication of the Buenos Aires Stock Market, a conspicuous mouthpiece of the most affluent businessmen in the nation: "The stock market has always been opposed to any state intervention that could damage the freedom of commerce...but it also understands that while facing the terrible present moment, full of uncertainties, in which the economic science's basic rules have been subverted...we have to try new factors and methods."[102] But overall, state intervention was positive because it was devised to take care of the economic elites' interests. "We must point out that the national government has been active in all the difficult moments of the industries, by trying through [the creation] of organizations and by any kind of measures to favor the producers."[103] These favorable state policies could be understood as a "side payments" or selective incentives to the affluent groups in society whose cooperation was essential for the adequate functioning of the system and for the required increase in revenue.[104]

The taxation system became more progressive in the 1930s, and at the beginning of the 1940s. To some extent, this was the result of the growing efficiency of the collectors; but it was also linked to some intentional purposes. One example is the sales tax. The sales tax affected only the first sale of a product and allowed for the deduction of the expenses incurred in buying raw materials and other inputs. Thus, the sales tax was a clear antecedent of the modern value- added tax, and it is possible to describe it as more progressive than the usual sale or consumption tax.

The sales tax aroused considerable protest among the big industrialists in the Unión Industrial. The UIA tried to press the government by lobbying in Congress and through personal letters to President Justo and street demonstrations. They complained that the sales tax charged mainly the manufacturers, and they were right: in 1935, out of 6.616 individuals or firms responsible for the payment of the new tax, 4.047 were industrialists.[105] Also, they claimed that the tax was distributed unevenly:

> The former tax [*transacciones*] was paid by more than 200,000 merchants and industrialists, whereas the one that is now projected only affects 12,000 or 13,000 of them. We understand quite well that the fiscal criterion offers enormous advantages through that difference and that it will ease the collection, but we cannot understand what benefit the sales tax will bring...to those 12,000 or 13,000 merchants and industrialists who will receive all the burden of a contribution than had formerly been paid by 200,000 taxpayers.[106]

The manufacturers also complained that the new tax would produce an insurmountable fiscal burden, "a new charge that will produce between 50 million pesos and 70 million pesos."[107]

The industrial producers were right when pointing out that the new tax shrank the number of taxpayers and this made collection easier for the state. Nonetheless, the new tax affected mainly big producers (more than 60 percent of the revenue came from industrial firms in 1936, 1937, and 1938[108]) and was more difficult to transfer to consumers than was a regular sales tax. From that point of view, the new device was a progressive one. On the other hand, the manufacturers exaggerated the quantitative importance of the sales tax. In 1935, the amount collected by the sales tax was around 24 million pesos, and in 1942 it had not reached the 50 million mark yet (see figure 2.1).

The UIA offered the alternative of increasing tax rates in the income tax in lieu of the sales tax. Of course, given the existing mild rates, that was a feasible option. But, as the representatives of the government reminded the manufacturers, "It would be convenient to estimate in which proportion the rates have to be raised and at the same time to assess the possible effects in the collection of the tax."[109] That is, the resources collected through the new sales tax were technically more difficult to obtain through a revision of the income tax rates and perhaps even more harmful for the taxpayers. Minister Pinedo reminded the UIA that the government was acting on behalf of capitalism and recalled all the "favors" that the manufacturers had received from the national government:

> The majority of the industrial group [UIA]—protected by the federal customs—cannot ask with coherence for some taxes to be cut...Some of the traders and industrialists who today raise their voice against this project [sales tax] must recognize the effort made by the national government in order to maintain favorable bank interest rates for commerce and industry...The industrial and commercial circles that challenge this tax do not appreciate that [it] means the end of the nightmare of the provincial taxes.[110]

Economic elites in general, and manufacturers in particular, were well aware of the "favors" obtained from the national government. The conflict found an easy solution. In the Senate, the bill was reformed and the rate of 2 percent that had been applied to industrial sales was cut to 1.25 percent, appeasing UIA's complaints.[111] The sales tax was passed in December 1934 and implemented in 1935. This was a minor conflict in a decade that featured cooperation between businessmen and governments and was characterized by the economic elites' acceptance of the state's tax policies.

Did the tax reform have any impact on the distribution of income and wealth? This is difficult to say. Pablo Gerchunoff and Lucas

Llach, working with the ratio between wages and productivity, estimated that since 1920, the pattern of distribution of income became less skewed, culminating in an accentuation of this egalitarian trend in the first years of Perón's government. However, this trend was not related to a specific tax policy but rather to the decline of exports and the growth of the industrial sector and, as a consequence, a bigger return for urban workers.[112]Alvaredo offers a different picture. He does not look at inequality, but rather at the concentration of income among the richest groups in Argentina. His analysis has an additional interest for us, because it resorts to income tax statistics as his main source. According to this source, in 1933, the top percentile (the richest 1 percent) accumulated 17 percent of the national income, whereas in 1943, their income share was 25 percent.[113] Surely, among these upper income taxpayers there were many *estancieros* and industrial entrepreneurs. Pinedo was right when he claimed to be defending capital's profits.

Of course, without the income tax, that situation might have been even worse. In fact, the political game improvised by the conservative administrations of the 1930s had some risks for them and for the economic elites and offered some opportunities for the less well-off groups. Although manipulated, elections maintained their basic function of providing the political representatives of the nation. In spite of their alliance with the *fuerzas vivas*, the conservative deputies acknowledged their obligation toward their constituencies. Thus, the diversion from its main goal—namely, social justice—of the income tax in the 1932 act was apparent for its very defenders. In the Chamber, the conservative deputy Martínez stated: "Probably, with this system, we have moved away from its spirit of justice... as a genuine income tax."[114] José María Rosa, a conservative politician and rural entrepreneur, also observed: "Later on, and given the increase income tax turnouts, the taxation policy could be more social oriented, by gradually making the domestic burden upon consumption disappear, and by substituting [consumption taxes] with those levied on wealth."[115]

The search for political legitimacy and the small adjustments to the tax regime established in 1932 converged, making every new reform slightly more progressive. Hence, even if tax rates in the global personal income tax remained stable, the government was able to tinker with the details of the income tax scheme in order to increase revenues. By doing this, it also improved the lot of the less affluent taxpayers and, on some occasions, began to affect the interests of the business classes.

Through the first income tax law of 1932, corporations were allowed to issue nonbearer shares. At the end of 1934, the executive submitted to Congress—and obtained its approval—for a bill draft, which created an additional tax of 5 percent on the dividends distributed by corporations when the shareholders decided not to register themselves in a special list created by the government. If the corporation had its headquarters abroad, the additional tax was always applied. This tax was collected at source in order to prevent evasion. In fact, as the governmental draft stated, the main goal of the bill was to close an important loophole in the income tax legislation.[116] Even if this was not the original intention, by tapping on the shareholders' incomes, the system was becoming more progressive. Some conservative deputies and *La Prensa* attacked the law from a traditional liberal position, arguing that anonymous shares were an important stimulus to the creation of joint ventures and the development of the spirit of entrepreneurship, but Minister Pinedo and his economic team dismissed most critics and pursued their policies with determination.[117] The foreign chambers of commerce in Buenos Aires protested against the new measure and sent their grievances to Congress. In the Chamber of Deputies, their defenders among the conservative representatives resorted to the traditional sympathy of Argentine elites for foreign investors and capitalists.[118] Pinedo's bold rebuttal demonstrated the growing autonomy of the state's rulers: "The last thing we need is the Chamber of Deputies of the Nation to delegate its right to impose the nation's laws to the foreign chambers of commerce."[119]

In 1936, the issue of political legitimacy and tax reform became furtherer interrelated. The government submitted to Congress a bill that suppressed the *patentes* paid by retail merchants and raised the nontaxable minimum of the income tax from 200 pesos to 400 pesos. The measure was intended to benefit 50,000 employees in addition to professionals and small merchants. According to the American secretary of the embassy, the main goal of this reform was a political one: "Clearly, these unexpected tax reductions are a further shrewd move for public support of a government, which has become increasingly unpopular due to its interventions in several provinces, the highly irregular provincial elections in the Province of Buenos Aires and the damaging episodes of last July during the Senate meat investigation."[120]

The End of the Honeymoon

In 1942, the income tax was firmly established within the Argentine tax regime thanks to the quasivoluntary compliance of the taxpayers.

However, in 1942, a bitter conflict between the conservative government and the entrepreneurial classes arose out of a taxation reform launched that year with the purpose of reducing the fiscal deficit provoked by World War II. As in 1929, and during World War 1, the main problem was caused by the fall in customs revenues.[121] Thus, the government decided to revise direct taxation.

The executive projected three mechanisms. First: an increase in the higher rates of the income tax. Second: the creation of an excess profits tax. And third: a mobile duty on exports that tried to fix a maximum price for the export products and therefore created a surplus of income for the state.[122] The excess profits tax was already proposed in 1941, arousing the protests of business representatives. Between May and July, different associations, institutions, and individual firms solicited the nonapproval of the new tax. The Buenos Aires Stock Market and many other national and local commercial bodies pressed the Congress in this regard.[123] The three more powerful associations, the SRA, the UIA, and the CACIP, perhaps honoring their friendly relations with the national government, showed a more prudent attitude and only sent to Congress their "considerations" on the matter.[124]

In 1942, when the executive's plan was fully known, business campaigns achieved momentum, and for the first time since 1932, the government was facing an organized and strong opposition to its tax measures. The entrepreneurs analyzed the new reform in detail in several articles and manifestos. On the income tax reform, they applauded the possibility of carrying over loses and profits from one year's accounts to the next and also the increase in minimum taxable income. But they asserted that the taxing of incomes derived from industry or commerce in the same way as those derived from "capital" (from investments in public bonds, bank deposits, etcetera) did not make economic sense. Moreover, they argued that the increase in the higher rates was 100 percent and that the economic situation did not permit an attempt to raise rates to such a level.[125]

In fact, up to that point, higher incomes had been lightly taxed. In 1932, the upper incomes (those over 200,000 pesos) contributed to the income tax with 11.1 percent of their incomes, and their taxes represented 11.9 percent of the total income tax paid. Their contribution became more important as time went by, reaching 35 percent in 1941. But the burden they bore was not substantially different that year. Some examples are illuminating. In 1941, the most affluent taxpayer declared an income that amounted to 5,182,000 pesos and paid 622,000 pesos. In 1942, the richest taxpayer declared a taxable income of 4,163,000 pesos and paid 497,000 pesos in income tax. Furthermore, these figures do not include patrimony, which was largely untouched by the income tax. Hence, the burden of the income tax on the wealthy seemed to be light. Besides, as the national government stated, in order to justify the income tax reform, the most affluent Argentineans had multiplied their incomes during the 1930s.[126] With the reform of 1943, this situation was profoundly altered: that year, a taxpayer declaring 5,000,000 pesos of income would pay around 1,000,000 pesos (see table 2.3).

One important issue was related to the taxation of dividends and companies' profits. The entrepreneurs asked for an exemption for undistributed profits or at least for a minimum rate on them, on the grounds that these profits represented the capital accumulation required for future investments and that they therefore formed the economic basis of the nation's welfare. This petition was linked to a new disposition in the law that obliged the withholding agents (the firms) to retain 25 percent of the dividends paid to shareholders and those dividends paid abroad (the 5 percent tax of 1934 had not been sufficient to stimulate shareholders to identify themselves; therefore tax evasion through shares was still a major concern for the government).[127] The objective of the entrepreneurs, in addition to improving efficiency, was to obtain a compensation for the new burden on dividends.

The thorniest issue, however, was the excess profits tax. This tax was trying to tap on revenues that were largely untouched by the

Table 2.3 Income tax paid by the wealthiest in Argentina (annual income over 200,000 pesos), 1932–1944

Year	No. of Taxpayers	%	Income	Taxable income	%	Tax paid	%	Rate
1932	101	0.1	38,712,000	38,430,000	6.3	4,258,000	11.9	11.1
1933	122	0.1	47,528,000	47,174,000	7.7	5,425,000	14.5	11.5
1934	151	0.2	53,458,900	53,053,700	8.3	6,267,700	15.6	11.8
1935	169	0.2	65,184,300	64,689,500	9.6	7,595,400	17.7	11.7
1936	171	0.2	70,065,000	69,427,000	9.1	8,323,000	16.7	12
1937	305	0.3	117,447,000	116,201,000	11.1	13,660,000	19.4	11.8
1939	227	0.2	89,530,000	88,576,000	9.3	10,275,000	16.8	11.5
1940	333	0.3	127,074,000	125,619,000	11.1	14,762,000	19.4	11.7
1941	471	0.4	184,876,000	182,776,000	13.1	21,442,000	22.3	11.7
1942	878	1.0	378,006,000	373,942,000	23.4	43,909,000	35	11.7
1943	1,031	0.8	447,469,000	440,894,000	21.6	88,376,000	37.8	20
1944	983	0.8	401,118,000	394,779,000	19.3	79,183,000	34.8	20.1

Source: Dirección General del Impuesto a los Réditos, *Memoria* (various years).

income tax. Economic elites complained about what they perceived as a political objective in the new tax: "The new excess profits tax seems to propose that the state should pursue a goal of social and distributive justice...In fact, instead of arriving at that better social order, it creates a disorder because it provokes envy and promotes conflict among social classes."[128] The government also recognized the social objective in its new legislation or at least used the rhetoric of social justice as a justification: "The project also pursues—and this is one of its main concerns—a more equitable distribution of the fiscal burden."[129]

The problem went beyond the distribution of wealth and affected the elites' ideas about power and fairness. In fact, as the government emphasized, the new rates were moderate.[130] But tax rates were not the only concern of the entrepreneurial groups. The elites opposed the reform because it attacked some moral principles of fiscal justice that would alter the balance of power: "What is serious and certain is that this accumulation of laws is giving the ruling of the country to a new class, truly, a state within the state, completely divorced from its problems...The country runs the risk that its ruling forces become subalterns."[131] Who was this "new class, truly a state within the state"? The threat did not come from the popular or the working classes but from the economists who became increasingly influential during the 1930s. Ricardo Sidicaro has asserted that the conflict was the result of the increasing state's autonomy. This is an accurate analysis as far as the state's bureaucratic organization is concerned. As has been shown, the success of the tax collection during the 1930s depended, to an important degree, on the efficiency of a recently established bureaucratic body. Beyond fiscal policies, other economic policies and the state's growing intervention in economy demanded the improvement of the bureaucratic capacities. This bureaucratic autonomy was an important concern for the economic elites. In 1942, *La Nación* published an article with the title "El peso de la burocracia," later republished in the *Anales de la Sociedad Rural Argentina*. In that article, the author alerted its readers about the excessive power of the new bureaucrats: "A bureaucracy that has bigger attributions everyday, helped by experts, frequently theoreticians, with biased and artificial orientations."[132]

This technocracy was the same one that had designed most economic policies in the 1930s and whose results had been widely supported by businessmen. Yet, as Caravaca and Plotkin put it, "It was not the same to speak on behalf of the corporation as to do it on behalf of science, even if what was spoken was similar and sometimes even said by the same person."[133] Increasingly "bureaucrats" gained autonomy vis-à-vis economic elites. As the 1930s went by, the representatives of the state staffed the economic boards at the expense of the business representatives.[134] Furthermore, as the 1942 proposals show, in the field of taxation, technocratic autonomy was a full-fledged reality in the early 1940s.

Why did a government so committed to business-class interests pursue this policy? The governments of the 1930s faced an important problem of legitimacy. They had their roots in the coup d'état of 1930, and they could not entirely clean the spot of their original sin due to the persistence of the electoral fraud during the 1930s. The governments were conscious of this "legitimacy deficit" and try to offset it with a more progressive fiscal policy. Besides, bureaucratic efficiency, the idea that the conservative rulers had been able to weather the economic storm of 1929, must have played an important role. Since 1934, the Argentine economy was recovering. Argentina became the sole nation in Latin America that avoided the debt default.[135] To some extent, technocratic success offered an alternative legitimacy to the absence of democratic or even corporatist legitimacy.

Moreover, the political and social atmosphere was increasingly favorable to policies concerned with the distribution of wealth in society. The growth of industry and the obstacles of a not entirely legitimate government to deal with working class activism only through repression were becoming apparent. Furthermore, Roosevelt's government in the United States created a model that would be emulated worldwide. These aspects were clear at the end of World War II, when both Perón and his opponents toyed with social justice issues in the electoral campaign.[136] But, as has been shown, social justice rhetoric associated with taxation had a long history. Since the 1920s, the idea of altering the distribution of wealth through a specific fiscal policy motivated those who supported the introduction of the income tax.[137] This notion became increasingly important during the 1930s and the 1940s.

In some provinces, the very conservative party displayed a populist rhetoric and policy that led to conflicts with the upper classes. The best-known case is that of the Conservative Party of the province of Buenos Aires, which tried to gather popular support and at the same time increase the revenue of the provincial government. In 1942, the conservative government of Buenos Aires introduced a progressive tax on plots of land larger than 10,000 hectares, thereby arousing the landowners' ire. The economics minister of the province did not hesitate in proclaiming: "We understand [this is the way] of fulfilling the program of the political party we represent... a party of clearly popular origin, with positive roots among the working classes of Buenos Aires, unconnected to whatever means unfair privilege."[138] As in the past, the fiscal policies were aimed at maximizing revenue, but unlike in the past, the possible effects of any tax on the distribution of wealth among social classes could not be neglected.

In 1942, the Socialists supported the government in Congress and criticized the elites' discontent as a proof of hypocrisy: "When the state projects the needed taxes to face the expenses, such interventionism is resisted on behalf of the [defense of] property rights. But [the rich] forget the state interventionism that supports, feeds and increases the profits of Argentina's affluent class."[139] Socialists justified their sudden support of the conservative government by underlining the differences between the new policy and the former ones: "Fortunately, now we can say that our budget offers different features from the... past years. It starts to have a social purpose."[140]

In order to solve the conflict, the main entrepreneurial associations demanded the creation of a fiscal council made up of members of their institutions and representatives of the government in charge of dealing with fiscal issues. However, the political crisis would dictate the rhythm of the successive tax reform. In 1943, a new coup d'état ended the conservative period of manipulated democracy.[141] The last constitutional government did not have time to approve the fiscal reform in Congress, but the new military authorities decided to carry it out themselves. To some extent, they followed the social justice rhetoric displayed by the previous conservative rulers. Thus, the measure proposed to solve the issue of the nonidentified share bearers was justified by appealing to the unfairness of the system:

> In the Argentine legislation, the fiscal inequalities are often apparent... It is the Government of the Revolution [the *de facto* government of 1943] that accepts the responsibility and the satisfaction of fulfilling the task of rectifying the legal mistakes, correcting unfair situations and forcing those who enjoyed a comfortable freedom to make a bigger or a safer contribution... Today, this inequality has disappeared. The Decree 31712/43 has created a system through which the share bearers living in the country will pay the adequate rate or the maximum payable.[142]

Nonetheless, and beyond the rhetoric, there were still space for agreement between the new authorities and the economic elites. Unlike the 1930s, it was not easy for business associations to predict how the directions of the new government would affect their interests. In 1930, the UIA and the SRA had shown their support for the uprising against Yrigoyen, and they expected favorable policies in exchange. In 1943, the situation was different. The coup d'état was the result of tensions within the government and within the army regarding the international situation and the role of Argentina, and there were little concern with economic policy making. On the other hand, the insistence of the new government that fiscal reform should be deepened, threw dark shadows on its future relationships with business interests.

The government, aware of the distrust of the economic elites, pursued a strategy of appeasement. Only one month after the coup, in July 1943, it created the fiscal council that business associations had requested, the *Comisión Honoraria Asesora del Gobierno Nacional* (Honorary Advisory Commission of the National Government, hereafter *Comisión Honoraria*).[143] The members of this *Comisión Honoraria* were: Ernesto Aguirre, president of the Stock Market; José María Bustillo, president of the SRA; Eustaquio Méndez Delfino, president of the Center of Traders of National Products; Luis Colombo, president of UIA; Otto E. Frederking, president of the Association of Real Estate Owners; Nemesio de Olariaga, president of the Confederation of Rural Associations of Buenos Aires and La Pampa; Tomás Amadeo, president of the Argentine Chamber of Commerce; José Mazzei, representative of the CACIP; and Ernesto Mignaquy, representative of the League for the Defense of Commerce.

Labor representatives were absent from the *Comisión Honoraria.* The reasons for this absence are difficult to establish. On the one hand, despite a considerable increase in the number of industrial workers since 1935, the rate of affiliation to trade unions was still low, and the conservative government prior to 1943 had kept workers' leverage at bay.[144] On the other hand, the power of the unions was not negligible, as Perón's success, based upon their support, would demonstrate.[145] However, taxation was beyond the scope of labor representatives, due both to the workers' lack of interest in the matter and to the opposition from the elites. When the most important business associations addressed the government in 1942 to complaint about the new taxation reforms, they argued that they spoke on behalf of "*todo cuanto está vinculado al trabajo*" ("everything that is linked to work") and demanded "the constitution of an Economic Council made of members of the government, members of the Congress and the associations *representativas del trabajo* (representing work)."[146] Among the latter, of course, trade unions were not contemplated. In fact, one of the complaints of the economic elites, particularly acute among industrialists, was related to their assumption that they belonged to the "working class" rather than to the "capitalistic class."[147] They maintained that the income tax rates affected "industrial, commercial and pure labor incomes to the same degree as incomes derived purely from invested capital, thus obeying anti-economic criteria."[148] In their view, those involved with industry, commerce, and labor represented the productive side of the economy and had to be treated with benevolence by the fiscal authorities, whereas those who obtained incomes from bonds, bank assets, and so on, were "purely capitalistic" and deserved harsher treatment on account of their minor contribution to the welfare of the nation.

Despite the number of associations involved, the tax proposals issued by the *Comisión Honoraria* strictly followed the program of the traditional *fuerzas vivas,* demonstrating the influence of the SRA and the UIA within the committee. The conclusions offered by the *Comisión Honoraria* to the finance minister showed an interest in recovering the fluid communications that had characterized these relationships between government and business during the 1930s. On taxation and the possible solutions to the fiscal constraints produced by the war, the interest groups followed the ideas developed during the 1930s by recognizing the important role of the state in the economy and the obligation of supporting it: "[The Commission] considers that if the state has contributed to maintain economic stability, all labor and productive sectors should contribute, not with an equivalent effort, but with one progressive and proportional to their volume of income, and never inferior to the burden that at present they bear."[149] In other words, the economic elites recognized the important work accomplished by national governments in the 1930s and their commitment to continue paying taxes in order to maintain similar kinds of policies. At the same time, they criticized the income tax reform promoted by the previous administration because it widened the exceptions for incomes derived from salaries and lower incomes. According to the *Comisión Honoraria*, there was a problem of lack of equity in the reform.[150]

The *Comisión Honoraria*, therefore, proposed piecemeal adjustments to the income tax, postponing wholesale reform. However, perhaps reluctantly, the *Comisión Honoraria* conceded on the issue of rates increase. It recognized that the Argentine income tax rates were milder than others in the world, but this was related to the fact of the burdens that the war imposed on the belligerent nations. Moreover, "Although the Argentine taxpayer, who today pays an average rate of

8 percent, can bear a higher rate, we must emphasize the necessity of not exhausting revenue sources." But by saying this, the *Comisión Honoraria* acknowledged and finally recommended the increase in the income tax rates. Their main objection was a question of equity: if rates were going to be raised, "all sectors linked to work and production must contribute, not with an equal effort, but with one progressive and proportional to their incomes, but not inferior to the rates they presently bear."[151] That is, allowances and deduction for some categories of taxpayers should be eliminated as a compensation for the higher rates that the upper incomes were going to face.

Hence, the economic elites were willing to pay a higher income tax. As in 1932, this was probably a better alternative to other forms of taxation, such as the projected excess profits tax. In fact, the events of 1943–1944 might be interpreted as a process of renegotiation of the cooperation of the economic elites with the Argentine tax system. As in 1932, economic elites were disposed to pay the income tax, even with higher rates, given other economic and political circumstances. This shows that the cooperation of the economic elites did not depend exclusively on the mildness of the rates but that it was embedded in a broader framework.

As mentioned earlier, the main issue in the taxation debate was the excess profits tax, and here economic elites obtained an important victory. The members of the *Comisión Honoraria* wrote a new project of excess profits tax that eliminated those aspects of the former project that were considered more harmful. The main issue was the discussion of what was considered to be an extraordinary profit. In 1942, the excess profit was regarded as a fixed percentage over a supposed normal profit. In the proposal of the economic elites, the individual taxpayer would be able to choose a base year from a list of years before the war as the criterion for establishing a "normal" profit.[152] In December 1943, Decree 18,230 established an excess profit tax that turned out to be an exact copy of the project elaborated by the *Comisión Honoraria*. Proudly, its members declared: "The work of the Commission has been described by the Minister of Finance as hard-working, patriotic and conscious and its projects, as far as the taxation system is concerned... have been totally adopted."[153]

Therefore, rather than a complete rupture, the process opened in 1942 was an impasse. On the one hand, both the state and the economic elites perceived that they needed each other. The state had built a modern, efficient, and complex tax system, but it needed the support of the entrepreneurial groups to make it work. The economic elites realized that the amicable policies displayed by the 1930s governments were only possible if the state had a solid fiscal basis. On the other hand, the political turmoil accelerated because 1943 created a fertile soil for uncertainty and mutual distrust.

Conclusions

The income tax introduced in 1932 achieved a reasonable success in that decade and became an important source of revenue for the state. The case of the income tax is quite relevant, because it is one conspicuous example of a tax that depends on semivoluntary attitudes for its adequate working. Income tax—like democracy—is a complex device that demands citizen's cooperation. Of course, as power and resources are unevenly distributed within societies, some actors or groups are singularly important in the process of building voluntary compliance. The Argentine government that introduced the income tax was aware that the success of its system depended to a large extent on the cooperation of the most affluent classes in the country. Economic elites were—at least until 1942—mildly treated by the income tax. Furthermore, as the governments of the 1930s showed a clear commitment to the elites' necessities, that goal was fairly achieved.

However, that was not enough. The extension of an ideology presenting the income tax as a moral obligation or as a broad consensus surrounding the taxation system would have reinforced the reform. To deal with this problem entails dealing with the problems of legitimacy of the 1930s governments. Originated in a coup d'état in 1930, and surviving thanks to the rigging of elections, the 1930s rulers had a difficult task in convincing their citizens of their legitimacy. As far as the legitimacy of the tax system was concern, the government's intimacy with the upper classes made things more complicated. The authorities were aware of these hindrances and improved the income tax system by increasing its progressiveness as time went by. At the same time, they combined repression with some social policies to compensate for their lack of legitimacy. These efforts did not solve the question. At the beginning of the 1940s, the governments were considered illegitimate, and the state was far from being considered a neutral agent among social classes.

Besides these problems, World War II affected the Argentine public finances, and the government attempted to restore the fiscal balance by reinforcing the taxation system based upon progressive taxes on the wealthy. This attempt made the national executive vulnerable to the criticism of its main societal allies: the business classes. Since 1942, the national government and the representatives of the economic elites disagreed over the definition of the national tax system. That crisis was the result of the state's growing autonomy in economic matters. Despite the favorable economic policies, economic elites perceived that the government was managing tax policies and other issues in a rather autonomous way, as the increased progressiveness of the tax system proved. Economic elites renegotiated with the military government of 1943 their contribution to the tax scheme. The crisis of 1942 demonstrated that the issues at stake went beyond the definition of rates. They affected other areas of economic policy and also touched upon perceptions of social and political influence and power.

Chapter 3

Taxation and Peronism (1946–1955)

Introduction: Welfare Policies under Perón

In 1946, Juan Domingo Perón, one of the leading figures of the military regime established in 1943, won the elections for the presidency of the republic. Between 1943 and 1945, the then Colonel Perón increasingly strengthened his position within the military government. Perón outmaneuvered his mates and rivals within the government and built his own constituency in society. In late 1943, Perón took charge of the Department of Labor (later on the Secretariat of Labor). From that platform, the military man established an alliance with trade unions and workers through a policy of concessions. Workers and unions gained the state's support while bargaining with employers.[1] Besides, state's social protection, addressed to labor, became a reality.

In the presidential elections of 1946, Perón harvested the fruits of his strategy and obtained the massive support of the Argentine urban working class, which was persuaded that the military officer was a guaranty for the permanence and was even responsible for the improvements in social policy that had been carried out in the past two years. The growth of cities, in particular that of Buenos Aires, due to the expansion of industry in the 1920s and 1930s, and the arrival of immigrants from the interior provinces to Buenos Aires city and its outskirts, made the working-class vote—in the first truly democratic elections since 1930—decisive.[2]

Peronism altered the distribution of wealth and power within Argentine society. Workers ameliorated their economic position and gained unexpected social recognition and symbolical salience. This process was justified with the rhetoric of social justice. *Justicia social* became (and still is) the most conspicuous motto of Peronism as a political movement.

The program of social reform initiated during the dictatorship continued during the first years of Perón's democratic rule. Peronist policies enhanced the workers' position vis-à-vis employers in the factories and other workplaces. Besides, they redistributed income from capital to labor on an unprecedented scale. The most important tool employed in this policy was the general increase in the workers' wages, a process that began before Perón won the elections in 1946. Between 1945 and 1949, real wages grew 62 percent, which exceeded industrial productivity. This increase altered the national distribution of wealth. In 1948, for the first time in Argentina's history, wages represented more than half of the national income.[3] The results of Peronist distributive polices were well reflected in a significant reduction of income concentration: the richest 1 percent of the population saw their share in the national income dropping from 26 percent in 1943 to 15 percent in 1953.[4]

Distributive policies were not only based on wage policies but also on a gamut of social measures that led Argentina on the path of building a welfare state. On many occasions, the government continued the policies that had already been enacted under the military regime. Thus, rents were frozen from 1943 and evictions were forbidden. This, together with a wage rise, contributed to the improvement in the standard of living of the urban popular classes (between 1943 and 1955, rents rose by 27 percent, whereas prices grew by 700 percent).[5] Social security and pension policies also followed the path trodden by the previous regime: the number of people who were enrolled in the pension systems skyrocketed from 1943 onward—from 480,000 to 2.3 millions in 1947 and to 4.6 millions in 1954. In 1948, those citizens who were over 60 years of age, and who had never contributed to a pension fund, obtained a state pension.[6] However, the system never became universal and egalitarian: important differences among workers survived according to their different trades, and consequently, to the different pension funds that they were contributing to. The public health system also expanded during this period, doubling the number of hospital beds in the country.[7] Nonetheless, the health care system was still far from being universal and, as in the case of social security, the different medical providers offered by trade unions created unevenness in the quality of the services that workers received. Peronist policies also advanced into the field of education. The budget for education increased by 30 percent between 1946 and

1954. Popular classes' access to primary education improved: illiteracy rates dropped from 13 percent to 9 percent between 1947 and 1960. The number of students who enrolled in secondary schools grew even faster than did the number in the basic levels, and university students boomed.[8]

It might be said that Peronist welfare policies created some inequities, or that middle classes—and not the popular classes—were, in many instances, the main beneficiaries. But if Argentina ever had a welfare state, it was the Peronist state (and as in European welfare states, the middle class was among its main beneficiaries).

The redistribution of wealth and the development of welfare policies were eased by the economic cycle. Between 1946 and 1949, the Argentine economy benefited from the rapid growth of international prices of her main agricultural exports. The government controlled external trade and used that control to redistribute resources from the countryside to the cities and from rural producers to manufacturers and urban workers. The abundance of foreign currency allowed the government to maintain stable exchange rates and to avoid inflationary surges in those years. Until 1949, the Argentine economy grew at an impressive 8 percent annual rate. In 1949, the economic cycle began its downturn. Argentine net terms of trade plummeted, and high rates of inflation appeared as an omen of the distributive conflicts that would assail the country in the following decades. The lack of foreign currency halted the process of inputs imports, which were essential to continue the vast program of industrialization envisioned by the government. This was one of the first examples of the recurrent external bottlenecks that characterized Argentine economy in the second half of the twentieth century. Since 1949, and particularly since the *Plan de Emergencia* (Emergency Plan) of 1952, the government attempted to obtain foreign currency and to tame inflation through the encouragement of rural exports and greater fiscal austerity.[9] Nonetheless, the concern about the income of the popular sectors and their role in an industrial society remained important during the period.

What was the role of taxation in the industrial and socially just society that Peronism endeavored to build? The government followed the international trend toward a greater participation of the state in economic affairs, and public expenses rose at a rate of 40 percent per year—in real terms—between 1945 and 1948. Since then, state expenditure slowly decreased, but it was augmented anew from 1952. Overall, in pesos of 1945, the state spent roughly 3 billion pesos in 1946 and more than 6 billion pesos in 1955.[10] These figures were far from being excessive in international terms (in 1955, public expenditures represented 28 percent of the GNP).[11] Tax collection accelerated its pace, but it was not enough to match rising public expenditures. In 1946, tax collections amounted to only 33 percent of total national government expenditure. In 1955, taxes contributed with roughly 55 per cent of the total expenditure, according to official figures.[12] From a government committed to a fairer distribution of wealth within society, one might expect a wider use of taxation. Yet, the distributive policies of the period were not based upon direct taxes, but upon the maintenance of full employment and high wages in industry and upon the increase of public expenditures that were funded with alternative sources of revenue, such as social security taxes, foreign trade profits, or credit. In fact, the relationship between Peronism and progressive taxation, as will be shown, was surprisingly ambiguous. In the first part of this chapter, I explore the evolution of progressive taxation under Perón's administration. In the second part, some hypothesis that account for the coyness of Peronist government in the use of progressive taxes will be offered. Finally, I will make some reflections on the long-term consequences of these policies.

Progressive Taxation under Perón

Since an early moment in his administration, Perón had decided to carry out the fiscal reform initiated by the former authoritarian regime and to strengthen the Income Tax Bureau. In fact, Perón's first economics minister, Ramón Antonio Cereijo, had been an officer of the DGIR. Perón's administration tried to improve the mechanisms of tax collection by centralizing tax administration and reinforcing DGIR authority. Perón completed the process of centralization of tax collection under just one institution, which had begun in the 1930s.

In October 1946, Perón decided to unify the two main tax agencies, the DGIR and the *Administración General de Impuestos Internos* (Bureau of Internal Duties) under the umbrella of a brand new office, the *Dirección General Impositiva* (General Tax Bureau) known as DGI. In fact, the fusion was a takeover of the Bureau of Internal Duties by the DGIR, which was considered to be more adequate for the tasks of collecting and monitoring taxes. The DGIR had established a national network of tax monitors and offices that could easily be used as tools to control internal duties' compliance, and it therefore helped the government to save a significant amount of money.[13] The importance attributed by the executive branch to the income tax office over the Bureau of Internal Duties was apparent. Since the Federal Capital was the most important office, the former director of the DGIR, Alfredo Gómez Morales, was appointed its director. At the head of the interior district was placed Francisco Álvarez Méndez, former director of the Bureau of Internal Duties.[14] Like the DGIR in the 1930s, the DGI continued to be an ideal platform for pursuing a technocratic cum political career (thus, in 1949, Gómez Morales was appointed director of the Argentine Central Bank and, in 1950, economics minister). At the end of 1947, the government proposed a new modification in the structure of the DGI that further enhanced its capacities and reinforced the trend toward tax centralization. According to that project—passed in Congress in August 1948—the DGI was authorized to collect and monitor taxes that were still under the jurisdiction of other administrative departments.[15]

In addition to an efficient tax bureaucracy, Perón inherited powerful tax devices. Yet, most of the government tax reforms were launched as part of the Peronist agenda in favor of social justice, and Peronist politicians emphasized the difference between their fiscal policies and the ones implemented during the decade of 1930. The conservative governments had maintained an "anachronistic system" in "favor of the economic sector that ruled the country." The only novelty introduced by the "oligarchy" had been the income tax in 1932. But at that point, the income tax had only a fiscal meaning and not a social one.[16]

Under Perón's administration, the progressiveness of some taxes deepened. At the beginning of his rule, the highest rate in the personal income tax was 22 percent, and the rate for corporations was 10 percent. In 1948, the higher incomes paid an effective tax of 26 percent; in 1949, the highest rate was 32 percent, and at the end of Perón's rule, in 1955, the higher effective rates were almost 40 percent.[17] In 1946, corporate rates were increased up to 15 percent, and in 1950, they went up to 24 percent.[18] Moreover, in the 1950s reform of the income tax, the government—following a proposal of the opposition in the Chamber—raised the minimum nontaxable income for the fourth category incomes—that is, wages and salaries—by 4,800 pesos annually, and by 1,300 pesos for the rest of categories.[19] This was also an adjustment to the price rising of the past two years.

The tax on extraordinary profits—implemented during the military regime in order to tap the increase of profits result of World War II—was repeatedly renewed under Perón's rule, despite the fact that the "extraordinary" circumstances that justified the tax had vanished. The goal of improving the distribution of wealth was explicitly stated as a justification for the renovation of the tax on every single occasion.[20] Thus, in 1946, the representative of the government asserted that there was no change in the "monetary income distribution among the different social sectors" after the end of the war.[21]

The main contribution of the new administration, as far as tapping wealth was concerned, was the implementation of the *impuesto a las ganancias eventuales* (capital gains tax) in 1946. This tax, originally drafted by General Farrell's government in March 1946, was considered a complementary tax to the income tax because it affected those incomes that were not already taxed by the income tax. It was contemplated as a temporary device that was due to expire in 1955. The tax aimed to tap profits resulting from the sale of assets and real estate properties. The targets were profits obtained in a single operation or nonrecurrent profits—unlike the ones that were affected by the income tax. Its peculiarity lies in being a proportional—20 percent of the profits—in lieu of a progressive tax.[22] The tax was based on equity criteria: "There is no reason why someone who in a single operation or in any circumstantial event earned $ 100,000 must be exempted from paying whereas some other, who has obtained the same profit thanks to their profession, trade or current activity must suffer the burden of taxation."[23] Notwithstanding the desire to tap on the wealth that profited from the legislation loopholes, the definition of the taxable matter of the new capital gains tax remained elusive.[24]

Peronist policy regarding death duties seemed to evolve along progressive lines as well. In Argentina, the Supreme Court had established that the so-called *impuesto sobre la trasmisión gratuita de bienes* (gift tax), which integrated both donations and inheritances, could not be used as a device to confiscate property. Several attempts of the provincial government of Buenos Aires of the early 1940s to fix a higher rate of 50 percent were pronounced to be confiscatory and therefore unconstitutional by the Supreme Court.[25] By underlining the confiscatory side of high taxation, the Supreme Court refers to the right to enjoy full proprietorship. The doctrine was interpreted as follows: the tax was not on the property but on the transfer of property—as an equivalent to the sales tax for those transactions that did not imply the exchange of money for goods.[26] But the transfer of property was inherent in the full right of property. In order to be considered a true owner, one should have the right to sell one's property, mortgage it, give it away, etcetera. The question is complex in a double sense. First of all, high death tax rates did not impede the free use of property in life. In other countries, high rates of death duties were not considered to be a threat to private property.[27] Second, the idea of a tax on inheritance was based upon the individual character of property. That is, property was the reward for personal effort. By bequeathing property, personal merit was discouraged, and property became a privilege. On the other hand, those who opposed any increase in the rates argued that patrimony had a familial, not an individual character.[28]

This discussion reveals a conception about the ways of achieving property and wealth, distinguished by their social legitimacy. Death duties—to some extent—are equivalent or even a substitute to a capital levy; they represent a tax on the accumulated wealth over a long period. Thus, in Britain, which was facing the threat of a capital levy, Winston Churchill proposed, in 1924, an increase in the rates of death duties because they punished the "idle rich" in a better way than did a capital levy, which might harm efficient entrepreneurs.[29] A tax on inheritance stimulated the entrepreneurial mind to develop new ideas and guaranteed the equality of opportunities that were embedded in the liberal philosophy, whereas a tax on capital punished a deserved accumulation of wealth. This distinction between earned and nonearned income, and between deserved and nondeserved wealth was also felt in Argentina. In the important parliamentary tax debate of 1950, the leader of the opposition, Arturo Frondizzi stated: "We are not worried about tax increases as far as they affect incomes not earned through work."[30]

The government shared this view, whereas the Supreme Court doctrine defended the idea that "inheritance is not a privilege."[31] With a new and favourable Supreme Court, the government imposed its view and in 1950 approved a law that contemplated a higher rate of 45 percent for donations over 1 million pesos between parents and siblings plus a fix amount of 260,000 pesos and a higher rate of 75 percent when the inheritance or donation was made between distant relatives or to a person without familial ties. The law also stipulated that, in any case, the rate could not surpass 80 percent of the amount donated.[32] Nonetheless, the federal government could not touch succession taxes that had been collected in the provinces.

The most important attempt at redistributing income was addressed to the rural world. In an early phase of Perón's administration, the government transferred wealth from rural producers to the cities through the workings of the Argentine Institute for International Trade Promotion (IAPI). This institution controlled rural commodities exports, buying them from national producers at a price that was lower than the world market price. During the first years of Perón's rule, the high prices of food products in the world market allowed the government to transfer resources from the rural to the urban sector in order to accomplish its goal of industrial promotion and working-class welfare. (Nonetheless, prices fell very soon, and the government looked for other alternatives). Besides, the freezing of rents meant an important shift of income from proprietors to tenants; a process that was taking place both in the countryside and in the city and which caused enormous concern among rural and real estate owners. This transfer of income was sharpened by inflation, as labor and other sectors were more able to adjust their incomes to price movements than were small- and medium-sized landowners.[33] Yet, these distributive mechanisms were not exactly taxes.

How were rural producers treated by Peronist tax measures? The income tax did not distinguish among sources of revenue, and therefore landowners (the first category of taxpayers) paid as much as did other categories in proportion to their incomes. Nonetheless, landed incomes received less deductions and allowances than did wage earners and manufacturers.[34] Absenteeism was one of the many features that marked Argentine landowners as the target of intense moral and social criticism since the 1920s.[35] Peronist legislation included a special surcharge of 30 percent for absentee proprietors. This measure was, to some extent, symbolic, because it defined absentee owners as those who lived abroad most of the year, whereas the notion of absenteeism was not necessarily linked to that of living in a foreign country. Yet, the law was addressed to landed incomes as can be seen by the definition of revenues that were subjected to the surcharge—individual incomes from the first category, individual incomes derived from farming, joint-stock company incomes considered to belong to the first category, or corporations' incomes derived from farming.[36] Only revenues from pensions, superannuation, and retirement benefit, also subjected to the surcharge, were not directly linked to land, but they were easily understood as part of the traditional sources of a *rentier* lifestyle.

The main aim of taxes on land was to encourage property fragmentation, as latifundios (large landed estates) were traditionally regarded as one of the main obstacles to Argentine progress. The idea of reforming ownership structure was still the most conspicuous argument in order to encourage special taxes on land during Perón's rule.[37] The conservative antecedents of Perón had already displayed taxation policies in several provinces with the aim of obtaining resources from beleaguered landowners. Perón and Peronist provincial governors continued that policy "in order to get [those plots of land] divided, sold and put in humble hands."[38] Hence, the national government imposed a tax on wasted land of 72 per 1,000 on the value of the land for those plots of over 1 million pesos, which was accompanied by more aggressive tax policies toward landowners in some Argentine provinces, in particular, Buenos Aires.[39]

Despite these seemingly progressive measures, the opposition argued that the social justice motto was a smoke curtain to hide an enormous tax increase and the administration's inability to control public expenses. For instance, they considered that the minimum taxable income fixed in 1950 was insufficient to match the price rise. A Radical representative accused the government of using a "*banderín populachero*" (popular flag) and of having, as its real intention, the collection of funds from no matter what source.[40]

Were the Radicals right and were the progressive taxes designed by the Peronists nothing but a pretense? To say so would be an exaggeration. For some sectors, which did not share the politicians' enthusiasm about social justice, the new taxes were indeed distributive, although this was not necessarily seen as a positive feature. In 1950, on the occasion of this tax reform, *La Nación* complained that the increase in income tax rates, both personal and corporate, and the wage increases were placing entrepreneurs under dire straits.[41] Besides, fourth-category taxpayers obtained important family allowances and tax cuts: "For this category of taxpayers there is an apparent improvement. It is not the same for the rest."[42] Therefore, for the conservative daily, Peronist tax policies were clearly biased in favor of labor and against capital.[43]

Yet, Perón's taxation policies cannot be characterized as straightforwardly distributive.[44] These policies showed some contradictory features, and they fully embraced ambiguity, both in discourse and in practice.

Perón's taxation policies were symbolically embedded in the constitutional reform of 1949. The Constitution of 1949 replaced the article 16 of the 1853 Constitution, which stated: "Equality is the basis of taxation and public burdens," with article 28, which said: "Equity and proportionality are the basis of taxation and public burdens." This reform was aimed at legitimizing fiscal discrimination and progressiveness and was bound to the social justice program developed by the government.

But very often, *justicia social* or the need to improve the distribution of income played a secondary role in the government's justification of its tax policies. Peronist politicians resorted to intellectual sources that were more committed to the protection of private property than to its distribution, mainly to economists who were related to marginalism. Among them was Edwin R. A. Seligman, one of the American reformist economists of the Progressive Era, who had had a great influence in the transition of taxation thinking from "benefits" to "faculty," that is, from the idea of paying taxes in order to receive some benefit from the state to the idea of paying taxes according to the faculty of the taxpayers.[45] The Argentine constitutional reform of 1949 was—according to one deputy—inspired by Seligman, who "made clear that equality, as far as taxation is concerned, does not mean identity but proportionality."[46] The other influential thinker was the Italian economist Benvenutto Griziotti, also a follower of the marginal school and of Paretian utilitarianism. Griziotti had been influential in Argentine taxation thinking since World War I.[47] As in the case of Seligman, Griziotti was a defender of progressive taxation that was based on the idea of the ability to pay.[48] But ultimately, both Seligman and Griziotti believed in progressive taxation—and, in the case of the Italian economist, even in a capital levy—as an emergency barrier against socialism.[49]

Nevertheless, even as a barrier, these ideas recognized the need for further distribution through taxation. Yet, in other cases, the Peronist rulers made clear their defence of property. Article 38 of the new constitution stated that the social utility of property extended previous considerations that were related to state capacities to confiscate property and established that "confiscation of wealth is abolished forever in the Argentine law."[50]

It is revealing that for some conservative critics of the government, the taxation spirit embedded in the new constitution protected private property and individual entrepreneurship. These critics seemed to be particularly concerned about taxation policies because these policies were considered to "jeopardize private property."[51] However, the new constitution meant a guarantee, because of its insistence on equity and proportionality: "Proportionality means rational incidence of the tax burdens upon wealth . . . Equity means substantially guaranteeing the right of property and the right to freely work."[52]

Hence, even if the government had declared the social utility of property, taxation was not the instrument for implementing that constitutional principle. By doing this, the new constitution was following several sentences of the Supreme Court that put limits to the threats to private property. Part of this defense of property was based upon the arbitrary decision that any tax that "absorbs more than 33 percent of the normal result of the efficient exploitation of the taxed estate" was considered confiscatory.[53]

It is revealing that Perón's administration, which was committed to an increase of collections and expenditure, did not challenge this doctrine of the Supreme Court (save in the mentioned case of the gift tax, which was not nationally applied). In fact, the Supreme Court that firmly established this doctrine regarding confiscation was composed of government-appointed judges.[54] To some extent, the administration's coyness was due to a commitment to private property, which was as strong as its defence of social justice.

Another important dimension of the Peronist discourse on taxation was the topic of the moderate rates. In 1948, Miguel Miranda, president of the National Economic Council (a sort of ministry of economic planning),[55] stated: "In general, our policy is not to increase taxes, because *no se puede gravar el trabajo* (work cannot be levied on)."[56] In 1955, the director of the DGI recognized this: "The burden of our taxes on labor, commerce, and on corporations as well is inferior to [the burden of taxes] in the main countries of the world."[57] President Perón himself, discussing the problem of evasion, was proud about the low level of taxation in the country: "Not long ago, a foreign visitor chatted with me about tax collection. When we dealt with the economic aspects of that topic, I, with natural pride, told him that our taxes were not very high and that they would be even less so if people paid them."[58]

Peronist taxation praxis was as ambiguous as was its discourse. Whereas in the early phase of its tenure, the government had deepened the progressiveness of the income tax scheme, after 1948, tax policies seemed to become increasingly regressive. For instance, a phenomenal increase in the sales tax rate was decided. This was a tax on the first sale of some industrial products and on some exports. Since its implementation in the 1930s, the tax on exports was inferior to the rates applied to the industrial goods. In 1943, the government increased the tax on exports from three per 1,000 to 1.25 percent of the value of each sale. Perón's administration increased the rate of the sales tax twice in 1948, bringing it up to 8 percent.[59]

This 8 percent rate that was applied to exports was considered to be beneficial as far as the world market was absorbing Argentine commodities and foreign consumers were paying the tax.[60] Moreover, for economic or ideological considerations, the government's attitude toward export trade was rather negligent.[61] To transfer income from the rural or the export sector to industry or urban workers was one of the centrepieces of Perón's economic policies.

The sales tax for industrial goods was a different matter. As it was said in chapter 2, sales tax conspicuously affected manufacturers among the different business sectors. The manufacturers' reaction toward the tax increase is difficult to assess. Industrialists who were close to Perón seemed to receive the measure as a good alternative to other forms of taxation.[62] Yet, rather than the possible consequences on industrial development, it was the apparently regressive feature of the rate increase that occupied centerstage during the debate. It was held that the sales tax could easily be transferred to consumers and that it therefore perverted the social justice goal of any tax policy. In fact, in 1951, the DGI expanded the 1948 measures and drafted a plan aimed at expending the increased collection from the sales tax in education and the building of the social security funds.[63] Despite earmarking the new revenue for social goals, the national government could not avoid a controversy on the regressive character of its policy. Although most basic goods were exempted from payment, clothes and shoes were affected by the tax hike, which aroused the outcry of the opposition representatives in the Chamber.[64]

Since the reform of 1948, the sales tax rapidly increased its contribution to the total revenue. In 1948, sales tax accounted for 5 percent of the total collection, while in 1949 (the first year of application of the reform), the amount collected by this item climbed to more than 18 percent of the total revenue. In 1955, sales tax and internal and oil duties made up the bulk of Argentine taxation system, representing almost half the tax revenues. Yet, the sales tax was not entirely regressive. The tax was able to tap on luxuries or other forms of status consumption. Marcela Harriague has estimated that in 1949, with a rate of 1.25 percent, sales tax absorbed 0.34 percent of the average working-class family income. When the tax rate climbed up to 8 percent, working-class families paid 2.17 percent of their income in the form of this tax.[65] Despite the substantial increase, the impact of the sales tax on the popular classes did not seem to have been enormous.

As far as the progressiveness of the tax system was concerned, other measures might have had an even deeper impact than did the sales tax. The role of corporate companies within the income tax and the gift tax was particularly controversial. In order to encourage the formation of incorporated companies, Argentine legislation offered a series of advantages, among them the possibility of realizing operations in any place outside the city of foundation. This prerogative allowed many affluent people to avoid the payment of the federal gift tax by transferring the donation of some amount of the gift under the form of capital assets to any province in the country. To tackle this, the military government of 1943 approved a law aimed at tapping a proportional amount of these operations.[66] The disappearance of anonymous shareholders since 1944 made this collection easier. Nonetheless, in 1950, Perón's government returned to the prior situation, re-establishing the right to issue nonidentified shares. Furthermore, also in 1950, the government suppressed the required inclusion of dividends in tax returns in order to solve the problem of shareholders' evasion of the income tax. But, as the government was aware, the reform opened new possibilities of fraud: "The reform introduced by the law 13.925, by establishing anonymity... quashes any possibility of controlling the existence of those shares and therefore opens up the possibility of heavy evasion in the gift tax."[67]

The administration found an alternative to the tax on donations as far as the corporations were concerned in the so-called *impuesto sustitutivo del gravamen a la transmisión gratuita de bienes aplicable a las sociedades de capital* (tax replacing the gift-tax applicable to capital corporations), implemented in 1951 for a period of ten years. This tax had the advantage of being applied in the whole national territory. Yet, the *impuesto sustitutivo* was a mild one. Like the capital gains tax, it was a flat tax of 1 percent on the capital and reserves of the corporations. The corporations were allowed to deduct from the capital the distributed dividends that, as it was said, were exempt from inclusion on the tax returns. The mildness of the rate and the generous measures regarding dividends were aimed at gaining entrepreneurial consent. Along with this, the sale or any transaction of shares, debentures, etcetera, were exempted from the capital gains tax. The nonobligation of identifying shareholders made this measure inevitable.[68]

The treatment of joint stock companies reveals the government's disregard for the improvement in tax collections. This policy was justified for the sake of efficiency. In January 1949, the Buenos Aires Stock Market plummeted. The government attempted to revive it with the new measures.[69] The control of shareholders limited the necessary flexibility of the stock market and hence meant a major hindrance to economic growth.[70] Yet, by doing this, an important tax inequity arose. Incomes that had been derived from stock companies assets—no matter the amount—were exempted, whereas those not derived from stock companies' assets were levied with a progressive duty.[71] This erased the progressiveness of the system for one of the most significant groups of taxpayers and contradicted the spirit of social justice.[72]

Due to these and other features, critics of Perón's rule pinpointed the regressive character of his tax scheme.[73] We can explore this issue by looking at the evolution of tax collection during Perón's administration. In figure 3.1, the contribution of the main taxes since 1943 (in current pesos) to the Argentine Treasury is shown. Income tax (personal plus corporate) continued to be the main source of tax revenue for the state during the whole period. Income tax revenue rose from 259 million pesos in 1943 to more than 4,500 million pesos in 1955. Nevertheless, inflation played an important role here. On the one hand, prices increased seven times between 1943 and 1955,

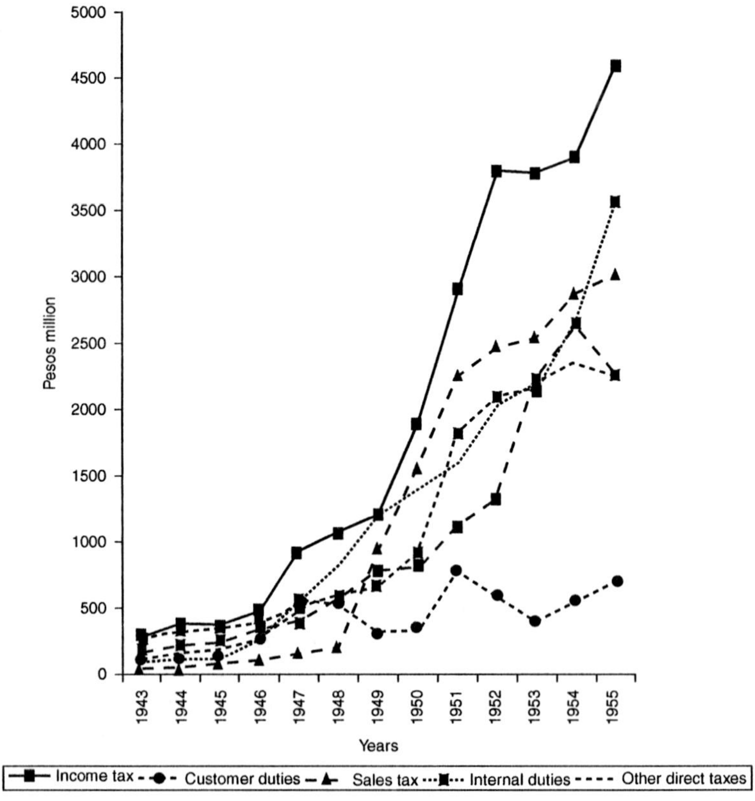

Figure 3.1 Tax collection in Argentina, 1943–1955

Source: *BDGI* (1955 and 1956).

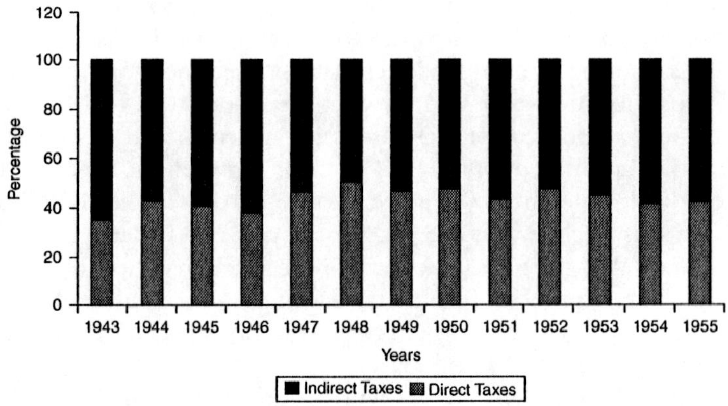

Figure 3.2 Indirect and direct taxes in Argentina, 1943–1955
Source: *BDGI* (1955 and 1956).

pushing up nominal revenues. On the other hand, inflation was a powerful incentive to avoid or postpone tax payment, and therefore, real collection was increasingly below potential collection.

Second—and related to the decline in customs revenues—sales tax and internal duties gained growing salience. Together, sales tax and internal duties exceeded the revenues that came from the income tax. In 1945, internal duties meant 25 percent of the total tax collection of the state, whereas sales tax represented a little over 6 percent.

Despite its shortcomings, it is worth looking at the traditional distinction between direct and indirect taxes due to its prestige among politicians of any tendency and among the officials of the DGI. In fact, Peronists and anti-Peronists alike defended the ideal of a taxation system that was based primarily upon direct taxes, such as the income tax. The question then is, how did reality contradict the ideal model? Figure 3.2 shows the evolution of direct and indirect taxes between 1943 and 1955. Data are not conclusive. Yet, it seemed that in the early years of Perón's government, between 1946 and 1948, direct taxes gained salience. The implementation of the new sales tax at the beginning of 1949 might have changed the tendency. At the end of the period, sales and internal taxes accounted for the growing importance of indirect taxes in the Argentine system. The relative significance of income tax and other levies on wealth at the beginning of Perón's rule might be explained also by the absence of any substitute to the declining customs revenues. But in fact, customs performed quite satisfactory between 1946 and 1949, doubling its importance in the total revenues compared to the last years of World War II. Therefore, the rise in the sales tax and the decline of the customs revenues were part of a deliberate Peronist policy to encourage the industrial sector.

Thus, as time went by, indirect taxation became more important. Yet, the problem was not entirely with the income tax. In 1950, taxes on income accounted for 4.2 percent of Argentine GDP whereas in 1955, they accounted for only 3.4 percent. Between those years, taxes on capital declined from 0.6 percent to 0.3 percent of the GDP.[74] But, beyond this decline, income tax maintained its efficiency. Between 1943 and 1948, income tax covered up to 12 percent of total public expenditure.[75] In 1955, income tax accounted for 16 percent of total public expenditures. The other progressive taxes performed less satisfactorily (see figures 3.1 and 3.2).

One might wonder if the downturn of the economic cycle since 1949 might have influenced a shift in tax policies. The nation faced a shortage of foreign currency to fuel her next step in the industrialization process, and inflation became increasingly difficult to tame. The economic plan of 1952, which aimed at economic recovery, emphasized the necessity of producing more. Sacrificing consumption and encouraging savings was one of the mottos of the economic plan.[76] Yet, it is not clear that the increase of consumption taxes and the multiple allowances in the income tax could accomplish the mission of keeping inflation at bay. Furthermore, the new trend toward indirect taxation began before the symptoms of recession were apparent, and after that the government did not renounce the increase of expenditure, which followed a brief period of austerity.

The question is therefore whether the government still had room to maneuver and whether it could meet the rising fiscal necessities with greater resources from progressive taxes. And if so, why did it choose to do otherwise? Again, it is difficult to offer any conclusive answer but there is some—if limited—evidence that proved that the government consciously chose a fiscal path for the nation that led away from progressive taxation. Income tax rates were not so high as to disallow new increases. Between 1946 and 1949, the highest marginal rates were 27 percent (plus the basic rate of 7 percent), although since 1950, they climbed up to 40 percent. In Britain, the standard income tax rates were 45 percent in 1950. However, the excess profits tax charged rates that were as high as 60 percent, which were well over Argentine rates (which ranged between 10 percent and 30 percent in 1949) and the surtax on the income tax, which crossed 90 percent.[77] In the United States, in 1945, higher marginal rates of the income tax reached 94 percent.[78] Even in France, where a tradition of resistance against income taxation prevented its utmost utilization, higher marginal rates amounted to 65 percent in the aftermath of World War II.[79]

As mentioned earlier, corporation income tax rates shifted from 16 percent to 24 percent during these years, and the capital gains tax was fixed at 20 percent, regardless of the taxable amount. The relatively mild rates and their nonprogressive structure might have allowed an increase of these tax devices. In the United States—one of the countries where the corporate income tax played a major role in the twentieth century—corporate tax rates crossed 48 percent until Reagan's administration. In France, corporate income tax, which had been enacted for the first time in 1948, attained a 50 percent rate.[80] Furthermore, the extension of allowances granted to stimulate reinvestments caused concern within the DGI and the Ministry of Economy, who were aware of the sacrifices that these deductions imposed on tax collection.[81]

As revealing as the government's reluctance to deepen the progressiveness of the tax scheme was its unwillingness to extend the tax base. The government raised income tax rates during the decade, but what about the number of taxpayers? This is something difficult to estimate, but some hints would indicate that the number of actual payers of the income tax grew at a slow pace during Perón's government. Between 1946 and 1954, the number of tax returns filled grew from 189,000 to 545,000, yet the number of potential taxpayers in 1954 was over 10 million.[82] It is true that wage earners (fourth-category taxpayers) had their taxes withdrawn by their employers and therefore did not have to fill in returns. However, it is possible to assume that there were still many nonwage earners who did not fill in any tax returns.[83] Moreover, retentions diminished during the decade as the minimum nontaxable income—and, particularly, workers' allowances—were repeatedly raised. In 1955, fourth-category taxpayers' allowances reached 15,000 pesos, and since 1950, workers earning less than 3,000 pesos annually were not subjected to any withdrawal from their payrolls.[84] This meant that many potential taxpayers were exempted from payment and their bonds with the tax system were severed.

Some international comparisons are revealing here. Taking advantage of the circumstances created by World War II, many Western nations extended their taxation systems, not necessarily making them more progressive but broadening the tax base. Sweden is probably the most conspicuous example. Since 1939, the Social Democratic government increased tax rates on income, wealth, and inheritances, and a war profits tax was introduced. (Yet, business obtained a substantial reduction in corporation tax). However, the main feature of the Swedish tax scheme was not its steep progressivity but its efficiency. In fact, and contrary to common knowledge, at the end of World War II, Swedish personal income tax was more lenient than was the British or the US one.[85] Swedish tax authorities have been able to collect more revenue than have most countries from the income tax, and the working class bore a growing burden of that tax.[86] Therefore, taxation in Sweden is not only progressive taxation but also "mass" taxation. In turn, this has allowed the Social Democratic Party to build a full-fledged welfare state.

There is, however, a more adequate comparison for Argentina than Sweden: the United States. Like Argentina, the United States was an economy of frontier and immigration, which supposedly discouraged high taxation. Both countries were organized in federal structures and in both cases, federal units (the states in the United States and the provinces in Argentina) became an important obstacle to the implementation of progressive taxation. Finally, in the United States and in Argentina as well, loopholes and tax expenditures for businesses made the tax system an intricate one.[87] Nonetheless, even the United States was able to broaden its tax base, thanks to the war. In 1939, 6 percent of US workers paid the income tax, whereas 70 percent did so in 1945.[88] In Argentina, there was no national campaign such as the one launched by the US government with the aim of "creating a taxpayer culture."[89]

The reluctance to create a "mass tax culture" by Perón's administration, (a government so committed to indoctrinate society) is striking. It is possible to argue that this was aimed at protecting working-class interest. But the beneficiaries were probably others than workers. In fact, Peronist welfare and expenditure policies created more middle-class jobs than it did employment in the industry. According to Juan Carlos Torre and Elisa Pastoriza, between 1947 and 1960, government bureaucracies, the white-collar salaried and the middle class self-employed were the most dynamic social groups in the country.[90] No matter who benefited from this policy, the government's unwillingness to make the tax system a broader one had momentous consequences. It is here and in the economic troubles of the succeeding years, not in a supposed gender bias of Argentine welfare policy, [91] that the reasons for the permanent ailing condition of the welfare state in Argentina must be sought.

The reluctance to broad the tax base is also shown in the governmental attitude toward tax evasion. Tax evasion increasingly called for politicians' and bureaucrats' attention since 1953. In 1953, the DGI expressed its view on the necessity of "intensifying external monitoring," that is, the control of taxpayers beyond the mere acceptance of theirs sworn returns.[92] In 1954, the DGI established a system of *inspecciones domiciliarias* (home monitoring), in order to curb major evasion.[93] In 1955, while facing a tax reform, the DGI, although it claimed that home monitoring had been successful, solicited from the government new weapons against income tax evasion.

To what extent was evasion of the income tax widespread? It is difficult to establish this, because under the label evasion, different behaviours are included, from plain fraud or noncompliance to other perfectly legal mechanisms to avoid payment by taking advantages of the law loopholes. Moreover, it is almost impossible to assess the behaviour of different actors and social groups as far as tax compliance is concerned. Nonetheless, it is possible to infer the magnitude of the problem by looking at some hints. First of all, in 1954, the DGI assessed the performance of the home monitoring system and reached the following conclusions: "It has been determined that in 80 percent of the [inspected] cases, responsible taxpayers had never submitted their returns...or they had submitted returns stating amounts that were lower than the real ones. Besides, it has been demonstrated that 50 percent of the registered taxpayers have submitted erroneous tax returns."[94] In 1960, the Central Bank carried out several studies on the levels of tax evasion, by calculating the difference between actual income and declared income. In 1952, income that had not been declared reached 49 percent of actual total income, and at the end of Perón's government, the rate rose to 51 percent. The same statisticians from the Central Bank estimated that in 1956, had unreported income been declared tax collections would have increased by 109 percent.[95]

One of the main reasons for the growing levels of noncompliance seems to have been the inflationary features that the Argentine economy acquired after World War II. In 1945, the rate of inflation was close to 20 percent. In 1948, it had fallen to 13 percent, but in 1949, it climbed again to over 30 percent. Since then, until the 1990s, inflation became a chronic Argentine malady. Because most taxes, particularly the income tax, are collected after a time lag, inflation has an impact on real collections. In situations characterized by long time lags and low elasticity of revenues with respect to income, this impact might be negative. That was a common pattern in "developing" nations, including Argentina.[96] Furthermore, inflation provided a new stimulus for tax evasion, as many people realized that as their nominal income increased, so did the tax rates.[97]

As prices grew, the advantages of delaying payment of the tax were greater, which encouraged those who wanted to take the risk of evasion. In turn, evasion created a vicious circle, as those who still paid believed—reasonably—that the system treated them unfairly and considered the possibility of joining the club of evaders, if they had the capacity to do so.

Several clues point to the relationship between the surge of income tax evasion and the rise of inflation in Argentina or at least the coincidence of both processes. Between 1950 and 1955, income tax collection was unable to tap a permanent proportion of the national income's increments.[98] Apparently, the divergence between the national income and tax collection became evident since 1952.[99]

The governmental reaction toward evasion might have reinforced that tendency. Since 1952, the government attempted to enforce several stricter monitoring systems in order to curb evasion. Nonetheless, stricter monitoring seemed to respond to the demands of the DGI, which was concerned about losing revenues, rather than to the executive's preferences.[100] For Perón and his cabinet, the main goal was to demonstrate the noncoercive character of Argentine taxation, which entailed proving its own legitimization through tax policies. This was reflected in the light-handed policy toward tax debtors. The government considered that a lenient treatment of evaders might encourage taxpayers' voluntary compliance. In 1949, the tax reform passed by Congress introduced the possibility of *blanquear* (laundering) capital being sent abroad. According to the reform passed that year, nonjustified increases of patrimony were exempted from the income tax (although not from the capital gains tax) if the rate those increases were supposed to pay was less than 20 percent. For the opposition, this measure and the exemptions for shareholders constituted the legalization of the flight of capitals and fraud.[101]

For the government, the reform "actually seeks to protect not those who had taken capital out of the country, but those capitals that used to be in the country, in order to give them the opportunity of returning and consolidating our economy."[102] Overall, this discussion shows the importance already achieved by the flight of capitals in an inflationary economy such as Argentina.

The lenient policies displayed by the national government were apparent in the concession of fiscal pardons. In 1949, a Law of Pardon was passed. The DGI, making virtue out of necessity, asserted that this had eased the judicial claims on tax debts and fees by reducing the number of cases. However, the main consequence was that open processes of monitoring and claims were cancelled, damaging the credibility of the agency as tax collector.[103] In 1950, a decree exempted from the payment of any fees those who "spontaneously" presented their declaration or normalized their situation as far as income tax and other duties were concerned.[104] The deputy in charge of defending the project in the Chamber argued that writing off the fee was "a reasonable compensation for those who prove, through self-denunciation...their willingness to comply with rules."[105]

Fiscal pardons might stimulate a further wave of evasion and fraud. Taxpayers could interpret the government's message not as an invitation to cooperate but as a symptom of weakness. Therefore, they could assume a new amnesty as the logical outcome of that weakness and noncompliance as a rational strategy to pursue. Yet, the government neglected this factor and presented itself as a benevolent tax collector. By doing this, it was attempting to woo middle-income groups, which were the main foci of tax grievances and equity claims. In fact, the measure favouring capital comebacks was addressed to middle-income groups—those who fell into the 20 percent income tax rate category.

Hence, Perón's government took a mild stance toward tax collection and preferred not to deepen the progressiveness in the tax scheme or to broaden the tax base. To accomplish this, it had to find financial alternatives to achieve mass income taxation. Thus, it resorted to the control of foreign exchange, inflationary monetary policy, social security taxes, and the expansion of public debt. Perón's administration deepened the use of the control of exchange as a source of revenue. The system became increasingly complex, adding new discriminatory measures in order to encourage different economic sectors. According to Roberto Cortés Conde, the government, through the control of exchange, obtained revenues that amounted to 3.7 percent of the GDP between 1946 and 1949 and to 0.5 percent of the GDP between 1949 and 1955.[106] In 1946, the Central Bank was nationalized and the government exerted greater control over private banks and monetary instruments. The government raised the monetary offer by expanding discount and lending to industry. As interest rates were lower than the rate of inflation, real interest rates were, on many occasions, negative ones, which virtually transformed credits into subsidies. The government used the Central Bank discounts as a source of public financing as well. While exports performed satisfactorily, the government employed its control of the export trade (through control of exchanges and IAPI) in order to maintain broad credit facilities without pushing up prices.[107] This situation did not last beyond 1949.

The most important alternative, as far as the discussion about fairness and progressiveness is concerned, was the extension of the social security system. During the first years of Perón's government, the social security system, which was based upon contributions of both employers and employees, became almost universal. As industrial production boomed and the number of workers increased during this period, the revenue collected through that mechanism became a valuable source of income for the national Treasury.[108] In 1945, social security revenues accounted for 19.9 percent of total expenditures. In 1955, they covered up to 29 percent of the Argentine budget.[109] It is worth comparing the collections coming from the social security system with those derived from the income tax. In 1950, the social security contributions accounted for 6.2 percent of the GDP, whereas the income tax amounted to 3.8 percent of the GDP. At the end of Perón's rule, the social security revenues represented 6.9 percent of the GDP, whereas the income tax collection fell to 3.2 percent.[110]

Social security taxes were taxes that were earmarked for specific areas such as the health system, housing and, most important, pensions. The rate for these taxes was 21 percent of the wage, 15 percent of which was paid by the employer and 6 percent by the employee at the onset of the system. These figures, however, do not tell the entire story. The remaining question is: were the employers able to transfer the burden of their social secutiry contributions to wages? Although there is no statistics to support any final conclusion, it is possible to make some inferences from the theoretical debate. If the labor market had a low elasticity of labor supply, a tax on wages (and therefore an increase in labor costs), such as the one caused by social security taxes, might not produce a decrease in labor employed but a decrease of real wages. This was the case in most industrial economies after World War II. The situation was different for underdeveloped countries, where the labor supply is elastic. Therefore, a social security tax could not affect wages but could affect employment rates. Perón's Argentina, which had low rates of unemployment (in fact the government promoted a fast, labor-intensive industrialization), was closer to the situation of the industrialized countries. Therefore, as Jorge Macon has asserted, it is probable that ultimately workers paid most of the social security contributions.[111] Besides, the 6 percent tax paid by employees might add up to a significant amount because the national pension system used to obtain surpluses during the early 1950s, diminishing the positive impact on the income distribution of the Peronist wage policies.[112]

That social security taxes were regressive was apparent to contemporaries as well. Dino Jarach, an economist exiled from Italy and living in Argentina, asserted that if the goal was to distribute wealth, a mandatory "social insurance" paid by workers was not the response. "The only solution is funding [pensions] with the personal progressive income tax or with a special surtax on the income tax...or with an increase in the rates of the income tax."[113]

Explaining the Rationale behind Peronist Tax Policies

Progressive taxation did not become the fulcrum of Peronist tax policies. The income tax and other progressive duties gained relevance in the first two years of Perón's government, but after that, indirect duties and even alternative ways of financing the Treasury prevailed. As shown, this was, to some extent, the result of deliberate decisions by the administrators. Nonetheless, this does mean that the entire Peronist movement supported a step backward from progressive taxation.

In 1948, within the framework of the Third Conference of Ministers of Economy—which gathered the economics ministers of the provinces—a representative of the Central Bank, the economics minister of the province of Buenos Aires, and Miguel Miranda, the president of the National Economic Council carried on a bitter dispute about taxation that revealed not only the internal divisions of the Peronist block but also the central notions that supported the Perón administration's tax ideas. Inflation and the overall increase of public debt were two sources of concern for the monetary authorities. During this conference, the Central Bank representative expressed his opinion on the necessity of increasing tax collection in a progressive way. The dispute revolved around the issue of taxing manufacturers. For the official of the monetary authority, a healthy and equitable tax policy could not dispense with the manufacturers' contribution. Moreover, the high rates established for the sales tax not only meant a deviation of the tendency toward direct taxation but also "affect[ed] consumption and inflate[d] the prices of merchandise." Miranda responded with the old argument that every tax device was ultimately levied on consumers: *"Dele toda la vuelta que quiera*. (Talk about this as much as you want.) Every tax is on consumption."[114]

The other dissident voice was that of the economics minister of Buenos Aires, who believed that manufacturers' profits should be taxed with the aim of improving social policies: "The state takes [those profits] away to distribute them with a social criterion."[115]

Miranda—who seemed to control the meeting even in the presence of Minister Cereijo—blantantly dismissed the critics. First of all, Miranda underlined the ideas about earned and nonearned income and justified the necessity of deductions in the income tax for industrial producers:

> This is why in the income tax law we established that the profits devoted to the expansion of factories are exempted from taxes. The future Constitution will have to recognize the existence of two classes of capital: the parasite capital and the productive capital...We are a country producer of raw materials, we do not have capitals and we are not going to have them if we punish them.[116]

Miranda further developed his argument by defining productive capital as the one devoted to manufactures:

> I am one of the manufacturers who earned a lot, and how did I do so? I did it, as did everyone else, by exploiting workers, because, what is capital but accumulated labor? But I pose this question: if the capitalist, the manufacturer, earns a lot of money and makes factories, what damage does he cause to the country?...This capital must not be punished...On the other hand parasite capital must be punished in order to force it to be active.[117]

According to Miranda, higher taxes on the wealthy and particularly on the industrialist were not necessary: "If more factories are set up there is no need of expending money abroad. This is why we must industrialize the country and once we are industrialized we will do as in North America."[118] By this, he meant that a full-fledged process of industrialization would make Argentina a prosperous nation, so prosperous that either taxation or further distribution of wealth would become superfluous.

The issue of the capital gains tax aroused some friction within the Peronist movement as well. Some representatives of Argentine interior believed the capital gains tax to be a levy on patrimony and a first step toward a greater taxation of capital. These representatives asked for differential and even graduated rates for the tax on patrimony according to its origin (capital assets, rural activities, labor, etcetera).[119] Yet, as has already been shown, the Argentine capital gains tax was based upon a single flat rate, and it was levied on nonrecurrent income rather than on actual patrimony. The capital gains tax was not the Peronist's way to a socialist society. In fact, it was closer to be the opposite. The new tax would allow the government to avoid an increase on the higher rates of the income tax by diffusing tax objectives. The government's defense of the new measure by linking capital gains to income and profits, and not to property, reinforces this interpretation: "We are in a similar situation to the majority of nations that have evolved from a restricted notion of income tax toward a general taxation on any kind of incomes, no matter if their source was permanent or accidental."[120] Ultimately, the argument of the Argentine government echoed the US policy that considered both recurrent incomes and capital gains as part of the same concept: income.[121] Hence, this was far from being a tax on property or on patrimony.

Despite the conflicts, the government imposed a tax agenda, which limited the reach of progressive taxation. Was this a coherent agenda? Was it backed by the Peronist rank and file? As the above-quoted words by Miranda show, the Peronist government was committed to thoroughly industrializing Argentina. In turn, this hampered the extension of the tax system. In addition to the exception of dividends from tax returns and the permissive policy toward anonymous shares, Perón's government deepened the economic approach to taxation begun under military rule. In fact, economic aims seemed in many circumstances to precede the fiscal and social goals of taxation policy. Of course, ultimately, this also had a social meaning because industry created jobs and hence reinforced the welfare of the Argentinean urban working class.[122] Since an early date, Perón's government consciously used fiscal tools to stimulate industrial production and to soothe manufacturers' fears. After bitter disputes with the government, in May 1946, the UIA had been *intervenida* (taken over) by the national administration and its activities almost halted.[123] Nonetheless, even under the control of the government, the UIA fulfilled some advisory roles in fields such as labor safety and health, transport, raw material supply, and taxation.[124] After the *intervención* (takeover), the UIA's director (a governmental appointee) justified his role by showing his contribution to the analysis of the income tax and tax exemptions that stimulated new industrial investments.[125]

This policy, initiated by the military government in 1944, responded to manufacturers' demands.[126] In 1946, facing the economic situation of the aftermath of World War II, which supposedly would open up international markets of industrial inputs, the government of general Farrell attempted to encourage a new phase of industrialization through a reform of the income tax.[127] The decree 15,921 of June 1946 introduced generous allowances of up to 38 percent for those profits that were reinvested to increase installed capacity in the factories, given a minimum investment of 30 percent of the taxable profits. The law was specifically addressed to manufactures, defined as "those industries that make or transform goods whose form, aspect, consistency, kind or use is different from those [goods] that served as raw materials or basic elements."[128] Moreover, in March 1945, the secretary of commerce and industry within the Ministry of Economy had drafted a bill that exempted from the payment of the tax on extraordinary profits those incomes that were devoted to the acquisition of capital assets for industry. However, the DGIR rejected the project in 1946, once Perón was in power, on two grounds. First, the end of the war would make technological imports easier and cheaper and second, the tax on extraordinary profits meant a minor influence in the building of capital reserves.[129]

Although in 1946, Minister Cereijo accepted the DGIR's advise—probably for the sake of maintaining collection—Perón's government strengthened the industrialist bias of the tax policy and at the same time built up a complex structure of discriminatory allowances. Tax policies were not isolated, but they were embedded in the growing interventionism of the state in the shaping of Argentine industrialization.[130] In 1952, and as far as the income tax was concerned, the amounts that it was permissible to deduct as compensation for the depreciation of capital assets were raised. The value of the machinery acquired before 1941 could be entirely deducted from the taxable income, and those equipments bought between 1949 and 1959 were permitted an allowance that went as high as 45 percent.[131]

Beyond the general allowances for the manufacturers, the government established a system of exemptions and incentives to specific sectors.[132] This economic approach to taxation meant that taxes were flexible in order to encourage production or exports. The income tax and the sales tax laws incorporated the possibility of partial suspension of the measure to ease the economic life of a sector or firm. Thus, in 1950, in order to encourage the supply of energy, oil producers were exempted from the sales tax. Some other goods, such as sugar, had been exempted for their regional significance or others, such as tobacco, enjoyed a deduction on the internal duty.[133]

These policies caused two kinds of problems. First, they had a negative impact on the collections of both corporate and personal income tax, and it was difficult to compensate for those losses with other taxes. As shown in figure 3.1, customs revenues dropped to a great extent due to the strong protectionist stance adopted by the administration.

Here, as elsewhere, taxes were, according to the Ministry of Finance, subjected to "economic and social goals."[134]

Second, these policies aroused problems of horizontal equity. Once a specific allowance was approved, those who were excluded attempted to obtain the same benefit. For instance, wheat and maize flour were exempted from the sales tax. In turn, rye flour was also exempted on grounds of the manifested inequity that levied only on this kind of flour.[135] More significant was the case of the building sector, which claimed to be treated as manufacturers—as far as the income tax was concerned—in terms of the benefits derived from the allowances for reinvested profits. In 1950, they achieved their goal: "It is apparent that, as other industries, construction transforms materials."[136]

The problems of inequity affected rural producers as well. This point was clearly highlighted and was also behind many of the arguments displayed by rural representatives. The SRA protested against the "disproportion between industry and cattle ranching as far as taxes are concerned," owing to which ranching was forced to bear a burden four times higher than that of manufacturing.[137] Rural entrepreneurs recognized the importance of industry in the new Argentina, but they believed that this development should be encouraged with a "sense of economic integration," because "The consolidation and prosperity of agrarian production constitutes the indispensable base for the development of industry and commerce."[138] Therefore, a harmonic economic development demanded equitable taxation. But the argument was beyond this balance between economic sectors and pointed out to a further demand for equity, which was based upon efficiency. If rural producers did not deserve the tax burden they bore, it was due to "Argentina's features, and particularly Buenos Aires province's features... essentially adapted to extensive cattle ranching and agriculture... We can state, without fear of erring, that we are the country [enjoying] the best conditions in the world for meat production."[139] Rural producers were remarking on one of the main drawbacks of Perón's economic policy: its repression of the activity with the greatest international comparative advantage. They were also shaping an alternative tax discourse that associated tax equity with economic efficiency.

On the other hand, rural owners played a familiar chord for Peronist rulers. They defended *estancias* as mechanisms for the improvement of social life, similar to big factories: "Like a big factory, the big *estancia*, [thanks to] resources that are not available for the small exploitations, [is not] an obstacle, but the best way to bring prosperity to the countryside and to improve the social condition of workers, thanks to the diversification of tasks and the technical advances employed in every phase of production."[140] This chant to the *estancia's* virtues resembled the Taylorite utopia of industrial affluence for everyone and thus attempted to fit into the Peronist view of Argentina. Thus, *estancias* deserved the same tax benefits, such as the introduction of deductions in the income tax for "improvements" in the lands and for cattle producing, as did factories.[141]

In 1949, the government modified its economic policy in order to obtain foreign currency by stimulating agricultural production for exports. The change of policy was met with a cold response in the countryside. The fiscal reform of 1950 provided rural producers with the opportunity of underlining the contradiction between the call for greater efforts and an unfavorable tax scheme. The Radical Party assumed in the Chamber the defence of landed interests.[142] Of course, the opposition claimed to protect the interest of the *chacareros* (small and medium farmers) and did not mention the demonized *estancieros.* But both *estancieros* and *chacareros* probably shared the arguments developed by Radical congressmen. First of all, policies promoting industrialization, as it had been carried out so far, were accused of encouraging the depopulation of the countryside.[143] Besides, rural producers did not get any fiscal compensation for those policies: "*Chacareros* are thoroughly squeezed." And tax pressure meant that the countryside was unable to recover its productive levels, to renovate the equipment, and to capitalize, as the government was demanding.[144]

Thus, the impossibility of obtaining income tax special allowances for capital reinvestments constituted for the rural sector a manifested tax inequity and a source of permanent grievance. This inequity became more apparent as the government attempted to solve the external bottleneck of the Argentine economy by stimulating agricultural exports. Finally, land incomes received tax exemptions for asset depletion and obsolescence and for depreciation on the value of any building on the rural property; they were also authorized to receive the special depreciation rates, that is, the incentive for reinvestments that manufacturers enjoyed.[145] So, what did make the difference? The problem was that landowners maintained that allowances for rural producers should be adjusted to their special circumstances. Thus, part of the discussion was about the definition of fixed capital assets. Cattle owners demanded that pure-breed animals be considered fixed capital and that their purchase should therefore be deducted as a reinvestment. (This was a controversial issue because, unlike equipment, cattle do not suffer unavoidable price depreciation). In 1955, just a few weeks before the coup that overthrew Perón, they obtained the special depreciation rates applied to breeding cattle.[146] Besides, the special rates of depreciation were associated with the rates of profits, and these were proportional to capital assets. Thus, a pure-breed animal was at the same time an investment and part of the capital/profit ratio. Yet, cattle owners asked for the special depreciation rates without any link to profits and they got these as well in the same reform. *Estancieros* obtained some other important advantages. In order to pay both income and extraordinary profits tax, landowners were authorized to declare a fixed value on cattle in lieu of their current market price. This system was considered fair since the marketplace might not reflect the real value of an animal that was not sold. Nonetheless, the fixed price of cattle was based on 1933 prices, and in 1955, the government decided to revaluate those prices. However, the increased values of stocks that resulted from this revaluation were "just for this unique occasion" exempted from the payment of both income and extraordinary profits tax.[147]

It is revealing that the government agreed to modify tax treatment toward landed interest and extended special depreciation rates to the tax on extraordinary profits at the same time that it was passing through a major political crisis. Again, tax policy was not a distributive device but a conciliatory arena in which even rural producers might be included. But this meant that exemptions and allowances created in order to stimulate industrial activities had become the rule undermining the universal aspirations of the tax scheme.

Peronist tax policies, which were aimed at building a thoroughly industrialized society that would distribute wealth for everyone without harming any interest, ultimately made the system more regressive. Where did the Argentine working class fit into the Peronist tax design? Labor was supposed to be the privileged sector in the Argentine tax scheme. Even the probusiness conservative governments of the 1930s designed an income tax that dealt leniently with the lower-income sectors. Recurrent raisings of the minimum taxable income to catch up with prices and an extra deduction for fourth-category incomes (wages and salaries) was not a novelty brought in by Peronism. Nonetheless, it is true that Peronist ideology reserved a special place for workers within Argentine society and, that to some extent, people, nation, and working-class became almost synonymous with one another.[148]

Rebates in the income tax for wage earners were repeatedly raised by Perón's administration. Of course, these modifications were an attempt to catch up with prices. For example, a worker earning 18,000 pesos in 1950 (and around 12,000 pesos in 1949) had been ratcheted up from the lowest income bracket to the second one. Without deductions and allowances, their income tax would have reached 221 pesos in 1949 and 590 pesos in 1950, that is, it would have more than doubled, whereas inflation reached 31 percent in 1949.[149] But, according to *La Nación,* an individual taxpayer from the fourth category, who was earning 18,000 pesos annually in 1950, would pay 252 pesos in income tax in lieu of the 530 pesos they used to pay before that year's reform.[150](Therefore, the income tax rose by 14 percent for this worker, whereas prices rose by 31 percent. If, as we are assuming, they were able to adjust their wage, the net result would have been a positive one). The last of the increases in workers' allowances that had been carried out by the Peronist administration took place in 1955. The modifications of the tax structure carried out in 1955 emphasized that the system was becoming more equitable and at the same time that workers deserved a special treatment. Thus, nontaxable incomes of all categories of income tax payers were equalized and raised up to 7,200 pesos annually.[151] But fourth-category taxpayers received special treatment. Their maximum allowance was also raised from 12,600 pesos to 15,000 pesos annually.[152] Some figures demonstrate the importance of this allowance. The average annual wage in Argentina was 11,897 pesos in 1954 and 13,025 pesos in 1955.[153] We have more detailed information for 1956—a year after Perón's fall—but it could provide a good picture of workers' positions, as far as the income tax was concerned. That year, salaried employees declared a total taxable income of 3,575,415 pesos. The taxable income of those earning less than 10,000 pesos annually (not necessarily employees, but it is reasonable to assume that condition for most of them) amounted to 2,934,702 pesos, that is, more than 80 percent of total income from labor. Of that amount, 2,258,283 pesos were exempted due to family allowances and minimum nontaxable deductions.[154] Even with inflation, the burden of income tax seemed to have been inexistent for an important section of the Argentine popular classes.

This policy of exemptions was defended by the government as a culmination of the Peronist doctrine, the "*justicialismo* (Justicialism, that is, Peronism) in action."[155] The main goal of these rebates was not to redistribute burdens, but to respect workers' achievements. According to the Peronist self-image, the state's goal was to increase the workers' standard of living and the government "cannot accept to appropriate through taxation that increase."[156] The new taxation measures reinforced social justice more by stabilizing previous achievements than by enhancing the redistributive side of fiscal policy.

Beyond this, were there other reasons for the Peronist regime's reluctance to include workers in the income tax system? First, the loyalty of the working class was not fully guaranteed despite the electoral success of 1946, and it is possible that the government fretted about the possibility of shattering its alliance with this social group. Workers and trade unions truly identified with Perón, but this was a contested and conflictive identification.[157] Second, historical paths between the European countries and Argentina had diverged. Many Europeans were used to paying direct and complex taxes in the nineteenth century, which included the income tax in Britain and similar taxes on wealth in the Scandinavian countries. In Argentina, nineteenth-century taxation was based upon indirect duties. But perhaps this was not as significant as were other historical reasons. Two devastating wars—mainly World War II—made a mass taxation politically feasible in Western Europe, the United States, and even Australia. War sacrifices encouraged the extension of income taxes that were based upon more or less durable social agreements with workers and trade unions.[158] Since Argentina was neutral or not directly affected by those conflicts, Argentine rulers did not feel the same urgency about overhauling the entire tax scheme. Still, some European countries remained neutral during the wars, and yet their income taxes became mass taxes. The most conspicuous example was Sweden. Here, since an early date, workers' representatives strove for the extension of suffrage, believing that their political participation would allow them to shape a more favorable tax policy.[159] Therefore, as in the case of the United States, taxation and representation were strongly linked and helped to create the notion of the citizen as a taxpayer.

It is significant that taxation issues were almost entirely absent from labor concerns during most of Perón's rule. Beyond asking for taxes that were committed to social justice, labor leaders did not pay much attention to technical details in the design of the Argentine tax system. Workers maintained, as their main idea about progressive taxes, the old Socialist demand of general exemption for wages. In 1953, the CGT adhered to the Five-Years Plan and published a document explaining the main consequences of the government's economic policies as far as labor interests were concerned. In a long discussion about wages, production, industrialization, and so on, taxation merited just a few lines, which focused on exemptions for workers: "Personal work will receive special tax exemptions or deductions due to the fundamental importance that the Peronist Doctrine assign it [to the personal work] in the social and *justicialista* (just) order," or "basic popular consumption goods will receive tax exemptions or deductions."[160]

In 1954, facing an economic downturn, the Peronist government organized the National Congress of Productivity (CNP), which was aimed at improving Argentine industrial productivity by formulating a general agreement among manufacturers and trade unions.[161] Taxation played a secondary role in the CNP, but the *Boletín de la Dirección General Impositiva* paid special attention to the Congress and showed the connections that the government attempted to establish between tax policy and a general agreement between workers and employers.[162] The social peace would not be based on a redistribute tax policy but, on the contrary, social peace would allow further tax exemptions, thanks to the increased productivity: "As an important result of the greater productivity, bringing the state more revenue, the increase of public burdens will be avoided."[163] In fact, this was one of the results of the CNP. José Gelbard, the leader of the employers' association, the Economic General Confederation (CGE), asserted that an increase in productivity would depend, to some extent, on the renovation of industrial equipment.[164] But this renovation demanded the rise of exports in order to obtain international modes of payment. Argentina was not prepared to expand her exports immediately and, therefore, some alternatives had to be found. These included an increase in the productivity of present equipment through the exertion of a greater control over the labor force and a prudent wage policy.[165] The government responded to the entrepreneurs' demands by offering new tax advantages. Thus, the Congress, following the finance minister's suggestion, proposed in its conclusions an initiative to "improv[e]the income tax scheme and the tax on extraordinary profits in order to face bigger costs of replacements."[166] Among these improvements were larger deductions in the income tax for reinvested profits; the application of the same policy to the tax on extraordinary profits; and income tax rebates for those profits that were "exclusively derived from the increase of productivity."[167] There was no discussion on the difficulty of distinguishing between profits derived from productivity gains and those derived from other sources, particularly for manufacturers. Ultimately, Perón's administration did not have the time to apply this policy. What did workers obtained in exchange for this concession? "Greater allowances for those incomes derived from personal work and for the popular consumed goods, in order to increase social welfare and the *capacidad de compra del pueblo* (people's ability to expend)."[168] This meant that employers and employees agreed—or at least agreed to try—to build an affluent industrial society.

Social agreements, such as the one attempted in the CNP, were frequent in the postwar Western world. Many countries, such as Argentina, whose governments were now committed to full employment policies and who were aware of trade unions political significance, sought to establish corporatist arrangements that maintained wage restraint by offering some compensatory income policies to workers (such as a progressive tax reform).[169] Through these income policies, European governments aimed to tame inflationary surges and to grant incentives to productivity and encourage economic recovery after the war.[170] The Argentine situation was radically different. Wage restraint was difficult for Peronism, because Perón's symbolic legitimacy was strongly associated with wage increases for the working class. Moreover, Perón's Argentina seemed to face a much more promising economic scene than did European nations, and recovery was not a necessity.

Progressive taxation was a major concern for labor representatives worlwide. Nonetheless, Argentine workers seemed to neglect taxation issues. Why? First, they were the main beneficiaries of exemption and allowances, and therefore they could consider the tax system as fair and socially oriented. However, critics could possibly argue that workers were not aware of the regressive features of the tax scheme. As progressive devices slowly lost ground vis-à-vis indirect taxation and (mainly) social security duties, the system was becoming silently less progressive. In fact, social security taxes, as mentioned, worked as a sort of invisible tax on wages. Besides, the government displayed strong propaganda mechanisms that were aimed at obtaining popular consensus, which insisted on the progressive features and redistributive achievements of Perón's regime.

But is it possible to explain the workers' disregard for tax matters as a blatant example of *false conscience*? The explanation is probably more complex and implies practical and strategic options along with the understanding of an ideological frame that extended itself beyond taxation issues. Let us first explore the problem of social security or payroll tax. As in Argentina, taxes such as these have been widely used in the welfare states of Western Europe and have been criticized by academics for their regressive features.[171] However, in Argentina and in Western Europe as well, the legitimacy of such taxes is related to the service they provide rather than to the source of collection. In Perón's Argentina, the social security system expanded successfully. In 1943, 481,837 people contributed to the system; in 1954, there were already more than 4.5 million workers in the system, including rural workers and the self-employed. In 1948, people over sixty, who had never contributed to the pension system, were covered by an earmarked fund that came from the national lottery.[172] As already stated, Perón's government resorted to social security funds to finance the budget and to subsidize other activities. This might eventually have delegitimized this type of taxation and led to greater evasion. However, since full employment and the age structure of the nation (a relatively low number of retirees) guaranteed the regular payment of pensions, social security taxes were mostly accepted.

Despite their success, social security taxes were also affected by problems of evasion since an early date. The rate of compliance of urban wage-earners diminished from 86 percent in 1950 to 55 percent in 1955.[173] Nonetheless, because the tax was withdrawn by employers, this does not reflect the workers' reluctance to pay but reflects the entrepreneurs' desire to retain their payments in order to finance themselves. Therefore, employers, rather than workers, were the main evaders with regard to the payment of social security taxes. Trade unions complained about employers' lack of compliance with social security contributions.[174] Because the social security system was fragmented into several funds that were run by the unions, their complaints were self-serving. Nonetheless, there is no reason to believe that their rank and file maintained a different view: pension funds meant an important achievement for many workers.[175] Funds, by guaranteeing that lower-income workers obtained important benefits, solidified workers' solidarity within the same trade.[176] Moreover, to some extent, payroll taxes were compensated for by the allowances that workers received in the income tax. Labor opinion on this tax must be understood within the framework of a tax system that was not thoroughly regressive and that offered workers a valuable position in keeping with their aspirations and social ideals.

Furthermore, workers' pressures shaped to some extent the actual workings of the tax. In the draft for the First Five Years Plan of 1946, the government proposed to reform the social security by transforming the existing fragmented system (every trade maintained its own scheme) into a universal one that was based upon the graduated contributions of workers, which was paid by both employers and employees. This system benefited those workers with inferior income who would obtain the same benefits (pensions, unemployment subsidy, health insurance, etcetera) from the common pool of social security contributions. However, workers who were already participating in the system resisted this proposal, and the government preferred not to challenge the most powerful unions, thus preserving the existing structure.[177] Moreover, the opposition of trade unions to the extension of pensions to the entire population was not only an attempt to protect unions' control over pension funds but also to defend the amount their constituencies received after retirement.[178] Thus, the trade unions' distrust of the provision of universal welfare ran parallel to the absence of universal mass income taxation.

Payroll taxes, even if regressive, were associated with full-employment and rising wages. In this sense, we should look at the economic ideology of the urban working classes in order to understand their consensual attitudes toward the government tax policies. In a recent essay, Lucas Llach and Pablo Gerchunoff have developed a suggestive hypothesis about Argentine economic development. They argue that one of the reasons for the (in)famous Argentine cycles of stop-and-go during the second half of the twentieth century was the contradiction between equity and growth. That is, Argentina was a country with a comparative advantage in rural goods from the Pampas, but the specialization in agricultural exports raised inequalities and did not provide enough jobs for the Argentine population. On the other hand, industrialization was an inefficient choice as far as international specialization was concerned, but it helped to preserve full employment, high salaries, and one of the main features of Argentine society since the nineteenth century—relative social equality.[179] Therefore, the Argentine popular classes welcomed a process of intense industrialization. In fact, unlike in many European countries, protectionism, even if affected workers as consumers, seemed to benefit them more as the industrialization process advanced and an open economy seemed to conspire against Argentine proverbial equality.[180] Thus, if the tax system was orientated toward encouraging industrialization, not only through protectionism but also through advantages for manufacturers as far as income tax or other progressive taxes were concerned, workers were not disposed to challenge this process by demanding a further redistributive step with the aid of taxation. Like the government, workers believed that distribution did not depend on taxation. When taxes were discussed, income policies seemed not to be at stake.

The important battles seemed to be in other fields. Thus, the tax advantages conceded to business groups in the CNP proposals were not challenged by CGT representatives. In fact, trade unions focused on diluting some of the employers' demands of greater workers' efforts and on protecting workers' positions within the factory. Thus, the CGE claimed that any obstacle to increase productivity, including any interference in employers' management of their business, should be removed. The entrepreneurs were referring to the so-called *comisiones internas* (internal commissions) of the factories. These were workers committees that exerted a variable but important form of power within every factory with regard to issues such as labor discipline or application of labor rights. Despite employers' pressures in 1955 to obtain internal commissions suppression, labor representatives successfully resisted the attack.[181]

Labor attitudes were not only part of a strategic logic, but they also had ideological roots. Daniel James has demonstrated that the Argentine workers' mentality was a blend of nationalist and industrialist ideas. Workers never disputed the right of employers to enjoy private property nor did they challenge capitalist economy. However, they believed in a full-fledged industrial society where workers could live with dignity. Both, workers and industrialists should fulfill their roles in harmony. As an acknowledgement of their dignity, workers were entitled to high wages and to some control of labor discipline and organization within the factories.[182] Therefore, it is not unreasonable to think that for many workers, tax privileges for manufacturers were a natural way of building up the cornucopia of Argentine industrial society. Moreover, since workers remained mostly exempted from income tax and other progressive levies, the system was equitable and respected the harmonious features that the taxation system should comply with. The workers, like Perón himself, did not believe in progressive taxation as the ultimate weapon of wealth distribution. Of course, this also had a negative side. In the long run, the growth of fiscal fraud was not favorable for those who received less income. The system became increasingly regressive after the 1950s. Exemptions and allowances encouraged a tradition of working-class absence of concern about taxation. In fact, this reflects the peculiarities of the inclusive process of shaping a social citizenship under Perón's rule. Horacio Gaggero and Alicia Garro noticed that the welfare services provided by the state during Peronism were not linked to citizenship but to labor: those who did not work were not entitled to social benefits.[183] In the same fashion, workers were becoming full citizens, who were entitled to rights and protection through their work (and their support of the truly national political movement, Peronism) but not through the payment of taxes. Citizenship and taxation diverged.

Consequences of the Peronist Tax Policies

Perón's administration deepened the progressiveness of the tax scheme between 1946 and 1949. However, this trend was quickly reverted, and the government chose alternative paths to taxation in order to finance its expenditures. This was related to two goals: the development of extensive industrialization and the preservation of working class' standard of life achievements. Yet, the moderate attitude of the government in the field of taxation might have had momentous consequences, such as the increasingly regressive character of the tax scheme and the growth of inflation, and it ultimately might have hampered the survival of the Argentine welfare state. Besides, Perón's administration conceived taxation as a field for social harmony, which made it difficult to resort to taxation as a source of greater distribution of wealth.[184] Despite this, the government was unable to gain the confidence of wide sectors of the upper and middle classes, which in turn caused the tax system to become increasingly fragile and assailable through evasion.

Financing the state with sources other than those that came from taxes had significant consequences. As mentioned, social security tax collections provided the government with an important alternative source of revenue. Moreover, high rates of employment and a young population created a big surplus that was used by the government to finance public debt issues. Yet, the system did not always work as smoothly as the government wished it to, and when inflation rates were high, the payment of pensions became severely strained.[185]

Another alternative to taxation was the rise of public debt, which gave rise to a short-lived debate on the government tax policy. Critics resorted to the same Keynesian arguments that the government had used and stated that increasing public deficit did not make sense during a period of prosperity, such as the one Argentina was living through, which was characterized by the absence of unemployment. Increased public expenditures were only legitimate with a countercyclical goal.[186] Moreover, Perón had argued, when he was the vice-president, that debt had not increased but had decreased, because the only real debt was the external one. The issue of domestic bonds, that is, internal debt, was, for Perón, tantamount to other forms of financing the Treasury (such as taxes) since both were ultimately paid by Argentine taxpayers. Perón's argument echoed David Ricardo's idea of the economic equivalence between an extraordinary tax (for a war, for instance) and a loan.[187] However, for some critics like Dino Jarach, that equivalence was spurious if the tax system was not equitable: "A fundamental premise of the theory...is public debt to be sufficiently democratized, that is, evenly distributed among categories of taxpayers, as to equalize tax burdens for paying the public debt and dividends obtained by bondholders."[188] In other words, if there was no correspondence between taxpayers and domestic creditors, the system was ultimately unfair.

Of course, the most insidious alternative to taxation was inflation. Inflation imposed dramatic redistributions of income within social groups and stimulated evasion. Between 1946 and 1955, annual inflation rates were over 10 percent (save in 1953 and 1954) and in 1949, 1951, and 1952, this rate crossed 30 percent. Yet, the relationship between inflation, tax evasion, and the decline of the income tax as a major source of revenue for the Argentine Treasury is a complex one. In 1953 and 1954, when the inflation rates were momentarily under control, evasion levels remained.[189] This shows that once tax evasion is allowed to go unchecked, it is difficult to contain at a later date. Moreover, the influence of inflation on tax compliance does not mean that inflation was the only reason for rise in evasion levels.

The problem of the perception of unfairness coupled with a lack of confidence in the state played an important role in the surge of evasion. In fact, inflation and the perception of government fairness might intertwine. Let us consider the case of middle-class retirees or people who obtain their main revenue from a fixed or difficult-to-adjust source. This last was the case of owners of urban property who did not have other major investments or incomes, save rents. They had to face not only the price rises but also government social policies. In order to solve the housing problem, Perón's administration continued the military government's policy of control of rents and prohibition of eviction, which limited the possibilities of the proprietors to adjust their incomes to inflation.

The complex system of discriminatory allowances, as it was mentioned above, created difficulties of horizontal equity among economic sectors. Merchants, professionals, or rural producers were among the nonfavoured groups and resorted to evasion as an economic strategy.[190] According to Central Bank estimations, the nondeclared income of independent professionals amounted to 51 percent in 1952 as well as in 1955.[191] The extension of deductions for the sake of industrialization aroused, to some extent, a sentiment of suspicion about tax policies—that they might be considered tax privileges. This was well expressed in the opposition discourse against tax reform in 1950. On that occasion, Frondizi challenged the income tax allowances for assets replacement: "Related to the problem of capitalization, it would be necessary to develop the concept of social capitalization and private capitalization in order to know to what extent the country is being capitalized in favour of the whole community or [to what extent it is being capitalized] in favour of some sector with some privileges within the national economy."[192]

Moreover, the professional and middle classes might have felt abandoned by the government in favor of both the working classes and the manufacturers. The 1950 reform, in particular, benefited those incomes that had been derived from participation in joint-stock companies, whereas middle- and upper-income groups that were not involved in corporate industry received the main burden of progressive taxation. Income tax might particularly affect middle-income groups. There were several reasons for this. First, inflation was pushing them up into higher tax brackets and making negligible the minimum nontaxable income. Thus, among the new taxpayers of the Peronist decade, those coming from the middle classes were a large majority.[193] Second, although nontaxable income and family allowances were updated during the decade, middle-income groups did not benefit as much as did the fourth-category taxpayers from this policy. Special deductions and allowances in the income tax were always addressed either to industry or to labor. Third, most of the fiscal measures were passed in the Congress without major discussion and without allowing the opposition to check government procedures. In tax matters—as in the case of other issues—Peronist rulers increasingly disregarded parliamentary procedures.[194]

This might have had momentous consequences, because some social sectors perceived Perón's rule as being increasingly authoritarian and illegal what undermined the legitimacy both of his tax and welfare policies. A good example is what Mariano Plotkin refers to as the "Cinema Agreement" between the administration and several movie theatre owners in Buenos Aires. Through this agreement, the entrepreneurs contributed with funds to the *Fundación Eva Perón* (a public-sponsored foundation in charge of some social policies addressed to popular and marginal sectors) whereas the government "forgot" to pursue an investigation on possible tax fraud against them and promised them future tax advantages.[195] The collection of monies and the provision of social benefits by a foundation that was personally linked to the president's wife should have had a deleterious effect on the trust of some sectors of the society regarding the neutrality of the state bureaucracy. This helps us to understand how taxes, even if moderate, were perceived as unbearable and were linked to privilege and to corruption.

Finally, Peronism meant a cultural and social subversion.[196] A plebeian élan took over Argentine streets, assaulting the traditional attitudes encapsulated in the phrase "oligarchy." Embedded in the antioligarchy rhetoric of the Peronist rank and file was a challenge to Argentine middle-class mores.

Of course, these are psychological factors that are difficult to assess and even to demonstrate. Nonetheless, some hints are worthy of mention. In a survey of Argentine taxation written in 1960 (with similar tax rates to those of 1955), Professors Surrey and Oldman asked professionals and businessmen about their opinions on tax rates. They concluded: "The feeling that the rates were too high seemed on the whole to to the entire tax, except the very top brackets. This attitude extended as well to corporate rates, though with somewhat less intensity." Moreover, the persons interviewed by the American professors manifested their "feeling that the trend toward investment incentives [as far as the income tax was concerned] may have gone too far."[197] These statements are related to 1960, when new incentives had been added to the income tax law, particularly regarding the import of agricultural machinery. Yet, the trend toward sector allowances was already fully developed under Perón's government. In any case, some middle-income groups seemed to hold particular grievances against government (mis)management of taxation affairs. The perception of unfairness was linked to a growing distrust of the government: "In the Perón regime, there was very little tax litigation since the taxpayers did not appear to trust the courts."[198] The justification of evasion and criticism of Peronist policies acquired moral overtones that, to some extent, reflected middle-class "moral economy." In 1956, after the coup that overthrew Perón, an Advisory Commission on Tax Issues, which was in charge of dealing with the problems created by the sheer volume of noncompliance and the possibility of a general tax amnesty, asserted:

> The disdain for principles, the power without balances, created a general scepticism about the convenience of complying with a series of laws whose inspiration in the common good was doubtful...The non-compliance of multiple and luxuriant rules was sometimes truly a self-defence or survival mechanism for the economic interests and, in general, a non-reprehensible solution, at least given the moral behaviour of the very rulers.[199]

Noncompliance was not only a matter that involved merchants, lawyers, or doctors. Large manufacturers, although receiving more lenient treatment, cheated as well and as much.[200] It is true that corporations, like wage earners, were submitted to automatic controls. However, the exemption of shares in individual tax returns probably encouraged a transformation of goods into corporate shares in order to launder nondeclared capital gains, benefiting both noncompliant taxpayers as well as corporations. Why did economic elites avoid tax payments? Of course, opportunity and inflation were powerful incentives to do so. The increase in the burden of taxation upon the upper-income groups might have encouraged further evasion. However, as has been shown, tax levels for big industrial businessmen were far from being unbearable, and deductions and allowances softened their burden even further. Moreover, manufacturers took advantage of the transfer of rural income to urban income and of the government's desire to encourage industrialization. As a result of these desires, the industrial sector obtained easy access to credit at low rates of interest, even negative ones, as the rates were inferior to the inflation rate.[201] Let us pose the question in a counterfactual fashion: Would the economic elites—or at least manufacturers—have boycotted the tax system if the government had taken a more cooperative or friendly stance? The most probable answer is: No. The apple of discord between Perón and business groups was not taxation policies (not even some industrial measures) but the empowerment of the working classes in the factories and the wage policies that were implemented by the government.[202] The policies displayed by Perón since he occupied the Secretariat of Labor modified the elites' image of the state and eroded the tax cooperation achieved in the 1930s.

The rural world demonstrated a permanent animosity toward the government as well. In November 1943, the military government carried out what Roy Hora has labeled an agrarian reform from above, by imposing agrarian contracts that favored tenants by freezing rents. These measures eroded landowners' revenues—that were trapped between almost fixed rents and inflation—and stimulated a broad movement of land sales and of massive access of tenants to ownership. Nonetheless, neither land tenants nor new farmers became attached to Peronist policies and from early on displayed the same grievances toward the industrialization-committed government as had been displayed by the traditional rural classes.[203]

The government was aware of this and of the vital role played by industrial entrepreneurs in a tax system that was based upon withdrawal at source and sworn returns. The cooperative bond was being broken by the entrepreneurs' distrust of the government. The government permanently sought to re-establish consent. This is well reflected in the suppression of certain activities that businesses could carry out as part of the tax system, which revealed the government's impotence in ensuring that the economic elites fulfil their role and/or an attempt to recover the trust of those elites by sending a message of confidence. In 1953, the Ministry of Finance eliminated the requirement of enclosing with their tax returns the accounting books of corporations with capital and reserves over 1 million pesos. The government argued that the resources and personnel that had been employed in the inspection of the accounting books were better used in the monitoring of taxpayers.[204] This was, to some extent, contradictory: revising book accounts was a way of monitoring taxpayers. But by exempting firms from showing their accountability, the government was sending a message of confidence to business groups. Inflation was playing a part as well, because what used to be medium-sized companies became the target of the law. Yet, the government could have updated the legal amount rather than make a general exception. In any case, big corporations could have easily complied with this disposition.

In 1954, the DGI launched a campaign aimed at recovering economic elites' cooperation.[205] The DGI summarized its efforts in this way: "The DGI...is making an intense effort to approach the people...It has found in the mentioned economic forces an efficient cooperation."[206] The mentioned economic forces were the representatives of the CGE. Its cooperation was a practical one: economic elites helped the government to collect income and other "declared" taxes: "Diverse associations such as the Stock Market, the Rural Society, the Association of Real State Owners, and the Center of Grocers of this city; the Chamber of Commerce, Industry and Navigation of San Isidro...offered on that occasion their premises to receive the tax returns."[207] To a limited extent, the state was "delegating power" with the aim of legitimizing taxation.[208] Allowances and economic incentives were not enough to dispel the economic elites' fears.

The Peronist's advanced social policy provoked the economic elites' animosity, both in the cities and in the countryside. This ended with the period of cooperation between the state and the upper classes that characterized the 1930s and inaugurated a period of bitter class conflicts. In addition to this, the working class, the main beneficiary of Perón's policies, was excluded from the income tax system and showed little regard for taxation issues, although it paid for most of its benefits through the social security system. Very soon, the system was perceived as unfair by those who did not have any other alternative but to pay, or by those who did not dare to take the risk of evasion.

Ultimately, taxation could not be used as a redistributive mechanism because wealth taxes depended on the willingness of the middle and the upper-income groups to cooperate. Furthermore, it is far from clear that the Peronist government had the political willingness, the social support, and the ideological framework to make taxes the nerve center of the state. The government's unwillingness to create a mass income tax reflects well the reluctance to tax workers and to use the income tax as the pillar of a welfare state. Moreover, a step forward to greater progressiveness conspired against the ideal society (one without class conflict) that Perón aimed to build in Argentina. As Louise Doyon has said of the right to strike, taxation as a distributive weapon was incompatible with Peronist fundamental philosophy.[209]

Chapter 4

Into the Labyrinth (1955–1976)

The conflict between economic efficiency and a fair income distribution has never been sharper in Argentina than during 1955-66. Unfortunately, even as the need for reconciling efficiency and equity became more acute, the main instrument that could be used for that task, the tax and expenditure system of the central government, became weaker[1]

After the overthrow of Juan Domingo Perón in September 1955, and until the return of Perón himself to power in 1973, Argentina's tax policy makers tried out several devices in order to increase revenues for the Treasury and to help in economic development. The tax system, which had been designed between 1932 and 1946, crumbled, but no major fiscal reform was implemented. In spite of a rhetoric that emphasized Peronist corruption and deviant fiscal policy, the different governments—Radicals or military—that ruled the country between 1955 and 1973 showed remarkable continuities with Perón's regimen. The period was characterized by a struggle and alternation in power between those who strove for the end of interventionism and a greater role for markets in the economy and those who believed that state intervention was needed in order to advance the process of industrialization in the country. To some extent, the latter were following the Peronist industrial creed, even if some of them, such as the so-called *desarrollistas* (developmentalist), encouraged a quite different distribution of wealth between capital and labor or emphasized the need for a different, capital-intensive type of industry.[2] In a lax sense, most politicians and economists were *desarrollistas*, that is, they thought that a powerful industrial sector was needed in order to make Argentina a modern nation. They believed taxation to be an instrument to promote industrial development and, at least in theory, committed themselves to the use of taxes as redistributive tools.[3]

Taxation reflected the economic and political difficulties that Argentina faced during those decades. The state's financial troubles became endemic as a result of the stop-and-go economic cycle. Every period of industrial growth was followed by an economic slump that was caused by the scarcity of foreign exchange and the monetary devaluation that was aimed at recovering competitiveness in the world market. The unstable economic cycle sharpened the distribution conflict among social groups and this, in turn, reinforced inflationary pressures.[4] Policy makers often reacted in a chaotic way, creating emergency taxes, adding new burdens to the same sources, or adjusting tax rates to inflation without considering equity issues. New taxes and levies multiplied, while old taxes survived. The result was an intricate palimpsest of rules and practices, growing and untamed tax evasion, and no improvement for the Treasury.

This does not mean that economists' and politicians' diagnoses were always flawed or that their medicine was completely inappropriate, but rather that they faced structural obstacles that were difficult to surmount. The first of these was high rates of inflation, which eroded tax collection, stimulated evaders to defer their payments, and undermined public confidence in the state. Second—and related to the first feature—the social and political conundrum that was created by the attempt to exclude Peronism and working-class representatives from the political arena, while maintaining social peace and economic growth, made the government structurally weak, and inflation became a feasible political alternative.

Argentine politics between 1955 and 1976 were characterized by intense instability and conflict. Military and civilian regimes alternatively attempted to govern a mobilized and fragmented society. In order to help the reader to follow the present narrative, a brief summary is needed. Between 1955 and 1958, a military government replaced the Peronist regime and tried to establish new rules for the country. These goals were unattainable due to the internal fractures of the ruling coalition and to the opposition of important sectors of the civil society. In 1958, Arturo Frondizi, heading a dissident faction of the Radical Party, the Intransigent Civic Radical Union (UCRI), won the first elections after Perón's overthrow. Perón and the Peronist Party were banned from the electoral contest, which would become a permanent feature of the electoral processes since that moment. Democracy was flawed in Argentina since its restoration. The discussion about the place of Peronism in Argentina political life was one the most contentious issues of the period and one of the reasons for the constant instability. Another source of instability was the permanent interference of the military in politics. Civilian rulers were always under the threat of a coup d'état. In 1962, Frondizi was removed from power by a coup, although the military allowed a civilian, José María Guido, to assume the presidency. In 1963, Arturo Illia, leading the main branch of the Radical Party, the Civic Radical Union of the People (UCRP) won the presidential election with only 25 percent of the votes. Again, Peronists were excluded from the contest. In 1966, Illia's elected government was overthrown by a new military coup. Juan Carlos Onganía's dictatorship, inaugurated in 1966, was an original one in the nation's history: the new rulers did not present themselves to society as provisional ones, but they aimed to transform Argentine structures deeply, which meant that they had to remain in power as long as the country needed them. Nonetheless, since 1969, social mobilization and economic troubles challenged the military regime. Onganía was replaced by other military men and, finally, amid growing economic chaos and political violence, the army was forced to transfer power to civilians in 1973, when a Peronist coalition won the—now truly democratic—election and opened the door to Perón's return as president in September. However, the old caudillo was unable to restore stability, and the democratic experience ended in a tragic way in 1976 with a new coup d'état that inaugurated the bloodiest dictatorship in Argentine history. The demise of democratic rule was accompanied by political violence, social mobilization, hyperinflation, and enormous fiscal imbalances.[5]

During the whole period, social and political conflict made the state an arena of dispute among social actors and not a neutral field. In turn, this eroded public trust and, therefore, tax compliance. Every attempted tax reform faced phenomenal obstacles posed by untamed inflation and permanent political instability.

The tax creed developed during the 1940s and under Perón's rule survived largely untouched for most of the period, and very few claimed that indirect taxes might be as fair as was the income tax or that it was at least more efficient. Moreover, the tax system was becoming so complex that nobody dared to reform it, and rulers fretted about the economic and fiscal consequences of a major overhaul. Yet, this does not mean that nothing changed during these years. The frailty of the Argentine tax regime and the economic problems made critics of the idea of progressive taxation more outspoken than they had been in the past. The protracted social and political conflict and economic instability subtly but deeply undermined the basis of the progressive Argentine tax system. The trust among taxpayers vanished, and the working class began to lose its unique position within the Argentine tax discourse as the most deserved social group. At the same time, noncompliance was increasingly legitimized by Argentine society. Without this legitimacy, we cannot understand the collapse of the fiscal system since the 1970s. This chapter explores the process of unravelling the Argentine tax system after Peronism, with attention being paid to issues such as evasion and inflation.

Times of Inflation...Times of Evasion

Inflation became endemic in Argentina in the aftermath of World War II.[6] It became part of day-to-day life and, therefore, most actors learnt to adapt their behavior to price movements by developing complex mechanisms of indexation, by postponing payments, including tax payments, or by reducing their cash assets. Between 1945 and 1976, prices went up by over 10 percent every year, except in 1953, 1954, and 1969. During some years, prices skyrocketed: in 1959, the inflation rate reached 129.5 percent; in 1975, prices for consumers rose by 182.4 percent, and in 1976, they skyrocketed by an unbelievable 444 percent.[7]

The relationship between inflation and tax collection was a major concern for contemporaries.[8] This concern was embedded in the political and academic debates of the epoch, particularly in Latin America. One of the sides of these debates was the controversy between the so-called monetarist and the structuralist schools on the origins of inflation. To put it simply, monetarists believed that the monetary policy was enough to correct price movements, whereas the structuralists thought that inflation was the result of deep economic bottlenecks that had to be removed before dealing with prices themselves. Of course, both approaches implied different views on issues such as state intervention in the economy, taxes, or redistributive policies.

Structuralists—who defended the state's enhanced involvement in economic and industrial development or who even advanced distributive policies—recognized the links between inflation and the weak performance of tax collection. Nonetheless, inflation might have been legitimized to some extent by resorting to economic theory. Keynes's theory that under certain circumstances, public deficit was preferable to unemployment, was widely discussed—and vulgarized—in Latin America and in other underdeveloped regions.[9] This does not mean that structuralist authors refused to recognize inflation as an evil and taxation as a possible way to tackle it but, rather, that both inflation and the unsatisfactory performance of the tax system had deep roots in Latin American social and economic structures. In an influential conference on Latin American tax policies, the famous British tax expert Nicholas Kaldor, stated that "Latin-America countries, far more than other countries of the free world, have a tremendous dead burden to carry in the form of maintaining the 'idle rich'" and proposed "to tax effectively the benefits derived from property ownership, either in the form of income, in the form of capital gains, or in the form of any other benefits which the ownership of disposable wealth confers."[10]

Many Argentine economists shared this view. Taxation was not a mere remedy against inflation but part of the needed structural reform of Latin American societies. First, inequality was one of the major problems. One of the main goals of tax policies and government expenditure was income distribution.[11] Second, Latin American countries, and Argentina among them, needed important infrastructures to continue their steps toward development. This was the best way to curb rising prices:

> I think that insofar as it is possible to increase tax returns or other government revenues, it is convenient to do so, but great care must be taken that the reduction of government expenditures does not imply the postponement...of those government expenditures which are investments...fundamental to development...The elimination of rigidities or bottlenecks is...a way to reduce basic inflationary pressures.[12]

These economists emphasized that taxes did not work adequately due to the lack of cooperation of entrepreneurs and the upper classes with tax collectors. Tax collections were falling down not only because inflation or high rates were encouraging evasion but also because of the lack of commitment of the well-to-do classes.[13]

Liberal critics asserted that inflation depended on governmental expenditure and that budget parsimony was therefore the solution. Inflation opened avenues of criticism to the idea of graduate taxation. In the above-mentioned international conference, another foreign expert suggested that in a period of high inflation, income taxation might be the wrong solution: "In an inflationary period, the greatest danger of a massive application of the income tax is that it becomes very rapidly a wage tax." According to this analyst, Argentina (or Brazil) already had a high level of taxation, but a "distorted pattern of the tax structure," public expenditure, and inflation were damaging economic activities.[14]

This criticism was also appearing in Argentina among some economists and entrepreneurs. Some businessmen, lawyers, and intellectuals complained that higher rates were affecting moderate incomes due to price increases: "Taxpayers pass from one bracket to another led by inflation, without their real incomes being any higher."[15] Some economists argued that high marginal rates were encouraging evasion. Therefore, reducing progressiveness within the income tax structure could help the government to recover taxpayers' compliance.[16] In some cases, those who considered that tax burdens had reached a limit emphasized that this produced flagrant inequities by favoring labor incomes versus those from the middle and the upper classes.[17] Nonetheless, the idea that labor was an undeserved privileged sector within Argentine tax structure was not widely accepted.

Most governments resisted pressures to modify the tax structure and argued that income tax and other forms of progressive taxation should be maintained as a means to constraint private expenditure and, therefore, as a palliative for rising prices. For the critics, taxation itself was a problem, and the solution to inflation was to cut government expenditures, particularly "unjustified" ones.[18]

Structuralists (interventionists) and monetarists (liberals) agreed on several points. Inflation encouraged evasion and distorted the tax structure. Therefore, both emphasized that inflation provoked inequities and demanded important public measures to halt the price boom. Despite the success of Keynesian or developmental ideas in Argentina, inflation was perceived as a real problem, at least since the implementation of the Plan of Stabilization of 1958, and even before that date.[19] Not only did those who favored monetary restrictions, but also those whose primary concern was development, realized that the rising of prices was undermining both equity and the idea of the tax system as a tool for redistribution.

Inflation affected tax behavior by encouraging taxpayers to defer their payments. However, the connections between inflation and the failure of a tax system, particularly one based upon graduated progressive tools, are not evident prima facie. Richard Mallon and Juan Sourrouille estimated that there was a strong negative correlation between inflation rates and public revenues, but price movements only explained a 13 percent of the total variation in state's revenues.[20] Although difficult to calculate, income tax evasion rates in Argentina were around 50 percent since at least 1952 or 1953, whereas the performance of prices was rather erratic. In 1952, the inflation rate was 38 percent, and the evasion rate reached 49 percent. In 1953, while rising prices halted at 4 percent, income tax evasion remained

49 percent. The story was similar in 1959 and 1960: in 1959, income tax evasion reached 63 percent, whereas the inflation rate was over 129 percent. In 1960, inflation was temporarily controlled and reduced to 27 percent; however, tax evasion still reached 59 percent.[21] Between 1960 and 1964, evasion rates of the income tax fluctuated between 46 percent and 54 percent, that is, they were similar to the previous period.[22] Since 1966 or 1967, evasion increased and again reached rates that were over 75 percent.[23] These figures also show that once evasion reached a certain level it had an autonomous impulse and that the betterment of other variables, such as inflation, was not enough to correct that impulse.

There seemed to be a significant link between evasion and economic activity. In 1962 and 1963, rates of evasion were at their highest, coinciding with a period of deep recession. They improved slightly with an economic recovery in 1964.[24] Nonetheless, this was not always a functioning relationship. From 1953 to 1955, economic production grew, and evasion rates did not drop. In fact, in 1955, while national income increased, income tax evasion achieved its historical peak. In 1956, tax evasion decreased as a result of political—rather than economic—circumstances.

The complexity of the linkages among different variables is well reflected in the relationship between tax collections and economic activity in Argentina. Tax collections were never high in Argentina when compared to the international standards. In 1960, the total (federal, state, and local) tax collection in Argentina amounted to 19 percent of the GDP. In Brazil, it represented a 23 percent, in the United States, 25 percent, and in Sweden, 37 percent.[25] Furthermore, since 1952, Argentine tax collections began to decline or, at least, stagnated when compared to the growth of national wealth. Only in 1970 did federal tax collections seem to once again achieve 10 percent of the GDP after over a decade of stagnation. Nonetheless, this was an ephemeral illusion, one that was not related "to the adjustment of the tax system to the rhythm of economic activity, but the result of...temporary taxes in order to normalize the situation of taxpayers."[26] In 1971 and 1972, GDP rose, whereas tax collections declined. According to the DGI's own estimations, the Pearson Correlation Coefficient between GDP growth and tax collection growth between 1960 and 1973 was 0.72, which indicated a lack of elasticity of the tax system in response to income growth in the country.[27] This contrasts with the contemporary international experience, at least in the industrialized countries, where tax revenues (excluding social security taxes) climbed in regard to the national income.[28]

Inflation, economic growth, and tax collections influenced one another in complex and often indirect ways. As far as taxation was concerned, the taxpayers' decision to evade their fiscal obligations was not only an economic one but also a political and moral one, based upon ideas of justice, equity, and trust. Inflation influenced Argentine tax structure, but its influence was rather indirect, complex, and not unidirectional.

Liberals complained against excessive public expenditure, but, in truth, governments spent less money in the years from 1955 to 1973 than they did during the last years of Perón's rule. Perón's administration spent around 30 percent of GDP. Frondizi reduced this proportion to 25 percent. This was cut again during 1962 and 1963 due to the impact of economic recession. Illia's government raised public expenditures to 26 percent, and the military government that succeeded him cut it back to 23 percent. Perón's return to the government in 1973 expanded public disbursements, which reached 30 percent of the GDP in 1975.[29] Although public expenditure did not increase, the state was unable to obtain enough resources to meet its needs. Between 1956 and 1966, the central government obtained between 65 percent and 75 percent of their general revenue through taxes.[30] This meant that around 30 percent of federal income came from sources other than taxation. Moreover, this was not the entire picture. General revenue was just one part of the budget. There were other items in the budget; in some cases these were earmarked revenues, such as the sale of bonds, credits, and the so-called "special accounts," which were derived from assets and debt and not from tax collection. In 1962, for instance, these revenues represented 12 percent of total federal income.[31] Besides, between 1955 and 1976, the fiscal balance was always negative. In a period of recession, like 1958 or 1962–1963, it represented around 7 to 8 percent of the GDP. In 1975, the public deficit reached 12 percent of the GDP.[32] To make things worse, the Social Security system's surplus (which had allowed Peronist government to use it as a source of revenue through the forced sale of public debt) vanished. Since 1959, the system had a permanent deficit, which forced the Treasury to transfer monies to pensions.[33]

Hence, fiscal and tax performances forced Argentine governments to finance themselves through loans—either from the domestic or the international market—or with the support of international agencies like the IMF, or through the printing machine. Debt became an important part of every annual budget: in 1957, the annual payment of debt represented 0.6 percent of total state revenues;in 1959, it represented 1.1 percent; in 1962, it climbed up to 7.6 percent of total revenues; and in 1964, it reached 9.6 percent, due to the economic recession of 1962–1963 that depressed tax collections. Since 1964, the payment of public debt in every budget was cut, but it always represented around 5 percent of total revenues. In 1972, it again crossed 7 percent and since then, it boomed.[34]

Thus, tax collections fell behind the GDP in the third quarter of the twentieth century, and Argentine governments found alternative and potentially risky sources of revenue. But, how was the internal structure of the tax system affected by the rise of noncompliance, inflation, and the sharp economic cycle? Was evasion making the Argentine tax system more regressive?[35]

The impact of price movements on a tax performance is related to the tax's elasticity. In theory, as far as collection is concerned, progressive taxes can more adequately resist the effects of price movements than can, say, a tax on consumption. However, different taxes perform in different ways, and it is difficult to establish a general pattern for both direct and indirect levies. Graduated taxes, such as the income tax, are supposed to be automatic stabilizers, that is, they are able to counterbalance the economic cycle. Hence, in the case of rising prices, the income tax should absorb part of the impact through the automatic increase in tax collections due to the fact that higher monetary incomes fall "naturally" into higher brackets of rates. However, in Argentina, untamed inflation and the slow decline of progressive taxation were parallel processes. Oscar Oszlak argued that the counter cycle effect of progressive taxation becomes diluted when inflation rates are remarkably high and the number of taxpayers is small.[36] As we know, this number was not large, and it probably shrank as a result of mounting evasion. Moreover, income tax evasion should have distorted equity within the tax structure, encouraging the government to seek monies through regressive taxes or through non-tax resources such as debt or inflation.

Inflation might have a profound impact in the internal structure of taxation in other ways. Rising prices could have made all taxes, direct and indirect, more regressive. Lower- income families were pushed into higher brackets within the income tax scheme and were therefore forced to pay higher rates. In the case of sales taxes and domestic duties, inflation eroded the revenues coming from specific duties—which used to affect luxury or middle-class goods—whereas ad valorem duties were more elastic to price movements and were therefore able to adjust to inflation.[37] In this case, inflation caused the same effect in both direct and indirect taxes. Inflation could also be a stimulus to a shift in revenue sources. Despite the assumption about the elasticity of progressive taxes, these were particularly prone to evasion, and therefore governments could search for alternative modes of collection that were more invisible, less based on voluntary cooperation, and more regressive.

We can compare progressive and regressive taxation between 1955 and 1973. I will assume that the income tax, capital gains tax, tax on extraordinary profits, and others—such as the emergency tax or the tax on the sales of cars—are progressive taxes, whereas consumption or sales tax are assumed to be regressive taxes, save the tax on the sales of cars. This is, of course, a simplification. Some taxes on luxury items—such as the above-mentioned tax on the sales of cars—might be considered progressive. Moreover, some analysts regarded taxes on exports as progressive. Nonetheless, I believe this simplification offers a reasonable point of departure.

Regressive taxes represented over 60 percent of the total tax collection during most of this period. In some years, the gap between revenues coming from regressive instruments and those coming from progressive ones was reduced. Thus, in 1956, the proportion of revenues coming from direct taxes increased by 4 percent.[38] This was due to the "emergency tax," the surtax on the upper echelons of the income tax scheme, which reached almost 5 percent of the total collection that year. It is possible that upper income brackets—who were the main payers of this new tax—felt that the new government of the *Revolución Libertadora* was more trustworthy than was the old one of Perón, and they therefore showed a cooperative stance. In fact, tax evasion decreased in 1956.[39]

In 1959 and 1960, collections that were derived from progressive taxes reached a record high of the period, representing 40 percent of total tax revenues. This was, to some extent, related to the temporary success of the stabilization plan carried out by the Frondizi's administration and the control of inflation. However, an interpretation of this surge of progressive taxation is rather difficult. In 1959, the main factor responsible for the success of progressive taxation was income tax. (See figure 4.1) Yet in 1960, income tax fell slightly, and the main novelty was the tax on revaluation, a duty on the companies that were allowed to revaluate their assets in order to adjust their tax payments to inflation. Because industrial companies paid this tax, it might be considered a progressive one. But ultimately, this tax was compensation for an enormous deduction given to corporations and other firms. Most entrepreneurs gladly welcomed the measure and, according to Oscar Oszlak, this deduction might have cost the Treasury ten times the monies collected by the tax on revaluation. The size of the deduction is well

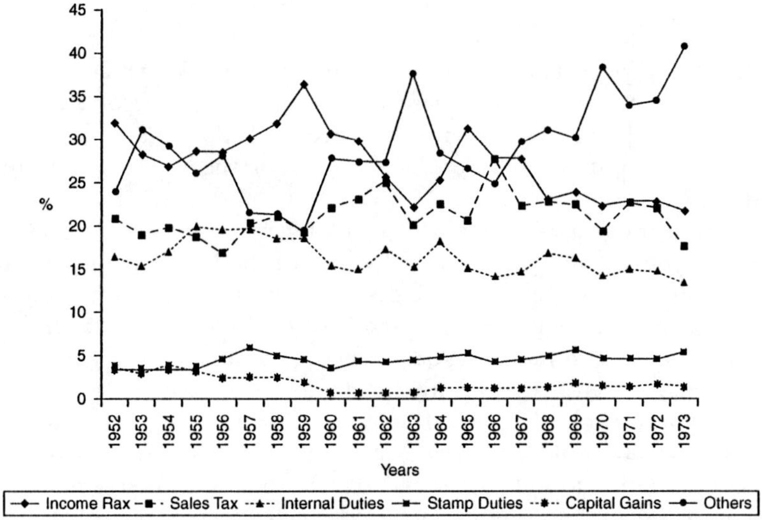

Figure 4.1 Distribution of taxes collected by the DGI, 1952–1973
Source: *BDGI* (1969), 416 and (1974), 789. (Income tax includes both, personal income tax and corporation tax. Social security contributions are not included).

reflected by the fact that the tax on revaluation reached over 5 percent of the total tax collection in 1960. Moreover, in spite of the lag between prices and fixed capital values, these compensations did not take into consideration the fact that inflation had not curtailed profits.[40] In turn, the loss of revenue caused by these deductions was a new impulse for inflation. This system was again implemented in 1967.

In some years, as in 1962 and 1963, regressive taxes achieved almost 70 percent of total tax revenues. Hence, economic depression would have deepened the unfairness of the tax system. In 1962 and 1963, in particular, income tax suffered a decline, whereas sales tax collections accounted for the same amount of money as did income tax. From 1964 onward, progressive taxes showed an erratic performance. Economic recovery and yet another emergency tax helped them to produce over 40 percent of tax revenues in 1965 and 1967. But the main factor behind this recovery of progressive taxation was the income tax performance between 1964 and 1967. This was related to a more effective tax collection during Illia's administration, and during Minister Krieger Vasena's tenure in office under Ongania's rule as well as to Krieger Vasena's policy of control of inflation. However, neither income tax nor overall progressive taxation maintained a sustainable recovery, and since 1968, both declined.

Since 1970, the inflationary surge further eroded progressive taxation. Inflation was getting out of control, and indirect taxes had the advantage of responded more quickly than did direct taxes to the movement of prices.[41] Therefore, the system had become acutely regressive when Perón returned to power in 1973. To a large extent, this was the result of the weak performance of the income tax during the 1970s.

Progressive taxes followed the turbulent Argentine economic cycle, the stop-and-go. As in the case of inflation, it is difficult to establish a single trend for the period as far as progressive taxation was concerned. Nonetheless, the crisis of 1962–1963 and the decline of income taxation since 1968 seemed to announce the demise of progressive taxation (See figure 4.1). In any case, as shown, taxes were increasingly losing their significance for financing the state, and the overall result should have been even more regressive. Furthermore, a growing deficit meant that social expenditures was increasingly difficult to expand or even to maintain, which affected the overall progressive features of budgetary policies.

Federico Herschel and Julio Rossi, in an article published in 1965, made a sophisticated calculation of the incidence of taxes on wage earners and nonwage earners between 1953 and 1961. They reached the conclusion that social security taxes were the key factor in making the Argentine tax system a regressive one, that is, in making wage earners the main taxpayers in the nation.[42] In 1955, social security taxes, together with other similar duties (such as the tax on apprenticeship) represented 6.9 percent of the GDP. In 1960, they declined to 4.2 percent, but then climbed up again in 1965 to 5 percent. In 1975, social security taxes represented 4.6 percent of the GDP. This was well over the income tax, which hardly achieved a 1 percent of the national product.[43] Herschel and Rossi, like many other economists, assumed that employers' contributions to social security funds could be passed to workers and that it was therefore a regressive tax.[44]

Nonetheless, the main problems caused by social security taxes did not arise from their regressive features. In fact, despite their importance, social security taxes as a percentage of GDP fell from the levels that had been reached during Perón's administration.[45] This was related to the growing deficit of the system. Under Perón, thanks to full employment and a large young population, the state used retirees' funds to finance itself by forcing them to accept public bonds. Social security taxes are earmarked taxes, and therefore, once the payments of pensions exceeded the collection, fuelling monies into the Treasury through this system became increasingly difficult. The deficit of the system was causing serious problems, because a larger generation of workers was retiring. To some extent, Perón's policy of financing public expenditures with retirees' savings was to blame for the situation. But this was also the result of inflation, as pensions could not keep pace with rising prices.

In March 1962, a demonstration of retirees, the so-called *Marcha del Hambre* (Demonstration of the hungry) in Plaza Once—a popular square in downtown Buenos Aires—-voiced the complaint that "the main cause for the instability of the [pension] funds is the enormous debt of the state that not only has withdrawn monies from the system but it was not making regularly its payments as employer."[46] Public debt and inflation were related. According to Manuel Belnicoff, a congressman from the UCRP who became the main speaker for the retirees, "pension funds are forced to invest their resources in state bonds. In that way, the assets of the funds dramatically suffer from the consequences of inflation."[47] Belnicoff, like most economists, believed that the system was ultimately a tax on wages, which made it an "anti-economic" one.[48]

The problems of the Argentine pensions system were the result of various factors: inflation, the ageing process, and the beginning of an economic slump that was causing serious trouble among Argentine entrepreneurs. Already at the end of 1961, the secretary of economy recognized in the Chamber of Deputies the alarming level reached by the debt of private firms to both the DGI and the social security funds: "It is known that many companies do not belong to their apparent owners but indirectly to the state because they accumulate an enormous debt with the DGI and huger ones with pension funds."[49]

But, unlike what most economists assumed, what made the social security tax system illegitimate was not its regressive features nor its inefficiency, but the deficit itself. In fact, Argentina was not exceptional in this. As Webber and Wildavsky remarked, the social security tax was a regressive tool if one considered it to be a tax. If one considered social security as a transfer of income, the picture was quite different.[50] Representative Belnicoff's popularity was not related to his invective against the regressive feature of payroll taxes but to his defence of retirees' incomes and his proposals for advances of money to the pensioners.[51] In 1967, the social security system was reformed, cutting pensions and benefits. The national government assumed control of pension funds in order to tackle this deficit. Between 1970 and 1975, the number of retirees who received the minimum pension climbed from 30 percent of the total to 80 percent of the total. That meant that the government was saving a lot of money;

but it also indicated that the rule of proportionality—the idea that the retiree should receive a reasonable proportion of their salary after retirement—was being broken.[52]

For most people, justice, in the case of pensions—and discussing progressiveness is, in the end, discussing justice—was not about who pays for but who deserves it, that is, about living with dignity after a life of hard work. If Argentine workers were not being paid a reasonable amount of money after their retirement, and they were forced to continue working, social security contributions were useless, and an essential part of the social contract was falling apart.

As in the case of social security contributions, export taxes too played an ambiguous role within the Argentine tax structure. Since the early twentieth century, Argentine governments had resorted to the withdrawal of revenues from exports, as a temporary device, in order to reduce fiscal imbalances. President Yrigoyen, who faced an important deficit in the aftermath of World War I and was unable to pass an income tax law, decided to levy on rural exports. The 1930s policy of control of foreign currency and Perón's IAPI were mechanisms designed to tax rural commodities. Argentina was a successful exporter of rural goods until the 1930s; the Pampas enjoyed comparative advantage in several temperate productions, and a tax on exports was supposedly easy to transfer to foreign consumers; hence taxes on exports were an attractive option for governments in dire straits. But these taxes affected the most productive sector, and therefore they threatened to kill the goose laid lays the golden eggs. Most critics insisted on this point and proposed alternative ways of financing the Treasury. However, between 1956 and 1970, export taxes were maintained and even increased. Export taxes became critical in some moments of economic adjustment, such as during the application of the Plan of Stabilization under Minister Alsogaray and Frondizi's, during the economic slump of 1962 or during the anti-inflationary policies of Minister Krieger Vasena between 1967 and 1968. During some years, taxes on exports represented an important collection for the Treasury. In 1959, export taxes amounted to 16 percent of the national government's total tax revenue.[53] Since Argentina's main commodities and consumer goods were the same, the movements of export and internal prices were strongly correlated. That meant that a tax on export might be a useful tool in the fight against inflation. For instance, in 1967 and 1968, facing increasing costs—due, in part, to the tax on exports—and declining profits, ranchers decided to sell stock. In turn, the massive sale of animals depressed beef prices in the domestic market and helped Krieger Vasena's price control measures.[54] Thus, in addition to their significance as sources of revenue, export withdrawals were also maintained as an economic tool. Yet, since 1969, domestic prices for the rural goods that were affected by the tax grew faster than did international prices, and therefore the duty became useless and was progressively cut.[55]

There were other issues at stake as far as taxes on exports were concerned. In 1955, in the period from 1958 to 1959, and again in 1967, export taxes accompanied a major devaluation of the Argentine peso. The goal was to make Argentine exports more competitive in the international market in order to obtain foreign currency to face the delicate situation of the balance of payments. This was part of the well-known stop-and-go economic cycle. As the Argentine industrial sector—the engine of growth and employment during most of the period—was based on the domestic market and therefore was a net importer, the level of foreign currency in the country tended to vanish during the periods of growth. The upturn of industrial growth was halted every few years by the lack of resources to import. At this point, the governments—mainly if the Ministry of Economy was in the hands of a liberal thinker—used to adjust the economy, that is, attempt to reduce Argentine aggregate demand to cool down the economy.

But devaluations, by making Argentine imports more expensive and exports cheaper, had other possible consequences. First, they might reinforce inflation, due to the price increases in imports and the fact that the instability of the peso made foreign currency, particularly the US dollar, part of the domestic references as far as prices were concerned. Second, devaluation meant a transfer of resources from the urban to the rural activities, from industrialists and urban workers to landowners and rural labor. Hence, a devaluation was perceived as causing distribute movements in favor of *estancieros.* In that sense, a tax on exports was both a barrier against inflation and a compensation for the transfer of income to the landed classes. In most cases, the tax on export was only a partial compensation.[56] Therefore, a tax on exports could be presented as a progressive device. This was the opinion of Herschel and Rossi. Because the tax reduced the profits of rural exporters, it helped to reduce the prices of agricultural goods in the domestic market. It was a tax on rural producers, and it helped to alleviate the burden of rising prices on consumers.[57] Nonetheless, taxes on exports were emergency devices rather than a permanent feature of the Argentine tax system. Using it as a normal tax and not as a special compensation would have meant preventing efficiency from playing any role in the design of the Argentine tax schema. The

Argentine tax system still had other instruments that made it possible to defend egalitarian principles, and it did not represent a direct attack on economic efficiency as did the tax on exports.

The Income Tax: The End of Trust

Income tax was still the main progressive tool within the Argentine fiscal system.[58] Between 1955 and 1964, income tax collections fell in terms of constant prices.[59] Income tax gradually lost its significance in total tax collections since 1952 (see figure 4.1). At the beginning of this period, income tax represented around 30 percent of total DGI collection. At the end of the period, income tax accounted for 22 percent of the tax revenues, which meant that the Ministry of Economy and the DGI had resorted to alternatives types of taxation.

This picture is even clearer if taxes on foreign trade, that is, customs duties, export withholdings, and other similar duties are included. Whereas in 1970, revenues from income tax were almost equivalent to revenues from taxes on foreign trade, both systems diverged since then. In 1975, taxes on foreign trade accounted for 30 percent of total revenues, whereas the income tax amounted to only 9 percent. In 1976, the income tax recovered slightly, but customs duties revenues grew at a faster pace, reaching 40 percent of the total collection. The performance of the sales tax was not more impressive than that of the income tax, and the final surge of 1975 and 1976 was due to the implementation of the VAT.[60] To some extent, this was an omen of the times to come. Argentina's tax regime was acquiring new features: foreign trade, as in the past, was becoming the fulcrum of the Treasury, supported in this new epoch by the VAT.

So far, we are assuming the income tax to be a progressive tax. But how were the progressive features of the income tax affected by inflation and evasion? One of the advantages of the income tax and of other graduated taxes is their elasticity, that is, their automatic response to national income variations, that is, when national wealth increases, tax collections must increase as well without any modification in the rates. However, evasion and delays in the payment of the tax might alter this basic feature of the income tax and thereby contribute to an increase in public deficit.[61] This was the case in Argentina during this period. Brodersohn demonstrated that income tax's income-elasticity for 1963 was less than one, that is, that the income tax was unable to tap into the increase in income.[62] In fact, this might reflect the loss of progressiveness in the working of the tax.[63]

Income tax did not perform quite differently from other taxes and, on some occasions, it performed even better. Tax collection seemed to be sensitive to the combination of high inflation and economic slump. Thus, in 1959, tax collection fell largely behind the national income growth. Nonetheless, the income tax performance was not particularly weak. In 1958, income tax represented 31.76 percent of the total tax collection, whereas in 1959, it amounted to 36.33 percent. Income tax revenues would not achieve this figure again. That same year, inflation reached its highest historical peak before the 1970s. A comparison with the sales tax is revealing. In 1958, sales tax accounted for 21.06 percent of total tax revenues, whereas in 1959, it dropped to 19.23 percent. Further comparisons are equally revealing. In 1963, in the midst of a deep depression, income tax revenues fell from 25 percent to 22 percent of total collections, whereas the sales tax dropped from 25 percent to 20 percent. In 1964 and 1965, income tax recovered faster than did other taxes. In other words, despite evasion and low elasticity, the income tax proved to be more resilient than did the other taxes. This might explain to some extent why governments refused to radically reform income tax. My argument is not that income tax was elastic or that evasion was not affecting it, but that its performance was relatively better than was the performance of other taxes—at least between 1955 and 1966.

This situation changed after 1966 or 1967, when income tax collection suffered from a sudden decline. In 1967, income tax revenues represented 27 percent of total tax collections. In 1968 it declined to 22 percent, and it did not go back to its former position during this entire period. In 1965, income tax collection represented 2.4 percent of the GDP; in 1970, it was only 2.1 percent; and in 1975, this figure fell to a meagre 0.8 percent.[64] Significantly, sales tax did not compensate for the loss in income tax. In 1966, revenues coming from the sales tax reached 27 percent of total tax collection. In 1967, they declined to 22 percent, and in 1975, they represented only 9 percent of total tax revenues for the national Treasury. Both the sales tax and the income tax were ready for reform.

Evasion was affecting income tax collection, and as has been said, inflation could have stimulated taxpayers to evade taxes. But in order to accurately interpret the performance of the income tax, we need to pay attention to other factors, such as the burden that the income tax represented for taxpayers, and, mainly, to the taxpayers themselves, that is, who paid the income tax? This issue is also related to inflation. Inflation might distort income tax incidence and therefore alter taxpayers' perceptions about the equity or fairness of the duty.

In that sense, inflation was not only an economic incentive to evade taxes but also offered moral grounds for noncompliance.[65] This is particularly relevant in the case of a tax, such as the income tax, which is based upon semi-voluntary compliance. Of course, some groups are more prone to tax evasion than are others, and some people perceived unfairness more deeply than did others. Distortions in the income tax arose out of different situations. For example, an inflation-related increase of income would move the taxpayer to a higher bracket and therefore they would be forced to pay a higher marginal rate of the income tax without having a real income increase. Also, some groups are better equipped to resist inflation than are others, even if their incomes are similar—for instance, to enjoy greater lags in the tax payment.[66] Hence, horizontal equity problems became more apparent. Moreover, in order to combat both inflation and economic disarray, the government introduced measures that aggravated distortions and inequities. For instance, increased marginal tax rates or the minimum nontaxable income—in order to tackle the fall in collections and to adjust tax rates to prices movements—might in turn create new groups of winners and losers and therefore renovate the animadversion toward the tax. Furthermore, whereas the different governments needed to maintain collections, they were also concerned about the necessity of encouraging economic development. The reconciliation of both goals proved to be elusive. But, in the short term, the tax policy makers combined higher rates in both personal and corporation income taxes with special deductions for investments as a way to solve this dilemma. However, this combination created a complicated web of exceptions, distorting the structure of income tax and creating new sources of complaint and noncompliance. Moreover, as an economic incentive, tax expenditures were to no avail.

Let us start dealing with these issues by looking at the tax rates. As it shown in table 4.1, higher marginal tax rates of the income tax grew from 33 percent in 1954 to its historical peak of 50 percent in 1969. Those increases mainly affected the Argentine upper classes. This might be interpreted not only as a deepening of progressiveness but also as an unbearable tax burden for the wealthiest people in Argentina and hence a new stimulus to avoid payment. As mentioned, several commentators emphasized that the income tax was becoming a burdensome duty.[67] Liberal-minded economists and entrepreneurs, who sought to reduce state intervention in the economy by reducing fiscal voracity, usually adopted this position. Nonetheless, they were not alone. Some authors who favored state intervention and the use of taxes as a redistributive tool saw in a reduction of higher rates one

Table 4.1 Income tax rates, 1954–1975

Year	Higher marginal rate (and basic rate)	Corporation tax	Foreign corporation tax
1954	33 (7)		
1955	33 (7)	30	
1956–1958	43 (7)	30	35
1959–1960	45 (9)	30	38
1961–1962	45 (9)	33	38.36
1963–1964	45 (8)	30	38.36
1965–1966	45 (8)	30	
1967–1968*	50	30	
1969	50	33	33
1970–1971	46	33	
1972	46	33	
1973	42	33	
1974	46	22	45
1975	46		

Source: *BDGI*, issues from 1954 to 1975.

*Basic rates were included in the marginal rates from 1967 onward.

measure—although not the only one—that might contribute toward halting tax fraud and regaining the taxpayer cooperation. Thus, the reduction of rates in 1963 seemed to have had a positive impact on tax collection. In fact, income tax revenues grew by 67 percent between 1963 and 1965, whereas real tax rates dropped by almost 50 percent in some cases. Therefore, a steeper graduation did not produce a greater collection, at least during a period of high inflation.[68]

The income tax rate structure changed during the period in a complex way: the Treasury attempted to maximize revenues and at the same time to preserve the progressive features of the system. The increase in the higher marginal rates was related to this dual goal. Nonetheless, tax rates affected different income groups differently and, at the same time, inflation, deductions, and allowances distorted income tax progressiveness. In figure 4.2, the evolution of income tax rates for four groups of taxpayers is shown. Every taxpayer was forced to pay a higher average rate of income tax between 1955 and 1962, no matter what their income was. However, higher income groups were more affected by the modification of tax rates than were lower-income groups. In 1955, incomes over 1 million pesos paid an average rate of 38 percent, whereas in 1962, they had to pay 48 percent. People earning between 250,000 pesos and 1 million pesos annually paid an average of 32 percent in 1955 and were charged a 38 percent rate in 1962. Those receiving annual incomes of 50,000 pesos

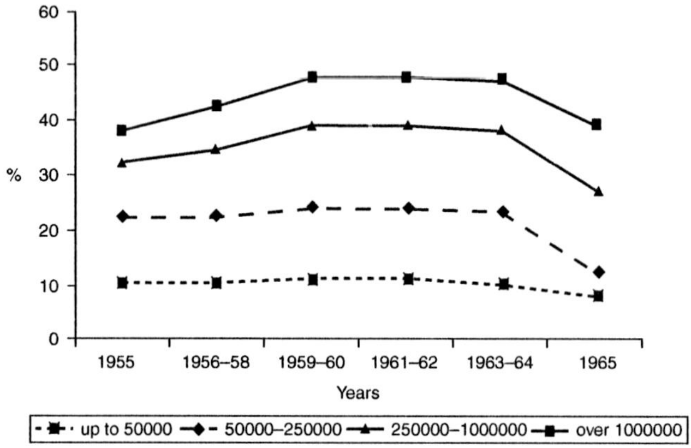

Figure 4.2 Net tax rates, 1955–1965

Source: My own elaboration based on 0. Oszlak, "Inflación y política fiscal", 14 and *BDGI* (Oct. 1962). Net tax rates are calculated as weighted averages for every category of income.

to 250,000 pesos paid an average rate of 22 percent in 1955, and only 24 percent in 1962. Last, lower incomes—those under 50,000 pesos—paid 10 percent in 1955 and 11 percent in 1962. Of course, this trend was inverted when taxes began to drop after 1962. Top income earners profited from a reduction of nine points in their rates between 1962 and 1965. Middle-income groups were the main beneficiaries of the tax cut: taxpayers of over 50,000 pesos of income obtained an average of 12 percent decrease in their rates. Last, lower incomes were also favored by a 3 percent decrease in their rates.

Hence, the tax rates design sharpened its progressive features, at least until 1965. However, this does not mean that income tax was become more progressive. Income tax was more progressive than were other duties, but it was affected by inflation and other circumstances that were making the Argentine tax system more regressive. First, the increase in the number of evaders caused problems of equity: the tax burden was increasingly distributed among fewer people. The same effect was the result of tax expenditures, allowances, and the intricate web of exceptions that dramatically shrank the universal aspirations of the income tax. Oszlak estimated that the average tax rate for the taxable income grew from 19 percent to 33 percent between 1955 and 1964. However, the average tax rate for the gross income fell. In 1956, 79 percent of registered taxpayers effectively paid income tax; in 1967, a meagre 26 percent of registered taxpayers were actually paying their income tax.[69]

The two most important deductions in the Argentine income tax were nontaxable income and family allowances that applied to every taxpayer and helped to establish taxable income and the special deductions for incomes of the fourth category, that is, wages and salaries. Nontaxable income was a significant part of the total net income: in 1964, it represented 57 percent of the total net declared income.[70] Of course, nontaxable income and family allowances, being fixed amounts, had a greater proportional significance for lower incomes than they did for higher incomes. Inflation made necessary constant adjustment in these allowances. Thus, in 1955, the minimum nontaxable income was 7,200 pesos, and family allowances were 4,800 pesos plus 1,800 pesos in the case of families with children. In 1969, the minimum nontaxable income reached 192,000 pesos. In 1970, due to inflation, the old peso *moneda nacional* was replaced by a new *peso ley* 18.188 (peso law 18,188). 100 old pesos converted to 1 new peso. Thus, in 1970, the nontaxable income was 1,920 "new" pesos. However, the change in currency could not halt inflation, and from 1971 to 1975, the basic allowance was reviewed every year and reached 28,584 pesos in 1975.[71] Although, in the long run, the adjustments in the minimum taxable income caught up with rising prices, in the short run, there was a lag between inflation and tax allowances, which caused a loss for taxpayers.[72] Personal and family allowances were universal, but lower incomes more profoundly resented their deterioration vis-à-vis prices.

The story was different in the case of special deductions for the fourth category. Deductions for wages and salaries were accorded due to the belief in a fundamental (moral and social) difference between earned and nonearned incomes and between workers and the rest of society. This special consideration for workers' income was sharpened during Perón's rule. This situation was criticized because, despite its seemingly progressive features, this measure created problems of horizontal equity. For example, in 1964, a married taxpayer without children who received an income derived from a salaried job could deduct 36,000 pesos as nontaxable income, 24,000 pesos for family allowances, plus 126,000 pesos for special deductions for the fourth category. Another taxpayer with a similar income, but one that was derived from nonsalaried activity, received only the benefits of the nontaxable income and the family allowances. Moreover, salaries—not just wages—were also included into the fourth category of incomes. Some professionals and business executives became salaried people and took advantage of these and other deductions (such as traveling expenses), which were allowed to be deducted from the taxable income.[73] Hence, under many circumstances, the beneficiaries of the special exemption for fourth-category taxpayers were not workers anymore. Many taxpayers probably considered that fourth-category incomes were undeservedly privileged. This inequity must have had a deleterious effect on the legitimacy of the system.

Nonetheless, workers' privileges were not the main source of losses for the income tax system nor were fourth category taxpayers the main evaders. Ultimately, salaried people had less opportunity to cheat than had other taxpayer categories.[74] Tax collectors' main source of worry, as far as evasion was concerned, were "incomes from the third category that include those derived from commerce, industry, agriculture, and some others of less significance...the cost of monitoring incomes from the third category is usually higher...and this cost probably grows at a faster pace connected to inflation."[75]

Furthermore, third-category taxpayers did benefit from tax expenditures as well. They did not receive a specific allowance, but the intricate system of exemptions and tax stimuli designed in Argentina since the 1940s was in fact oriented toward this type of taxpayer. Most governments during this period believed that Argentina's prosperity ought to be based on industrial development. Therefore, tax policies were designed to encourage industrialization. But that meant exemptions, deductions, and even a partial or total pardon of the debts (the so-called *blanqueos*). Sometimes these were general measures but on other occasions, they were accorded to a single firm. Thus, for example, incomes derived from shares, bonds, and other kind of assets that were devoted to finance projects and investments were exempted from payment of the income tax. This created problems of both vertical and horizontal inequality, since those taxpayers who invested in other kinds of assets did not obtain the same benefit and since most investors in this type of activity came from the most affluent groups of Argentine society.[76] The variety of exemptions was immense. As an analyst remarked, there were special deductions and exemptions in the payment of the income tax for almost everything: for the development of companies in the province of La Rioja, for toll-road companies, for those companies that were able to establish integrated stalls, and so on.[77]

Hence, tax loopholes and evasion by no means benefited working-class taxpayers. Business activity, which was usually associated with upper incomes, was probably the main beneficiary of the agonizing Argentine tax system. The treatment of corporations and shareholders exemplifies this.[78] The sale of shares, bonds, debentures, and other types of assets was exempted from income tax.[79] Furthermore, the highest rate for corporation tax was 33 percent, whereas the highest rate for personal income tax reached 50 percent. Dividends were exempted from income tax payment. To some authors, these were powerful stimuli to incorporate patrimony, and because that option was more feasible for upper incomes, it was part of the regressive features of the Argentine tax system.[80]

An analysis carried out by Fernando Tow at the end of the 1960s delved into this issue in some detail. Available data showed a deterioration of the percentage of national income received by wage earners and a growing concentration of wealth in the upper echelons.[81] This might have had a positive impact on income tax collection, as upper income groups were also the main taxpayers. However, the study concluded that between 1959 and 1967, income tax evasion (measured as the gap between potential and actual collection) had increased. Furthermore, that increase was not evenly distributed among taxpayers. Whereas evasion had fallen among taxpayers who earned less than 1 million pesos, it had increased among the most affluent taxpayers. The number of upper-income taxpayers decreased, despite inflation and growing income inequality as did the amount paid by these taxpayers.[82] The explanation for this process was that upper and middle incomes transformed their assets into corporate ones. Between 1959 and 1967 the number of Argentine corporations that declared their taxable income to the DGI grew by over 100 percent. Moreover, the difference between potential and actual tax payments made by corporations increased during this period.[83]

Tow's hypothesis was criticized by a liberal economist, Juan Vega. Vega underlined two problems of Tow's analysis. First, if tax rate differentials were stimuli to the transfer of assets, why did the transfer not begin earlier? "I believe this is not an explanation of evasion of upper brackets because such an alternative already existed in 1959."[84] However, this critique is debatable, and different interpretations are plausible as far as this matter is concerned. Inflation must be included in the picture. In 1956, when the higher income tax rate was raised to over 40 percent, very few people obtained incomes that exceeded 1 million pesos. In fact, in 1955, the higher income bracket crossed 750,000 pesos. That means that as inflation skyrocketed, more people began to earn more than 1 million pesos, and therefore the stimulus to change the form of their assets was also gradual. In 1963, corporation tax rate was cut, which increased that stimulus. Furthermore, in 1967, the higher marginal rate of the personal income tax was raised again by five points, thus broadening the differential with the corporation tax. Vega's second critique was also flawed. He noticed that the fact that some people were transferring their assets to a corporate form did not represent evasion in the legal sense of the word.[85] However, he did not take into account the fact that Tow was emphasizing both the transfer of assets as well as the growth of the differential between the potential and the actual tax that was being paid by corporations.

The significance of corporations, and of corporation-originated tax evasion, as far as the income tax was concerned, can be more accurately grasped by widening the scope of the analysis. Since Argentine governments—particularly Frondizi's developmentalist policies—were interested in promoting full-fledged and major industrialization, large companies increasingly received favorable treatment. Thus, they were the main beneficiaries of governmental plans for renegotiating the payment of firms' debts, including tax debts. In order to take advantage of those plans, debts had to exceed a certain amount, which benefitted large corporations.[86] This option was particularly available for companies after the deep recession of 1962–1963 and allowed corporate firms to indefinitely postpone their tax payments. In 1963, a recently created Honorary Committee for the Industrial Reactivation supported the idea of postponing the payment of tax debts for some companies that were in dire straits.[87] Moreover, in a very delicate situation in which the credit market tightened, tax evasion became paramount in the industrial companies' desperate search for cheap financing. During the 1950s, 16 percent of the total investment in manufacturing industries came from tax evasion. During the 1960s, the figure amounted to over 50 percent. In addition to fraud, industrial companies' debts became a serious problem during the decade: around three quarters of the total private debt owed to the social security system and the DGI lay with the industrial sector.[88]

The depression of 1962–1963 is crucial in this narrative because until that year, corporation tax and personal income tax diverged in their performances. Whereas personal income tax was falling as a proportion of the total tax collection, corporation tax increased its participation in the total (national, provincial, and municipal taxes included) tax revenues. In 1953, corporation income tax represented 3.8 percent of the total tax collection; in 1959, 5.05 percent; and in 1961, 6.07. The personal income tax that in 1953 reached 11.43 percent of the revenue fell to 8.57 in 1959 and to 7.33 in 1961.[89] The crisis of 1962–1963 halted this trend and caused major problems for the income tax system. The next turning point was 1967. Industrial companies run into greater trouble than they had in 1962. The number of bankruptcies skyrocketed. Since 1967, the government was studying different plans in order to help companies in a difficult situation to begin their recovery.[90] The crisis of the Argentine manufacturing sector and the decline of income tax coincided (see figure 4.1). Since 1966, the falling tendency is clear and unstoppable. In 1966, income tax collections amounted to over 27 percent of the total revenue; in 1973, to over 21 percent. This is not mere chance. Industrial production and income tax are historically strongly linked—not only in Argentina. The increase of evasion and delays by manufacturers were obviously affecting income tax feasibility. Moreover, industrial entrepreneurs were also withholding agents, and their lack of cooperation with the system, which was due to discontent or a desperate economic situation, was undermining the global income tax system.

Manufacturers' debts with the Treasury were undermining the DGI's efforts to keep the tax system afloat. The situation became a conflictive one during Illia's presidency. This was linked to Illia's attempt to strengthen governmental autonomy, which aroused what César Tcach refers to as "corporatist opposition."[91] In lieu of cooperation with business, Illia's administration sought to improve bureaucratic efficiency and to demonstrate toughness in the treatment of evaders. Alberto M. Caletti was appointed DGI's general director, and Antonio López Aguado and León S. Schwartzman were his immediate subordinate officers. The three were scholars, experts in the field of taxation.[92] At an early point in his tenure, Caletti launched a campaign of pressure on the tax debtors: phone calls were regularly made and telegrams insistently sent. The new director noticed that the debts had reached 44 billion pesos. The Tax Bureau was seeing to "actively manage" this debt, as Caletti put it.[93]

DGI's campaign continued in early 1964. That year, the Tax Bureau sent letters to 100,000 firms with the aim of collecting some of the 70 billion pesos owed by the companies.[94] For several weeks, the tension between business representatives and the Tax Bureau mounted. The UIA and the Argentine Chamber of Joint-Stock Corporations accused the DGI of focusing on big companies and forgetting small ones.[95] Director Caletti, in a television interview, warned that past abuses would not be tolerated.[96]

Tension, as usual, was the prologue to negotiation. Business representatives had a meeting with President Illia, who offered some credits to firms to help them pay their debts. Businessmen rejected the proposal, deeming to be insufficient. The DGI threatened them with confiscation of properties. Entrepreneurs responded that the government was going to be forced to expropriate all Argentine factories because all of them had tax debts. Illia gave up and declared an extension of payments until 1966.[97]

Ultimately, the executive power had the last word over the DGI. However, if the DGI had maintained such a firm position, it was due to the backing of a government committed to bureaucratic autonomy and to the enforcement of tax laws. The DGI's toughness in its relationships with the entrepreneurs continued during Onganía's authoritarian rule. Illia's extension did not solve the problem of the payment of debts. In order to tackle it, Ongania's administration passed in November 1967 the *Ley de Rehabilitación de Empresas* (Law for the Rescue of Companies). The law was an ambitious plan of bailing out those companies that due to "their social significance, economic size, technological development, or influence in the national, regional, or zonal economy" required financial aid to pay their debts to the DGI and the social security administration.[98] The DGI grudgingly accepted the bailing out of companies. The governmental help meant an important loss of revenues, and the Tax Bureau showed its disagreement even more openly than it did during Illia's tenure.[99]

During Ongania's authoritarian rule, as Ricardo Aroskind noticed, the state deepened its links to the large companies, which received important financial and tax relief, as the mentioned bailout demonstrates.[100] But the capitalist modernization envisioned by the new government demanded certain autonomy for the technocrats. Raúl Cuello, the new head of the DGI, emphasized the necessity of keeping private influence at bay within the DGI: "Within the scheme envisioned for this organism by the Revolution, there is no place for the influence of groups or sectors."[101]Minister Krieger Vasena, who had appointed Cuello as the head of the DGI and encouraged his reform of the institution, had begun his professional career as a young economist at the Tax Bureau, and he was probably aware of the importance of autonomy. But despite the autonomy and commitment of the DGI officials, the Argentine tax scheme stalled. No government was able to gather enough social support to carry out the needed reforms. The DGI was also an institutional victim of the failure of the tax system in general and of the military dictatorship in particular.

Inflation and tax evasion were related in multiple and complex ways. Beyond mutual influence, both phenomena might share some common origins. Some of the reasons that lead people to "cheat" the Treasury might be at the root of inflationary tensions as well. The above- mentioned Honorary Committee for the Industrial Reactivation that had proposed to allow companies to delay their tax payments also proposed the establishment of an Economic and Social Council, a "social agreement" that would put an end to workers' and manufacturers' demands and guarantee the possibility of designing long-term policies.[102] The committee was hence linking inflation, tax problems, and social conflict. Inflation in Argentina and in other Latin American countries has been interpreted as the result of the impossibility of achieving a consensus among social groups, mainly labor and capital (but also between rural and urban productions) and the necessity to reward contradictory interests at the same time. Both the cycle of wage and price increases and the repeated devaluations since the stabilization plan of 1959 reflected this elusive goal.[103] This policy of "gaining precious time," in Albert Hirschman's felicitous phrase, in turn caused greater problems.[104] Inflation, as has been shown, became a stimulus and an alternative to other forms of taxation. Moreover, inflation created the idea of ephemeral victory and then led to frustration. For instance, inflation allowed companies to obtain credit with real negative interest rates. The combination of inflation and the income tax was in truth provoking a transfer of incomes from lenders and savers to debtors, among them, industrialists. The higher the income tax rate was on interests, the lower were the real interest rates industrialists were paying.[105] When the rising of prices halted and the market credit tightened, businessmen faced a desperate financial situation and this—along with workers' pressures—exacerbated animosity toward the state's allegedly inefficiency.

Nonetheless, Argentine society was growingly complex, and labor and capital did not encapsulate the entire social world. Many other people—professionals, lawyers, doctors, retirees, independent workers, renters, civil servants—were affected by inflation without being its main beneficiaries. Those fixed-revenue groups, which included retirees on pension, renters, or those without the capacity to index their incomes, were in an even worse situation. They blamed the different governments for the inflation and became increasingly hostile toward public institutions. When the deficit climbed and collection did not allow the state to maintain efficient public services, frustration regarding public expenditure fanned out. Moreover, middle-class citizens perceived that the tax scheme was designed keeping in mind both fourth-category taxpayers (workers) and businessmen, who benefitted from multiple exemptions and deductions. Therefore, they had many incentives to evade their payment, and unlike what they believed, they also had opportunities to do so—at least as much as did salaried workers or industrial entrepreneurs. Yet the idea of the middle class as a victim of the tax system gained strength since the end of Peronism. In fact, it can be argued that the very concept of the middle class was shaped around this idea.

As early as 1957, an article published in the *Revista de Ciencias Económicas* emphasized that dishonest behaviors were spreading throughout Argentina as a result of governmental policies, particularly tax policies. The author of this article, Alberto López, argued that the tax regime was dishonest because it tried "to make people believe that solutions lay not with everyone, but with the few, the 'privileged ones,' the 'rich'."[106] Therefore, the solution to the Argentine fiscal problems was the income tax, because it made the affluent pay more. But, according to López, this was a dangerous mystification, based upon two misleading "slogans": "fiscal justice" and "social justice":

> Later on, the triumph of numbers arrives and every slogan repeats that the 'the rich must pay,' and thus, the income tax, the tax on the extraordinary profits, the capital levy, and so on, become the fulcrum of the speeches of those who aspire to guarantee not only 'fiscal justice' but also 'social justice.' (Even though A. Bevan has said that to believe that it is possible to achieve an egalitarian society through the fiscal system—only through the manipulation of taxes—it is a form of intellectual cowardice.)[107]

López's radical rejection of social and tax justice as praiseworthy goals was a rare one. Yet, his rejection was embedded in a wider framework of criticism toward state interventionism that would gain greater support. According to this critic, state intervention, during Peronism and afterwards, was harming private initiative and encouraging dishonesty. These two negative aspects of the state's interventionism were linked to the very idea of social and tax justice. In order to guarantee social justice, the state could not help but increase taxes and therefore undermine private activities.[108] Politicians had been dishonest for "announcing that the 'crisis must be paid for by the wealthy' without saying that this would mean the suppression of private property and therefore that the poor would pay later."[109]

López's idea—that the origin of corruption was the inability of Perón's and successive administrations to cut public expenditures—was not an original one among the critics of Peronism and business circles. However, his idea that tax policies were particularly harming "the incomes from the middle classes" and that this was part of a war of the politics against economy made an original contribution to the debate.[110] López was emphasizing that the main victims of what was already referred to as the Argentine crisis were the middle classes. Who were they? López did not specify, but from his words, we can infer that they were entrepreneurial people (those with economic initiative) whose field of activity was an economical and not a political one. According to López the political and the economic realm were separate spheres and the middle classes did not belong to the political realm.

The idea of a decline of the Argentine middle classes frequently attracted the interest of the press. In some cases, the members of the middle classes were more clearly identified. In a 1957 article, the middle classes appeared as the losers in a battle—the battle of inflation—that was won by wage earners and businessmen. But here, the middle classes were referred to as the "traditional middle class," those whose main source of income was fixed. This class included urban and rural proprietors, whose properties were rented as well as lenders and savers.[111]

Inflation and taxation were undermining the middle class. Some of the harsher critics of the Argentine tax scheme put the blame on the income tax:

> The middle class... used to be conservative and capitalist and it slowly grew richer and richer every year until 1930... Since that year, the income tax began to cut its income, and after 1943 it has been punished more severely, to the point of being deprived of the necessary means to have access to those things it used to enjoy: home, education, holidays. [The middle class] has been transformed into a white-collar proletariat.[112]

In the quoted passage, it is difficult to pinpoint precise who the middle class is. Yet, it is possible to observe some common features with other descriptions. Perhaps the idea that the middle class "used to be *conservadora y capitalista*" can be interpreted as meaning that the middle class was made up of the people who saved money (conservatives) and, at the same time, of entrepreneurial-minded people (capitalists). This image was becoming increasingly popular. In 1963, the executive justified the cutting of rates in the income tax by recalling that the hitherto high rates for middle incomes "weaken the middle class by shrinking their incomes, and besides it causes the voluntary migration of qualified technicians and intellectuals," that is, the loss of entrepreneurial talent.[113] A more surprising endorsement to this view came from trade unions. In 1965, the CGT urged the middle classes to accept a new social order, "to give up apathy and to catch up with the tone of the new times, which are characterized by the incorporation to the social, political, and economic system of the large popular masses."[114] But at the same time, the CGT acknowledged that the national economic development depended on "efficient investments" and, in turn, that these depended on the available capital, that is, the savings made by "the middle classes, mainly the most affluent ones, who have the greater capacity to save."[115]

Thus, the important presence of the "middle classes" in public disputes centered around taxation was linked to what some groups perceived as the need to "capitalize" Argentine society, that is, to encourage private savings in order to stimulate investments and future economic growth. The middle classes were allegedly the main savers in the country and the main victims of an aggressive tax system. To some extent, the role of savers and investors overlapped in this rhetoric. This is not surprising. Big entrepreneurs could be easily depicted as profiteers of the most insidious tax, inflation. Therefore, the public defense of private initiative against the intrusive activity of the state had to be cautious enough to avoid siding with corporations and large firms. Increasingly, the UIA identified itself with the middle class, whereas during the past decades, it had identified itself with labor. A 1963 speech of Dr. Oneto Gaona, president of the industrialists' association, is revealing:

> The increasingly heavier burden of the super tax [income tax] must be ended; it only serves to boost tax evasion, to encourage the emigration of technicians, to frustrate the middle class and the small savers; and to depress the economy even more by deterring the formation of capitals...From a humanitarian point of view, I contemplate particularly the situation of our middle class. Tax policy must take into account the possibility of encouraging the extension of this class...by allowing workers who aspire to progress to save and capitalize.[116]

According to the UIA, a heavy tax burden on the middle classes was preventing Argentine society from saving the monies that were essential for investments: "The Argentine Industrial Union is concerned about the serious problem of the *descapitalización* (loss of savings) of our middle class." However, workers were also victims of the high rates of the income tax. Fourth-category taxpayers deserved greater allowances:

> The modification of the law of the income tax, alleviating incomes from the fourth category, is a decision that our Legislative Power must take without further delay for the sake of the nation's economy...[The nation] will not be able to progress if the preparation, the technical and scientific improvement and the *capitalización* (savings) of this great sector of Argentine people [workers] is not encouraged.[117]

Hence, the UIA was playing a familiar chord in the Argentine discourse on taxation: the necessity to increase allowances and deductions for workers' families. For the UIA, income tax rates were becoming unbearable for Argentine taxpayers due to inflation. The DGI and the different governments "led by a mean spirit in order to collect more funds" did not adjust rates to keep up with prices. Yet, revealing enough, the solutions proposed by the industrialists were far away from the fourth-category taxpayers' strict interests. Family allowances were "sporadic palliatives." What was needed was a "reasonable modification of the graduated scale of the tax."[118] But the graduated rates affected mainly high incomes. This point is more apparent in the examples chosen by the manufacturers to demonstrate the negative impact of progressive rates on incomes due to inflation. The UIA stated that for an income of 300,000 pesos, the surtax of the income tax represented in 1943 0.63 percent, whereas in 1961, it took 25.85 percent. Incomes of 1 million pesos paid 3.90 percent due to the surtax in 1943, whereas in 1961, they paid 35.52 percent.[119] Nonetheless, incomes from 300,000 pesos to 1 million pesos were not the typical workers' wages. In 1959, out of 399,600 taxpayers only 16,166 obtained more than 250,000 pesos of taxable income, that is, less than 4 percent.[120] Therefore, the UIA was putting forward not only a defense of a more production-oriented taxation but also an attempt to protect upper-echelon taxpayers. In this defense, the UIA thought that tax evasion was "logical," considering the irrational fiscal policy implemented by the government.[121]

This noncooperative stance was even clearer in the case of the Argentine Chamber of Commerce. Like the UIA, the Chamber of Commerce insisted on the necessity of increasing the rate of *capitalización* (savings) and therefore that of private investment of the economy. Like the UIA, they considered that granting special allowances for fourth-category taxpayers was not enough: "We do not believe tax unfairness to affect only incomes from the fourth category."[122] The solution was to reform the graduated surtax within the income tax in order to adapt to rates to inflation.

The Chamber of Commerce displayed a harder stance within the same line of criticism that had been displayed by the UIA. Perhaps this attitude was due to the fact that the Chamber of Commerce represented some sectors that had never been considered particularly deserving by the Argentine tax ideology. For commerce—unlike for wages, manufactures, or even ranching—it was more difficult to obtain deductions and tax incentives. This tougher position was well reflected in the response of the Chamber of Commerce to the measures projected by the government in order to improve collection. For the association of merchants, the new policy was a "mechanism of coercion inadequate for democratic institutions." Furthermore, this coercion was useless. The government should strive for "the acquiescence of those obliged [to pay]." How to achieve that "acquiescence"? First, taxes should be fair and equitable among private actors, and second, expenditures should be cut. Moreover, the state itself should demonstrate its commitment to fairness through the "moralization of its acts." That is, tax collectors and the bureaucracy should comply with the law. At the same time, the state could not demand strict and punctual payments from taxpayers before fulfilling its duties toward its creditors.[123] This letter of the Chamber of Commerce presented a picture of an inefficient state that had broken its pact with civil society due to the corruption of the bureaucracy and unfairness in its treatment of taxpayers. The logical outcome was the lack of acquiescence—the noncooperative attitude displayed by many citizens.

The creation of a working-class identity, as far as taxation was concerned, was about a special and deserving group. This group received privileged treatment through the tax law. This was deemed to be legitimate due to the special place that labor occupied—or should occupy—in the progress of the nation. This identity, which began to be designed since an early phase in the history of the income tax, was reinforced by the Peronist regime, which placed workers at the top of a new and ideal social hierarchy. The creation of labor identity through taxation—the famous fourth-category taxpayers—was thus largely related to public policies; to some extent, Argentine working-class identity was being shaped by the state. As in the case of the working class, middle-class identity was also linked to taxation. But in lieu of benefiting from more favorable treatment, the middle classes, or at least those who spoke on their behalf, argued that they were the most conspicuous victims of fiscal policies. To some extent, this was also related to an image of the middle class as a special group (an entrepreneurial, creative, and saving class), which deserved better treatment due to its role within Argentine society. However (and unlike the case of the working class), the shaping of the middle-class identity after Peronism did not originate in the state but in civil society. Middle-class groups lacked clear political representation and were not as organized as were workers or employers; therefore, many wished to speak on their behalf and obtain political benefits with their support. Moreover, the identification of the middle class as the victims of tax policies reflected the increased independence of civil society and the growing feeling of distrust that the state's activities and institutions aroused in Argentine citizens.

In 1960, Jorge Mayer, a radical critic of the Argentine tax system stated: "Tax evasion was always a natural safety valve...and a healthy reaction of economic forces against the exactions of political organisms. Rather than condemn tax evasion History makes its apology."[124] Tax evasion was thus legitimized as a defense against an inefficient bureaucracy: "This bad administration provokes a defensive reaction against fiscal demands, similar to [the demands] of the American settlers against the bureaucracy of the viceroyalty. It is a new episode of the fight for rights."[125] Mayer alerted that the most possible outcome of the state's aggressive tax policy was "The lost of faith, the cauldron of distrust and their final consequences...the legal or illegal evasion of payment, and lastly, the rebellion of taxpayers, a process whose first symptom was the episode of Poujade in France."[126] Mayer did not realize that Argentineans found it easier than did the French to cheat the state, and therefore, tax revolt was not necessary. Still, his criticism reflected an increasingly successful credo among the Argentine middle-classes: the idea that they were paying for the useless bureaucracy and for the privileged ones in Argentina: "The minimum non taxable income seems to have been imposed due to the trade unions' pressure, creating a new privileged sector and the [minimum non taxable income] is notoriously insufficient, because it does not allow *la capitalización de la clase media* (middle class to save)" or "the modest shopkeeper is persecuted; the big company is exempted."[127]

Seen in the long run, during Frondizi's administration, the transformation of Argentine society from a quasi-cooperative tax state into an adversarial tax state was completed. In a cooperative tax state, the taxation system is based upon a few key (and usually direct) taxes,—such as those levied in the early 1940s in Argentina—and the support of economic elites. In an adversarial tax state—such as Argentina in the 1960s—taxes are disputed by civil society, mainly by upper-class groups. Taxes and exemptions multiply, and the system becomes more regressive.[128] At the same time, the complexity of the tax system and the distrust of the state legitimized noncompliance. Since the end of Perón's rule, many economists, politicians, and intellectuals justified tax evasion as a "natural" way to resist an authoritarian, arbitrary government. As already shown, some entrepreneurs justified nonpayment as a result of the oppressive nature of tax rates. Even the Supreme Court to some extent legitimized noncompliance. For instance, in the case of Santiago Graffigna, Vinery of Mendoza declared that under the republican system, a tax was legitimate only if it was devoted to the general welfare.[129] Therefore, it allowed taxpayers the possibility of evaluating whether or not the government was spending its money according to their ideas of general welfare. Of course, this sentence of the Supreme Court was based upon the notion of "no taxation without representation." The problem is that the Constitution established that tax laws and tax rates were to be designed by the Congress, as the legitimate representatives of the nation. The Congress was also in charge of passing the annual budget and thus of taking into consideration the "general welfare" of the nation in the allocation of public moneys. Hence, this sentence highlighted the lack of legitimacy of the Argentine representatives. This distrust was increasingly affecting not only politicians or bureaucrats but also the state itself.

Epilogue

Argentina was riding an economic roller coaster. The stop-and-go cycle, combined with high inflation and the consequences of a social and political conflict that was on the verge of becoming an open civil war, were formidable challenges to any type of tax system.[130] Under these extreme circumstances, the confidence mechanisms that a progressive complex tax scheme required could not survive. In turn, this had deep consequences, which became particularly acute since the end of the 1960s. Public deficit was increasingly difficult to eradicate. In 1966, it achieved 4.3 percent of the GDP. Between 1967 and 1970, due to the relative success of Minister Krieger Vassena in improving collection, the deficit was temporarily under control. Yet, since 1971, it quickly skyrocketed. That year, it reached 4.3 percent; in 1975, it amounted to almost 16 percent of the GDP.[131] The unraveling of the fiscal system is even more apparent if we look at the evolution of tax collections. In 1970, taxes covered up to 80 percent of total public expenditures, whereas in 1975, they only financed 25 percent of total governmental expenses.[132] The crisis of the Argentine state in 1976 was also a fiscal crisis.[133]

The collapse of the tax system had momentous consequences for the cohesion of Argentine society. The "breaking up of the fiscal pact," as Ricardo Carciofi aptly put it, meant that the state was unable to continue playing its role, that is, subsidizing private actors, transferring income from one sector to another, financing public infrastructures, and guaranteeing the welfare of citizens through pensions and other public interventions.[134] The social pact was broken.

Chapter 5

Searching for Solutions: The VAT

The feeling of permanent crisis haunted policy makers since the end of Peronist rule. Most politicians believed that the crisis was also affecting the Argentine tax system and that a reform was urgently needed. If the attempt to compensate for the losses caused by inflation led the governments to implement new taxes, the awareness of the necessity to gain taxpayers' confidence led policy makers to try out different approaches in the relationship between state and civil society as far as taxation issues were concerned. Nevertheless, every attempt failed and became a victim of either political instability or of its own coyness. Unlike what happened in the 1990s—when President Carlos Menem and his economics minister, Domingo Cavallo, were able to carry out significant reforms in the tax structure and the tax collection—the governments of the 1960s and 1970s lacked both the required political stability and a bold program of reforms. Furthermore, without taming inflation, any serious tax reform was doomed to failure.

Revealingly, any attempt at reform was embedded in other major economic or political goals. Some politicians believed that Argentina faced an economic bottleneck, and that a leap forward in the process of industrialization was needed. Others addressed the problems caused by a possible stagnation of productivity in the rural sector (the main source of foreign currency for the nation) or tried to enhance distribution by increasing capital contributions to the Treasury. Finally, the Peronist reform of the early 1970s tried to tackle social conflict, which was one of the main origins of political instability and a significant push factor in the inflationary process. Increasingly, the ideal world and reality clashed. Only at the end of the period—and paradoxically, under a new Peronist administration—did a timid reform subtly acknowledge the failure of Argentine progressive tax structure. This reform introduced the Value-Added Tax (VAT) in the country and unified the income tax and other progressive devices under a new tax, the *impuesto a las ganancias* (profits tax). To some extent, the Peronist reforms of the 1970s were an important precedent of those implemented by Menem in the 1990s.

This chapter explores the origins of the most important tax reform in Argentina after the implementation of the income tax in the 1930s—the introduction of the VAT in 1974. Although this reform did not halt the deepening of the fiscal crisis in the following years, it established the basis for the transformation of the Argentine tax regime in the 1990s. It also meant, implicitly, that Argentine policy makers and its civil society were renouncing their ideal—never fully achieved—of a progressively conceived tax scheme.

The "Social Pact"

Between 1966 and 1973, the military attempted to end Argentine permanent political instability and her turbulent economic cycle by perpetuating themselves in power. However, in 1973, the military government, assailed by social revolts and its inability to tackle economic troubles, decided to call for elections; for the first time since 1955, Peronism was allowed to participate without proscriptions.[1] The military seemed to have reached the conclusion that only Perón could reestablish social peace. However, the Peronist victory did not mean the end of violence. The Peronist government, in a first phase that was headed by Héctor Cámpora, was under severe strain. Among Cámpora's supporters, there were the so-called *Juventud Peronista* (Peronist Youth) and some guerrilla groups who saw in the return of Perón to Argentina the first step in the building of a socialist state, the "*patria socialista*." (socialist fatherland). The new government—and Perón himself—facing intense social mobilization and political violence, looked for channels of "institutionalization of the movement." As far as the economic situation was concerned, this process of institutionalization was embedded in the notion of a vast "social pact" between business representatives and trade unions.[2]

The idea that a broad societal agreement might solve national problems drew on many sources. General Lanusse, the last head of the state under the military regime before the return of Perón, had already proposed a—ultimately failed—"Great National Agreement." The success of the European recovery in the aftermath of World War II, based upon agreements between labor and capital, also had a permanent influence on the minds of many Argentineans, who aspired to reach some stability and prosperity for their country.[3] The idea of a social pact was also personally appealing to Perón, who had regained his influence in Argentine politics. The Justicialist leader linked the social pact to the first Peronist experience in power, which supposedly had been based upon a similar sort of class alliance.

The social pact was also part of the economic agenda developed by the CGE, which gathered small- and medium-sized companies, firms from the interior, and those whose main source of profit was the domestic market. The CGE held a more positive view on corporatist arrangements than did other business interest associations. Due to its secondary role within the Argentine business class, the CGE had greater expectations about the benefits they could obtain from economic councils and other kind of advisory bodies. Even before Perón's return was an actual possibility, the CGE had demanded the creation of an Economic and Social Council, whereas other business associations opposed the idea of this council on the grounds that it would hamper the free play of market forces.[4] But for the CGE, the social pact was the way to tame inflation, to control salaries and, at the same time, to improve the distribution of wealth.

Without making it explicit, the corporatist project of the CGE had, as a model, the income policies of the European social democracy and, therefore, became increasingly attentive to tax matters. Taxes should help to improve the distribution of income and to build a powerful domestic market. These were compatible goals: "The aim of the tax policy is the protection and the stimulus to labor, to investments, to production and consumption... It will intend to achieve an equitable distribution of income and to discourage those activities inadequate for the national development."[5] In fact, the tax system was unfair because its burden lay mostly on "those who have small and middle incomes." The lack of progressiveness of the Argentine tax system undermined a process of economic development based upon the domestic market, as the CGE advocated.[6]

What was the CGE's tax program? First, the CGE proposed to soften tax policies through "a wide tax amnesty; an extension of deadlines; the condoning of fees; and the cut in present rates."[7] Second, the role of corporatist agents in tax matters was to be clarified. That meant a minimization of state control on taxation and the participation of business and labor representatives in the tax policy making. This would help to make the system work. For instance: "The social security is an obligation of the community. This goal must be reached by the reorganization of the pension system in order to guarantee its efficient working." The key was shifting the control of the pension funds to the representatives of the social corporations: "The management of the funds must be in the hands of workers and employers, equally represented, and its working must be autonomous."[8] The General Tax Bureau (DGI) should be subjected to corporatist checks as well.[9]

The CGE's agenda limited state autonomy in tax matters. Yet their proposals were not inspired by the idea that the state was intrinsically inefficient—unlike what the liberal critics of the 1980s and 1990s argued—but by the goal of achieving the so-called "national development."[10] The CGE was launching its own program of government, and thanks to Campora's victory, they would have the opportunity to try their ideas. For a brief period, the CGE's leader, José Gelbard, was the economics minister; his main aim was to encourage the signing of the social pact.[11] The corporatist experiment headed by the CGE reflected the exhaustion of the social conflict and the distrust of private actors toward state autonomy.

The taxation ideology defended by the CGE was not radically different from the ideas held by the trade unions. However, for the General Confederation of Labor (CGT), the tax policy offered no solution to the dilemmas of Argentine society. Like the businessmen gathered in the CGE, the trade unionists believed that taxes should attain two goals: social justice and greater productivity of the national industry.[12] However, beyond a critique of the sales tax, the trade union did not have an alternative taxation policy. In fact, the CGT maintained a striking antitax rhetoric. Any plan to increase taxes was challenged on the grounds that it would only encourage evasion and that it would be useless in the fight against inflation:

> [The solution is not], from the point of view of this labor union, to increase taxes with the aim of getting higher revenues in order to diminish the deficit in the budget, mainly because those higher revenues are equal to the amount presently evaded; moreover, the higher the tax, the higher will be the level of evasion, and the new taxes will mean higher costs, which will be shifted to prices.[13]

Trade unionist even criticized the spendthrift behavior of the rulers: "There is no progress in the reduction of the deficit of the state companies... Besides the enormous national deficit, we have to add the provincial and the municipal deficit."[14] The solution, like the one proposed by the CGE, was the development of a powerful national industry that would be based upon the domestic market. The building of this domestic market was in fact a distributive policy, which demanded the cooperation of the affluent classes and the entrepreneurs: "Since economic development is about efficient investment, available capitals are needed. Naturally, these must come, in addition to what foreign cooperation can provide, from the upper-income sectors."[15]

How to explain this absence of a tax program among the leaders of a labor union that demanded a better distribution of income? First, any policy tending to promote the national industry helped to improve the distribution of income and, therefore, taxes were not needed.[16] Second, distribution for the trade unions was not only about income or wealth, but also about power. Their corporatist language referred not so much to the distribution of income as to the "democratization" of income. Economic development should be achieved through economic planning and the intervention of the state.[17] State intervention, nonetheless, was not the fulcrum for this proposal. The process of "democratic distribution" should take place mainly in the factories:

> Employers must understand that the times in which the company was exclusively in the service of its proprietors have ended. This has to be a community, to which workers feel that they belong...This will be accomplished when employers share with the workers not only profits...but the very management of the company...We, who believe in democracy as a system of life, must accept that democracy within the companies, that is, where men spend more of the useful time of their lives, is the real foundation of a truly democratic society.[18]

The goal was, hence, an ambitious one: to restore the workers' power in the factories. Since the second half of the 1960s, an independent and radical labor movement had developed in Argentina and had started gaining influence and autonomy from the CGT. This movement and the pressure of the unions' rank and file radicalized the agenda of the traditional labor representatives. Furthermore, the unionists' self-image as one of the "factors of power" led them to propose an economic agenda that included not only nationalization and industrialization policies, but also the comanagement of factories by both labor and capital.[19] Trade union leaders understood that this had been one of the reasons for the success of the European recovery:

> The organization of big and modern companies with different systems of co-management of the workers is one of the richest experiences of the postwar [period], particularly in countries that are usually taken

> as models, those which we should imitate. This is the example of the German Federal Republic, the origin of the 'German miracle.'[20]

In fact, many European societies were living through similar experiences. Inflation had push up workers' nominal incomes and therefore increased their income tax payments. During the 1970s, trade unions pressed for tax cuts or wages rises. In some cases, as in Denmark, a tax revolt broke out. In others, unions asked for a tax cut in exchange for wage restraint, and in yet other cases, they demanded the democratization of the factories. But by doing this, they were not showing their commitment to the postwar social pacts, as the Argentine unions assumed, but were challenging them.[21] There were, however, some differences between Western European and Argentine unions. First, Argentine unions were not fighting the impact of the income tax on their constituencies (which was not so important). Second, European unions—in a rather contradictory way—did not ask for a cut in (welfare) expenditures, but in their tax payments.

The 1973 social pact was not the one envisioned by trade unions. Nonetheless, they signed the agreement, under pressure from Perón, in an attempt to recover positions within the Justicialist alliance because they feared the influence of the radical left wing that was represented by the Peronist youth. This pact meant that the CGT was forced to abandon mobilization and to accept limits to the growth of salaries and the freezing—for two years—of collective agreements.[22] Union constituencies were probably disappointed with this result.

The CGT did not take advantage of its participation in the social pact to advance some general policies, such as tax policies, or other policies. Its strategy focused on outmaneuvering the other participants in the agreement in a search for some benefits for its rank and file. Thus, even though collective agreements were not allowed for two years, the trade unions were able to renegotiate workers' conditions through the *comisiones paritarias* (sector committees). Most significant, in late 1973, the Committee of Prices, Salaries and Standard of Life of the social pact conceded to the unions the right to go through the account books of the companies, something that European trade unions had sought to no avail.[23]

In March 1974, the social pact began to unravel. Unable to reach agreements on the limits to salaries and prices, employers and unions left Perón to take those decisions personally. Nonetheless, governmental decisions were constantly violated.[24] In July 1974, Perón died and Gelbard lost his main support within the government. In October, the minister was forced to resign. The CGT had never been completely happy within the frame of the social pact shaped by a minister who came from the business sector. The collapse of the social pact seemed to grant power to the unions. In fact, what happened was the acceleration of the process of political and social breaking down, which would have among its main victims workers and union leaders.[25]

Despite unions' negligence about taxation, they did not renounce the distribution of wealth. In fact, the government and the CGE were aware that the success of the social pact depended on the possibility of carrying out a policy of social justice. The return of Perón to power was surrounded by big distributive expectations. One of the main goals of the government's Three Years Plan was to increase workers' share in the national income up to 50 percent.[26] The Three Years Plan clearly referred to tax policy as a fundamental instrument in the search for this goal.[27]

Some progressive features of the tax system were accentuated at the beginning of the Peronist government. Progressive tax devices were unified into a single new income tax, the *impuesto a las ganancias.* Personal and corporate income taxes were separated in order to identify assets owners, and dividends were taxed with a graduated rate. Last, nondistributed profits were forced to pay higher rates. Nonetheless, the higher rates for the personal and corporate income tax were cut.[28]

Despite the egalitarian rhetoric and the clear pressures from below, the government and the DGI focused mainly on improving monitoring and collection.[29] There were good reasons for this. In 1974 and 1975, this search became almost desperate as the public deficit skyrocketed from 1.5 percent of the GDP in 1973, to 10 percent in 1975. According to one of the economic policy makers during the period, the main problem was not the deficit itself but the difficulties in managing it.[30] In the context of distributive conflicts, the deficit was rapidly monetized and it boosted inflation. Moreover, for the DGI, the problem was not so much the relation between the deficit and the GDP as were the absolute levels of collection and evasion, which cast a doubt on its contribution to the Treasury. The revenues collected by the DGI as a percentage of the national product reached 9.8 percent in 1970 but fell to 7.2 percent in 1973 and to a minimum of 6.6 percent in 1972. Rather than a continuous decline, tax revenues coming to the General Tax Bureau showed an erratic performance, like the Argentine economy itself.[31] However, as an internal report of the institution noticed, "The changes in the economic structure had not been accompanied by a similar evolution in the tax structure."

The tax regime lacked flexibility, and this was something "that an expansive fiscal policy cannot tolerate."[32]

The VAT

The most significant feature of the 1970s tax policy is that the DGI, some officials of the government, and representatives of business associations—that had played a secondary role in the social pact—began to conceive of the most transcendental tax reform in the country since the 1940s—the introduction of the Value-Added Tax. The government and the DGI had been seeking the advice of national and foreign experts, and they wrote different drafts of the tax since at least 1964, when the same debate was taking place in Europe. Although the government discussed the project with professional economists, it did not conceal its willingness to do so also with businessmen.

The reader might recall that the sales tax implemented in the 1930s was—since its very inception—regarded as the lesser evil (compared to the tax on transactions). The sales tax was essentially a turnover tax on industry (and on some exports).[33] It fell prey to two kinds of criticism: first, as an indirect tax, it was considered a regressive one; second, it narrowly targeted a small group of big manufacturers, thus arousing inequity issues. When the Peronist government made the sales tax its main tax device, complaints about the regressive feature of the measure skyrocketed. Raúl Prebisch condemned the tax and proposed an income tax on consumption as an alternative.[34] In a more specific manner, Federico Julio Herschel, inspired by the Indian model, proposed a so-called tax on expenditure that would encourage savings and, therefore, investments. The tax on expenditure would be based (as would be the future VAT) on the sales tax, the internal taxes, and the *impuestos a las actividades lucrativas* (provincial turnover taxes).[35]

The problem was not only the sales tax, but also the *impuestos a las actividades lucrativas*. Since the 1930s, the provinces had been deprived of many fiscal possibilities through the implementation of the income tax and the subsequent centralization process. In order to obtain new resources, they increased taxation on their local activities. This became a source of concern for the Argentine Industrial Union (UIA), which complained about the overlapping of taxes and demanded the suppression—or at least the unification—of these taxes.[36]

The international atmosphere contributed to the discussion of the new tax as well. In an international conference held in Santiago de

Chile, the VAT was suggested as the best alternative to sales and consumption taxes.[37] In a publication of 1964, one of the contributors emphasized the "great importance" of developing what he referred to as "a progressive system of indirect taxation" in Latin America.[38] In 1967, a Latin American nation, Brazil, became the first country to introduce the VAT as a replacement for an old turnover tax.[39]

As far as the Treasury was concerned, the sales tax had at least two important advantages. First, since it was paid by a reduced number of manufacturers, its collection was easy. Second, as Argentina increasingly became an industrial economy and industry replaced agriculture as the leading economic sector in the country, a tax on manufactures tapped into the most obvious source of wealth. However, in the mid1960s, many factories were going through dire straits and were facing significant amounts of debt with the DGI. Since then, the possibility of introducing the new tax was increasingly present for policymakers, entrepreneurs, and the media.[40]

In 1966, the Federal Council of Investments, an advisory institution created in 1959 to design and discuss development policies for Argentina provinces, debated on the possibility of introducing the VAT in the nation. The Federal Council noticed the advantages of the Value- Added Tax. Unlike the sales tax, the VAT was proportionally distributed throughout the entire chain of production and sale. But the institution also remarked upon potential difficulties in implementation. A tax on manufacturers made sense if the industrial sector was concentrated, the small number of taxpayers being an additional advantage for the tax collector. Moreover, the VAT was a cumbersome device, mainly as far as taxing retailers was concerned.[41]

When Krieger Vasena was appointed economics minister under Onganía in 1967, the VAT became a distinct possibility. The "modernizing" program of the minister underlined industrial development as one of its main goals. The VAT supposedly would reactive industrial production by suppressing the damaging sales tax and would modernize the tax system. The sales tax was not an entirely regressive levy. It had different rates according to the type of product, which ranged from 3 percent for basic consumption goods to 20 percent for durable goods. But this system might have encouraged industrial fragmentation, as some companies sought to avoid high taxation by buying some products or parts from other companies. As the tax on a certain product was paid by the selling manufacturer, that is, the last one in the chain of production, firms tended to avoid (at least in appearance) vertical integration and the incorporation of the selling phase to their structures.[42] The VAT would solve these problems and would encourage big industry to pursue the path of concentration. This was understood as part of the "modernizing" and "rationalizing" project launched by Krieger Vasena.

In January 1967, the minister announced in the venue of the Chamber of Joint Stock Corporations the inception of the new tax for January 1968.[43] The VAT aimed to widen the tax base. Thus, not only manufactures but also services were included in the new tax. Moreover, the project envisioned a progressive design for the VAT. Different products and services were subjected to different rates. The general rate would be 6 percent, but some products and services that were considered to be luxuries or nonessentials would pay 10 percent, 15 percent, or 20 percent.[44] Moreover, most essential consumption items, such as cereals, meat, and sugar, were exempted. As pointed out, the widening of the tax base meant that small businesses and retailers had to be incorporated into the scheme. However, forecasting technical problems, the project established a register system, and manufacturers who sold goods worth less than 6 million pesos and merchants and retailers who sold goods worth less than 24 million pesos were exempted.[45]

But the reform was not an easy one. The DGI and some economists recalled the technical difficulties that the new tax would involve. These were related to collection issues. Thus, the sales tax had become the most important single tax for the Treasury, representing in 1967 around 22 percent of tax revenues and more than 2 percent of the GDP. Hence, as far as collections were concerned, the sales tax was far from being a failure. This was related to the fact that the taxpayers were a small but easily target group. In 1967, there were only 60,000 registered taxpayers for the sales tax, which represented a meager 5 percent of Argentine firms. Furthermore, 80 percent of the revenues from the sales tax came from only 3 percent of the registered taxpayers, that is, "0.1 percent of the companies of the country paid a sixth of the current revenues of the national Treasury."[46] Thus, the sales tax was essentially a tax on big industry. Of course, there was a good deal of discussion about how easily manufacturers shifted the tax on to consumers. No matter where the truth lay, industrialists complained about the burden that the sales tax represented, particularly in those hard times. The VAT envisioned an alleviation of that burden by making other people contribute. However, widening the tax base was not easy, and Krieger Vasena's project sought to involve more "big" taxpayers in the process by extending the VAT to commerce and service rather than by making it a universal levy. Even in this manner, the number of taxpayers would increase substantially, which in turn would create new difficulties.

Collection was the main concern for the DGI. In fact, if Krieger Vasena's proposal was a timid one, it was due to the fear of a sudden loss of revenue. The entrepreneurs became impatient with the government's slow action. In 1968, the director of the DGI, Raúl Cuello, presented to the Buenos Aires Stock Market the reasons for the delay in introducing the VAT:

> But the increase in administrative costs and the administrative complexity of a tax that would incorporate such a large mass of taxpayers would make it practically unmanageable by our revenue agency... This is the reason why, facing the demands of entrepreneurial sectors... against the sales tax, I insist that the main problem created by it is a financial one. If so, the payment system should be discussed in order to allow for a greater flexibility... but the suppression [of the tax] should never be considered.[47]

The VAT introduction stalled, but it was permanently present in the debates. In 1970, the DGI still insisted on finding technical obstacles to its implementation.[48] Yet, the entrepreneurs, particularly the big manufacturers, did not give up. In 1971, the UIA requested from the economics minister a bold measure: to substitute the VAT and some new taxes for the sales tax, the export withholdings, and the income tax.[49]

In September 1971, the so-called Committee for the Study of the Tax Reform echoed the recommendation of establishing the VAT made by the Argentine Association of Tax Lawyers, the Association of Banks of the Argentine Republic, the Argentine Federation of Graduated in Economics, and last, but not least the Coordinated Action of Free Business Associations (ACIEL), the umbrella organization of businessmen.[50] This recommendation was not immediately followed, but the VAT was finally passed in 1974. The bill passed that year established that the new tax would begin to work in 1975, allowing taxpayers a reasonable time for understanding the new tax. Taxpayers had to be "educated." The goal was a challenging one because the number of registered taxpayers was expected to rocket from around 175,000 to more than 600,000.[51] As in most previous drafts, the law established different rates for different products and services: a 13 percent general rate and a 21 percent rate for luxuries. Most popular consumption goods were exempted. It also established a drawback system for the exports, which allowed exporters to get a refund on the VAT paid for those products that were sold abroad.[52]

Several associations of the civil society (most of them business interest representatives), such as the Association of Industrialists of Cordoba, the Association of Financial and Investment Firms, the UIA, the Argentine Chamber of Joint Stock Corporations, or the Buenos Aires Stock Market, participated in the design of the VAT bill.[53]

Of course, the DGI presented the VAT as an essential part of the economic program of the Peronist government: "The Value Added Tax...is framed within the global goals of the tax reform of 1974," and the objectives of the reform were "harmonic" with the "Three Years Plan for the Reconstruction and the National Liberation." Among these objectives was "a more equitable distribution of the national wealth."[54] It is true that the program designed by the CGE included the VAT, but the final outcome was beyond the control of this organization and of many of those who were in charge of the governmental economic policy from 1973 to 1974.[55]

Nonetheless, not every official and economist within the DGI showed a similar enthusiasm about the new tax. For two of the most well reputed Argentine tax experts, Jorge Macon and Pedro Pavesi, "The adoption of the tax on added value is not a priority for the Argentine tax regime, since other reforms, particularly those focused on personal taxation, are more urgently needed." This meant that before introducing the VAT, the progressive tools of the tax scheme had to be revisited.[56]

Yet, both defenders and detractors of the new tax concurred that the VAT might improve the existent system in two ways. First, it would replace two levies characterized by their inefficiency and high rates of evasion: the sales tax, and the *impuesto a las actividades lucrativas,* which were collected in some provinces. Sales tax was particularly onerous for manufacturers and encouraged evasion from taxpayers, who felt they were unfairly treated. By spreading the burden among a greater number of taxpayers, the new tax on added value would widen the tax base (one of the DGI's goals in order to increase revenues) and at the same time halt evasion and stimulate productivity and investments.[57] Macon and Pavesi agreed that the new tax would be "an important improvement in the field of consumption taxes."[58]

But beyond these improvements, the new tax was also praised for different reasons. The VAT had gathered an impressive degree of support amid the political and social turmoil of the period. Marcelo Lascano, one of the defenders of the tax within the DGI, enthusiastically celebrated this unusual consensus: "The support of the political parties or of the associations representing the national producers proves the sympathy for the tax reform and the VAT. There was, it is true, some disagreements on some technical details of the tax or on some administrative measures. However, there was no general challenge."[59]

But Lascano could not conceal that this new tax, which was based upon a pact supported by political parties and business associations, excluded the CGE and the CGT, and, even more revealingly, that it did not consider the possibility of submitting the new tax to the scrutiny of the social pact. Thus, Lascano had to forcefully integrate the VAT into the Peronist economic agenda: "The Three Years Plan, drafted in 1973, although it did not incorporate the VAT as a specific tool among its financial and economic policy proposals, gathered all the suggestions that had made the VAT a key piece in the new tax strategy."[60]

Macon and Pavesi were also aware that the VAT meant a rupture with the recent history of Argentine taxation. For the first time in many years, a tax gathered the support of several associations of the civil society:

> The VAT...will have important advantages...First, the tax seemed to enjoy a high degree of prestige among important sectors of public opinion, probably due to the valuable preachment of remarkable experts...this perhaps happens for the first time in the history of Argentina. Of course, this can be considered as a political and not a technical feature, but we have to keep on mind...that in order to make a tax work properly we have to get the approval of those who have to pay it.[61]

The enactment of the VAT was a sort of silent paradox of the third Peronist administration. The government tried hopelessly to achieve a lasting stability for Argentina, by arranging a broad social agreement between employers and employees. But the social pact never worked. Trade unions accepted it as an imposition of the political movement to which they belonged and which shaped their identity. Some members of the CGE were their main supporters, but they were overwhelmed by political turmoil. Other business interests—perhaps not as numerous as those gathered in the CGE, but equally or more powerful—half-heartedly accepted the pact, but only for a brief period. The VAT was passed by a noninstitutionalized social pact, in which neither the CGE nor the CGT participated. Policy makers were aware of the significance of the new tax. The director of the DGI, the accountant José Andrés Ballotta, underlined that the VAT would "become the axis of the tax reform."[62] The VAT was designed as the instrument that would provide the Treasury with enough revenue without interfering with entrepreneurial activities. The DGI did not recognize this image and asserted that the VAT was part of a wider plan to distribute income and to attain some of the objectives of the economic policy.[63] However, in the long run, the VAT was mainly a collection instrument. It would substitute for the sales tax and would provide greater revenue than did progressive devices during the coming years. In 1975, VAT revenues amounted to 1.73 percent of the GDP; in 1977, they represented 2.75 percent. The VAT's consolidation came in the 1990s, during Carlos Menem's administration. Whereas in 1991, it reached 3.75 percent of the GDP, in 1992, it contributed with revenues that were equivalent to 6.41 percent of the GDP. This level was maintained throughout the decade.[64] As long as the VAT was aimed at any social or political goal, it laid the ground for a detachment of the state from intervention in the market.

Epilogue

The decline—or at least the reshaping of the Argentine industry—and the introduction of the VAT coincided. A progressive tax system—with the income tax playing a pivotal role—had, in Argentina and elsewhere, been based upon the development of a fully industrial economy. I am not claiming here a strict causality. Britain was toying with the idea of the income tax during the Napoleonic wars, when, even if the industrial revolution had already begun, it would be difficult to describe the country as a full-fledged industrial society. When the income tax was introduced in Argentina in the 1930s, although factories were already a presence in the country, manufactures did not (yet) represent the main sector within the Argentine economy. However, in Argentina, in Britain, and elsewhere, industrialization reinforced the income tax and other progressive tax instruments. Since the 1970s, or even earlier, in Western Europe and the United States, a rapid process of obsolescence and technical change unfolded. Some had talked about deindustrialization; others preferred to speak about a "post-fordist" society, a modification of labor relationships, technology, and a shift in investments from heavy industry, mines and other to new sectors. The introduction of the VAT in Europe coincided with the beginnings of this dramatic process. The momentous consequences of this tax reform for Argentina had already been noted.[65] As we have already seen, Argentine industry was facing growing problems since the crisis of 1962. These problems were, without a doubt, affecting the Argentine fiscal balance.[66] Corporation tax revenues plummeted, tax evasion mounted, and the key role of manufacturers as tax agents was not properly fulfilled. The introduction of the VAT in 1974 was not the solution to Argentine tax crisis, but it meant an acknowledgment of its problems.

Paradoxically, the decline of income taxation was, to some extent, related to the very pattern of industrial development that was being pursued by Argentina and other Latin American countries. As E. V. K. Fitzgerald remarked, the "fiscal crisis" of the state in Latin America in the 1970s was related to the need to promote industrialization by providing subsidies, tax credits, and different public services for private companies. Ultimately, taxes on income, wealth, or even on foreign trade were going to be replaced by taxes on consumption.[67]

Therefore, the collapse of the Peronist government in 1976 was also a fiscal crisis. In the midst of the rampant inflation and political violence, it is difficult to perceive the contribution of the last democratic government before 1983 to tax reform in Argentina. Yet, to some extent, the introduction of the VAT and the unification of income and wealth taxes under the rubric of *ganancias* was a rehearsal of what Carlos Menem's administration would accomplish in the early 1990s. Domingo Cavallo's tax policy aimed at increasing collection by widening the tax base and simplifying the tax structure. The income tax and, mainly, the VAT became the cornerstone of the tax scheme. The government was able to reverse the declining trend of the income tax that had begun around 1952. As in the 1970s, the success of the VAT in the 1990s was the result of a consensus. This was not a corporative consensus that was forged behind the scene with business representatives, but rather a wide social support to Menem bold policies, as a result of his success in curving inflation after the dramatic experience of hyperinflation during the period 1989–1990. In fact, the hyperinflation meant that the inflation tax—as an alternative source of revenue for the Treasury—had to be ruled out. The persistent memory of the hyperinflation and the greater political stability of the decade changed the institutional setting and explained the success of Cavallo's tax reforms, at least in the short run.[68] Menem and Cavallo found a more fitful environment in which to carry out their reforms than the beleaguered governments of the 1950s, the 1960s, and the 1970s.

Conclusions

The trade-off between equality and growth is one of the big themes of political philosophy and economic thought. To some extent, this is a universal theme, which is always present in human affairs. Nonetheless, this dilemma became particularly acute in modern times, especially so in the twentieth century. John Rawls's outstanding classic, *A Theory of Justice*, was not only a timeless philosophical reflection, but also the product of a specific context. Rawls's essay might be interpreted as a defense of social democracy—when this ideology was both at the apex of its success and was being assaulted by economic problems and ideological renovation.[1] If the dilemma between growth and equality was so intense in the twentieth century, this was the result of the extension of democracy in the Western World, understood not only as an extension of political rights but also of the social and economic inclusion of the popular classes. Argentina was not foreign to this process. One of the classic accounts of Argentina's modern history is, in fact, a narrative of the progressive inclusion of social sectors into the category of *citizen*, as the term is understood in a broad sense.[2] But the process of democratization of Argentine society was a strained one, making the conflict between equality and growth particularly severe.[3]

In Western Europe and—to a minor extent—in the United States, the process of democratization during the twentieth century was accompanied by a complete overhaul of nineteenth-century taxation. Despite many national variations, it is possible to assert that graduated, personal, and corporation taxes became the fulcrum of the new tax regimes. The sacrifices imposed by two devastating wars and the growing state intervention in the economy account for this move toward progressive taxation. Nonetheless, pressures from below were also important. Working-class mobilization and democratization were an important part of the process of tax reform. After World War II, the creation of welfare states in many European countries and—to a lesser extent—in the United States demanded the generalization of the income tax and other progressive tools.

Latin America and Argentina were not strangers to this process either. Ideas about building a social democracy played an important role in early discussions on the income tax in Argentina. Still, in Argentina, as in other Latin American countries (such as Brazil), the introduction of the income tax was carried out in the context of nondemocratic governments, in an epoch of political exclusionary practices. Although it is only possible to speculate on the consequences of this fact, it is possible to argue that the income tax was stained with the lack of legitimacy of the 1930s governments. Under the advent of democratic rule, the income tax in Argentina might have had more progressive features and might have been widely accepted by most social groups. On the other hand, conservative governments of the 1930s, being elected through electoral rigging, employed progressive taxation as an alternative source of legitimacy. Ultimately, the income tax worked reasonably well during the decade, thanks to the cooperation of the economic elites and the creation of a modern tax bureaucracy. This was not unique. In the United States and in most European countries, upper classes' contributions were essential for the adequate functioning of the income tax in the early phases of its implementation. At the end of the period of conservative hegemony, the process of bureaucratic modernization clashed with the alliance with upper classes and showed some of the weakness of the process of tax reform.

The process of (social) democratization that had been interrupted in 1930, was restarted under the administration of Juan Domingo Perón during the mid1940s. Although his government was prone to authoritarian rule, his agenda became a radically inclusive one. In particular, the working class was given a new place in society and politics. Inspired either by the US New Deal or by the British Labour government in the immediate aftermath of World War II, the Peronist government committed itself to a general improvement of workers' and popular classes' welfare. Nonetheless, and unlike in the European cases, Peronist rulers did not resort to taxation as an essential instrument in the building of a fullfledged welfare state. A consequence of this was that the Treasury did not need to extend the tax base of the progressive scheme. The number of income tax payers remained surprisingly low in Argentina during these years. This had a lasting influence on Argentina's capacity to sustain ambitious welfare policies. In truth, European welfare states were based not on taxes that plundered the rich, but on almost universal progressive taxation.

Moreover, taxes did not play a major role in the political imaginarium of the Argentine working class—not even as a distributive weapon. To some extent, Peronism had helped to transform workers into citizens, but not into taxpayers.

Despite the mildness of progressive taxation during the Peronist era, the tax system began to be challenged by several social actors. This demonstrated the importance of the link between taxes and political trust. Economic elites and some sectors of the middle classes showed their discontent with Peronist social policies and authoritarian manners by boycotting the tax system. Later on, inflation and economic problems reinforced the trend toward tax evasion and fraud. These troubles not only had economic roots but were also related to social actors' growing distrust of the state and of one another.

The economic and social turmoil of the following decades (1955–1976) did not contribute to the restoration of confidence or to the reformulation of a more inclusive social agreement, which might have rescued the Argentine tax system. The income tax and other progressive duties lost their importance as a source of revenue for the Treasury vis-à-vis taxes on foreign trade, debt, and—most dangerously—inflation. Attempts at reforming the tax system failed; often, they were the victims of political instability. It must be said that the government, through these attempts, even the more conservative ones, never lost the hope of making the income tax the nerve of Argentine fiscal regime. The idea that a modern and efficient tax system had to be based upon progressive direct taxation still enjoyed an almost universal recognition (in Argentina and elsewhere). Yet, the ideal model and the reality were diverging more and more. The establishment of the VAT in 1974 was, to some extent, an attempt to reconcile reality to the tax law. It was also the first time that economic elites had a significant influence in the shaping of a new tax. This was an omen of the defeat of equality in its battle against growth.

Between 1976 and 1991 (or even until 2001–2002), Argentina lived through her particular fiscal crisis of the state, which was punctuated by a hyperinflationary episode in 1989, and that ended in an international default in December 2001. In the process, the economic structure was rearranged, and Argentineans witnessed the demise of the model of development that had been based on the manufacturing sector and the domestic market. During the first decade of the present century, Argentina had firmly reoriented her economic model toward the export of rural commodities, thus replicating the formula of the "golden years" of the beginning of the twentieth century. This process had been a painful one and has been accompanied by an increase in inequalities. The fiscal system has not been completely rearranged, though, as shown in the episodes of 2001 and 2008 that have been referred to in the introduction to this book.

In the 1990s, Carlos Menem's administration found a solution to monetary instability in the so-called convertibility law, that is, in a currency board system that fixed the value of the peso. This system weakened the competitiveness of Argentine exports and made the government resort to external borrowings in order to buttress the currency board. Nonetheless, at least for some years, the Argentine economy achieved reasonable economic growth, inflation was subdued, and there were some improvements in economic efficiency.[4] There were improvements in collection as well. The control of prices automatically led to increased revenues for the Treasury (the Olivera-Tanzi effect). Besides, the government committed itself to a stricter control of tax collection, at least until 1993.[5] Income tax collection recovered from 0.67 percent of the GDP in 1991 to 3.78 percent of the GDP in 2001, whereas the VAT, which amounted to 3.75 percent of the GDP in 1991, reached 5.71 percent in 2001.[6]

The reform achieved some lasting goals.[7] Tax revenues reached stability during the decade. Yet, problems persisted. Probably, the atmosphere of moral laxity that surrounded Menem's administration did not help to rebuild citizens' trust in their institutions, which included taxes (in fact, control of inflation might have contributed more significantly to the fiscal results than did the scarce governmental attempts to restore credibility in the institutions and trust). Despite some reforms in 1998 and 1999, the tax base remained small, save in the case of the VAT.[8] Taxes were not more equitable either. In fact, if we search for an egalitarian side to Menem's policies, we should look at monetary policies. The taming of hyperinflation improved income distribution early in his tenure; a strong currency (the peso was pegged to the dollar) preserved the illusion of a high-salary economy.[9] Late in the 1990s, economic recession played havoc with the Argentine fiscal balance. Revenues coming from VAT dropped by 20 percent in 2001; those from social security dropped by 11 percent; and income and property tax collection fell by 10 percent. The government experimented with new types of taxes. In 2001, it enacted a tax on bank accounts and transactions, which amounted to more than 10 percent of total state revenues in the second half of the year.[10] Late in that year, the currency board system was on the verge of collapse. The uncertainties and rumors led to a run on banks. In December 2001, the government of the Radical Fernando de la Rua limited the withdrawal from bank deposits, causing a popular revolt in the city of Buenos Aires and, ultimately, to its own demise.[11] In 2002, after devaluation and default, tax revenues kept falling. The critical situation led the new government, now again in Peronist hands, to impose duties on exports, as it had done during World War I.[12]

Default and devaluation were paving the way for a new epoch in Argentine economic history, for a return to an export-led growth. Taxation was reshaped in this new export era. The tax burden became heavier. Since Argentina was already an open economy and was fully integrated into the world market, taxes on imports lost their significance. Export taxes appeared intermittently and gained more importance from 2007 onward. Income tax and taxes on wealth in general have played a small role in the Argentine tax system. They have recovered since the early 1990s, partly due to the end of inflation, but mainly due to the fact that the recently privatized companies now have to pay the corporation tax.[13] Payroll and social security taxes gained salience. The main source of revenue for the Treasury came from consumption taxes, in particular, the VAT, which became the universal tax that the income tax aspired to be. The other novelty was the frequent resort to emergency and extraordinary levies, among them, taxes on exports. In 2004, emergency taxes represented an impressive 4.6 percent of the GDP.[14] One of these extraordinary measures, the raising of export retentions on soybeans, caused the 2008 rebellion of rural taxpayers.

The Argentine tax system looks incoherent and regressive (even if we consider the controversial export taxes as progressive ones). Argentina's tax history is not unique when compared to that of other Latin American or European nations. Since the 1970s or the 1980s, inequality rose worldwide. Since the 1970s, trust in the capacity of the tax system to redress economic inequality began to vanish. In the 1980s, international economic agencies recommended that inequality and poverty be tackled via social expenditures and not via progressive taxation. Since an earlier date—in the 1950s—the British Labour Party had developed a gloomier view on the possibility of narrowing the gap between rich and poor through income taxation. In the mid 1960s, a Labour government toyed with the idea of introducing the VAT as a response to the loss of productivity of British industry.[15] In 2006, François Bourgignon and Pamela Cox, president and vice-president, respectively, of the World Bank for Latin America, published a long article in the conservative daily *La Nación* on ways to deal with inequality and poverty in Argentina. Both authors praised Nestor Kirchner's government for Argentina's impressive recovery after the 2001 collapse and for making equity "a central theme in the [public] debate in Argentina."[16] What were the recommendations of both these international experts? First, the setting up of institutions that provided equal opportunities; second ensuring the right working of markets: "When markets do not work or when they do so in an imperfect way, the distribution of wealth and power influences the way in which opportunities of investments are defined."[17] Third, if market failures were impossible to correct—which was the "ideal" solution—the government had to carry out distributive policies, that is, "for example, provide better access to education, health or sanitary services."[18] Revealingly enough, taxation was not even mentioned. Probably, they were considered another distortion of free markets. Nonetheless, some studies demonstrated that progressive taxation still played an important role in improving the distribution of wealth in many European countries.[19] Would not inequalities have been greater in Argentina without the income tax? Will Argentina be ready to tackle social unfairness in the future without extensive progressive taxation?

Notes

Introduction

1. *La Nación*, October 4, 2010.
2. According to a recent study, more than 85 percent of Argentineans confessed to having commited some type of tax fraud in the past year. See Marcelo S. Bergman, *Tax Evasion and the Rule of Law in Latin America: The Political Culture of Cheating and Compliance in Argentina and Chile* (University Park: The Pennsylvania State University Press, 2009), 4.
3. As far as I know, we do not have many studies on the Latin American history of taxation. See Luis Aboites Aguilar and Luis Jáuregui, eds., *Penuria sin fin: Historia de los impuestos en México siglos XVIII–XX* (México: Instituto Mora, 2005) and Paula Azar et al., *¿De quién, para quiénes y para qué?: Las finanzas públicas en el Uruguay del siglo XX* (Montevideo: Fin de Siglo, 2009).
4. Roberto Cortés Conde, *Poder, Estado y política: Impuestos y sociedad en la Argentina y en los Estados Unidos* (Buenos Aires: Edhasa, 2011) offers a cultural approach to this issue for the nineteenth century. The notion of "budgetary cultures" is developed by Carolyn Webber and Aaron Widalsky's *A History of Taxation and Expenditures in the Western World* (New York: Simon & Schuster, 1986), chap. 1. It refers to the priorities chosen by a society in matters of spending and taxing. These priorities are part of a wider moral and cultural framework that holds together the social fabric.
5. Martin Daunton, *Just Taxes: The Politics of Taxation in Britain, 1914–1979* (Cambridge: Cambridge University Press, 2002), 8–13. On the concept of the tax state and its crisis, see Joseph A. Schumpeter, "The Crisis of the Tax State," *International Economic Papers* (1954): 5–38. On the historical formation of the tax state, see Kersten Krüger, "Public Finance and Modernization: The Change from Domain State to Tax State in the Sixteenth and Seventeenth Century. A Case Study," in *Wealth and Taxation in Central Europe: The History and Sociology of Public Finance*, ed. Peter-Christian Witt (Leamington: Berg, 1987).

6. See Sven Steinmo, *Taxation and Democracy: Swedish, British and American Approaches to Financing the Modern State* (New Haven & London: Yale University Press, 1993), 3–4.
7. The classical example of rational choice theory applied to politics is James Buchanan and Gordon Tullock, *The Calculus of Consent: Logical Foundations of Constitutional Democracy* (Ann Arbor: University of Michigan Press, 1963). See the perceptive critique of these approaches in Daunton, *Trusting Leviathan: The Politics of Taxation in Britain, 1779–1914* (Cambridge: Cambridge University Press, 2001), 8–10.
8. Richard Bonney, "Revenue," in *Economic Systems and State Finance*, ed. Richard Bonney (Oxford: Oxford University Press, 1995), 435.
9. Ibid., 472.
10. The "game theory" perspective, drawing on a contractual view of society, has expanded the notion of rationality that had been defended by the rational-choice approach by underscoring the influence of other agents' decision on individual behavior.
11. Buchanan and Tullock, *Calculus of Consent*, 34–35.
12. Of course, the problem of the "free rider" (the one who takes advantage of collective action without sacrificing anything) is a real one. But cooperation and trust might be a solution that is just as important as public coercion to this challenge. On this topic, the classical work is Mancur Olson, *The Logic of Collective Action*, (Cambridge, MA: Harvard University Press, 1965).
13. Jonathan Di John, "The Political Economy of Taxation and Tax Reform in Developing Countries," in *Institutional Change and Economic Development*, ed. Ha-Joon Chang (New York: United Nation University Press, 2007), 136–40.
14. Margaret Levi, *Of Rule and Revenue* (Berkeley: University of California Press, 1988), 10–13. Levy has been widely influenced by Charles Tilly's historical sociology and by Douglass North's institutionalist approach to economic history. See also Bonney, "Revenue", 434–35, for an institutionalist historical account that pays special attention to the relationship between taxpayers and rulers. Some authors, inspired by this perspective, have dealt with the problem of tax evasion in Latin America, focusing on the administrative cost of enforcing compliance and the cost of taxpayers not paying their taxes. They emphasize that citizens' perception of the possibility of being punished by tax authorities is by itself a powerful deterrent to the evasion. See Bergman, "Tax Reform and Tax Compliance: The Divergent Path of Chile and Argentina," *Journal of Latin American Studies* 35, no. 3 (2003): 593–624, and Richard M. Bird, "Tax Reform in Latin America: A Review of Some Recent Experiences," *Latin American Research Review* 27, no. 1 (1992): 20–21.

15. Evan S. Lieberman, *Race and Regionalism in the Politics and Taxation in Brazil and South Africa* (Cambridge: Cambridge University Press, 2003), 58–59.
16. Daunton, *Trusting Leviathan*, 7. On the aspect of voluntary or "quasi voluntary" compliance, see Levi, *Rule and Revenue*, chap. 3.
17. Margaret Levi, "A State of Trust," in *Trust and Governance*, ed. Valerie Braithwaite and Margaret Levi (New York: Russel Sage Foundation, 1998), 82–84. A similar argument has been made by Bergman, *Tax Evasion*, 26–49, in what he refers to as "noncompliance" and "compliance" equilibria.
18. Ibid., especially chap. 1.
19. World Bank, *Argentina: Tax Policy for Stabilization and Economy Recovery* (Washington, DC: World Bank, 1990), 53.
20. Direct and progressive taxes are not necessarily the same, but during the twentieth century, most people—reasonably—believed that there was a relationship between graduate direct taxes and a fairer distribution of tax burdens.
21. On the issue of trust, in addition to Levi's essay see the other chapters in Braithwaite and Levi's, *Trust and Governance.*
22. Daunton, *Trusting Leviathan*,12–8.
23. The long and puzzling twentieth-century Argentine decline has deserved wide scholarly attention. Among others, see Pablo Gerchunoff and Lucas Llach, *El ciclo de la ilusión y el desencanto: Un siglo de políticas económicas argentinas* (Buenos Aires: Ariel, 1998); Gerchunoff and Llach, *Entre la equidad y el crecimiento: Ascenso y caída de la economía argentina, 1880–2002* (Buenos Aires: Siglo XXI, 2004); Gerardo Della Paolera and Ezequiel Gallo, "The Argentine Puzzle" in *A New Economic History of Argentina*, ed. Gerardo Della Paolera and Alan Taylor (Cambridge: Cambridge University Press, 2003); Cortés Conde, *La economía política de la Argentina en el siglo XX* (Buenos Aires: Edhasa, 2005); Paul H. Lewis, *The Crisis of Argentine Capitalism* (Chapel Hill: The University of North Carolina Press, 1990); Carlos H. Weissman, *Reversal of Development in Argentina* (Princeton, NJ: Princeton University Press, 1987); Carlos Díaz Alejandro, *Essays on the Economic History of the Argentine Republic* (New Haven, CT: Yale University Press, 1970); Eduardo Míguez, "El fracaso argentino: Interpretando la evolución económica en el corto siglo XX," *Desarrollo Económico* 44, no. 76 (2005): 483–514; Richard D. Mallon and Juan Sourrouille, *La política económica en una sociedad conflictiva: El caso argentino* (Buenos Aires: Amorrortu, 1973) or Aldo Ferrer, *La economía argentina: Etapas de su desarrollo y problemas actuales* (Buenos Aires: FCE, 1963).
24. Levi, *Rule and Revenue*, 17–23.
25. This is Partha Dasgupta's argument in "Trust as a Commodity," in *Trust: Making and Breaking Cooperative Relations*, ed. Diego Gambetta (New York: Basil Blackwell, 1988), 50.

26. John Rawls, *The Theory of Justice* (Cambridge, MA: Harvard University Press, 1971) developed the concept of "veil of ignorance," referring to a hypothetical "original" position in which individuals do not know their social status, talents, luck, and so on. Therefore, in that position, an individual would prefer a social contract in which any increase in inequality should benefit those less better off. In must be said, nonetheless, that Rawls introduced his "original position" as an abstract concept and not with a precise historical meaning.
27. Buchanan and Tullock, *Calculus of Consent,* 78.
28. Steinmo, *Taxation and Democracy,* 7.
29. Daunton, *Trusting Leviathan,* 19.
30. Theda Skocpol, "Bringing the State Back In: Strategies of Analysis in Current Research," in *Bringing the State Back In*, ed. Peter B. Evans, Dietrich Rueschemeyer, and Theda Skocpol (Cambridge: Cambridge University Press, 1985), 7.
31. Ibid., 9, 14.
32. See Roy Hora, *Los estancieros contra el estado: La Liga Agraria y la formación del ruralismo político en la Argentina* (Buenos Aires: Siglo XXI, 2009).
33. Miguel Ángel Centeno, *Blood and Debt: War and the Nation-State in Latin America* (University Park: The Pennsylvania State University Press, 2002), 6, 130–37.
34. Evans and Rueschemeyer, "The State and Economic Transformation: Toward and Analysis of the Conditions Underlying Effective Intervention," in *Bringing the State* (see note 30), 49 and 54.
35. The classical account of the process of state building in Argentina is Oscar Oszlak, *La formación del Estado argentino: Orden, progreso y organización nacional* (Buenos Aires: Ariel, 2004). See also Tulio Halperin Donghi, *Proyecto y construcción de una nación (Argentina 1846–1880)* (Caracas: Biblioteca Ayacucho, 1982), prologue. I am not claiming any kind of Argentine exceptionalism as far as state capacities are concerned. A similar development can be found in the Brazilian case; see Kurt Weyland, *Democracy without Equity: Failures of Reform in Brazil* (Pittsburg, PA: Pittsburg University Press, 1996), 185–86.
36. Albert O. Hirschman, *Exit, Voice and Loyalty: Responses to Decline in Firms, Organizations, and States* (Cambridge, MA: Harvard University Press, 1970), 33.

1 Discussing the Income Tax (1914–1930)

1. Roberto Cortés Conde, *Dinero, deuda y crisis: Evolución fiscal y monetaria en la Argentina, 1862–1890* (Buenos Aires: Editorial Sudamericana, 1989).
2. Between 1890 and 1914, taxes on international trade represented around 53 percent of the Treasury's revenues. Juan Pan-Montojo,

"Los ingresos aduaneros y la formación de los estados nacionales: España, Argentina, Perú y México en el siglo XIX" (paper presented at the 14th International Economic History Congress, Helsinki, 2006); Jimena Caravaca, "Estado, economía y economistas: El caso del impuesto a la renta en la Argentina, 1890–1932" (master's thesis, FLACSO-Buenos Aires, 2008), 20 and Andrés Regalsky and Elena Salerno, "Financiamiento e inversión pública en la transición hacia el Estado empresario: Argentina 1900–1935" (paper presented at the 14th International Economic History Congress, Helsinki, 2006), 7.

3. The trend toward progressive taxation gained international momentum during the war and in its aftermath. The United States and some European countries established their income tax during this period or, like Britain, transformed their old proportional taxes into graduate income tax. Colombia, Chile, Brazil, and Mexico also enacted the income tax after the war.
4. The Radical Civic Union, founded in 1891, was originally seen by the historiography as the representative of the middle class against the conservative oligarchy that ruled the country. Today, this characterization has been widely disputed. See the traditional image in David Rock, *Politics in Argentina 1890–1930: The Rise and Fall of Radicalism* (London: Cambridge University Press, 1975); and two recent revisions in Paula Alonso, *Between Revolution and the Ballot Box: The Origins of the Argentine Radical Party* (Cambridge: Cambridge University Press, 2000) and Ezequiel Adamovsky, "Acerca de la relación entre el Radicalismo argentino y la 'clase media' (una vez más)," *HAHR* 89, no. 2 (2009): 209–51. The UCR was also known as the Radical Party, or simply, the Radicals. I will use these terms indistinctly in this book. Therefore, Radical will refer to the political party and not necessarily to an ideology.
5. Adriana Montequín, "Sector público y sistema tributario argentino, 1914–1932," *Ciclos en la historia, la economía, la sociedad* 5, no. 9 (1995): 144, and Rock, *Politics in Argentina*, 107–10.
6. Pablo Gerchunoff and Horacio Aguirre, *La economía argentina entre la gran guerra y la gran depresión* (Buenos Aires: CEPAL, 2006), 52.
7. Ibid., 48.
8. I analyzed this topic in José Antonio Sánchez Román, "Economic Elites, Regional Cleavages, and the First Attempts at Introducing the Income Tax in Argentina," *HAHR* 89, no. 2 (2009): 253–83.
9. On the economic consequences of the war in Europe and the rest of the world see Derek Aldcroft, *From Versailles to Wall Street, 1919–1929* (London: Allen Lane, 1977), chap. 2. For Latin America see Bill Albert, *South America and the First World War: The Impact of the War on Brazil, Argentina, Peru and Chile* (Cambridge: Cambridge University Press, 1988).

10. *DSCD*, 5, September 24–25, 1928, 453–54 and Daniel Díaz Fuentes, *Las políticas fiscales latinoamericanas frente a la Gran Depresión: Argentina, Brasil y México* (1920–1940) (Madrid: Instituto de Estudios Fiscales, 1993), 52.
11. *DSCD*, 5, September 24–25, 1928, table 8.
12. Regalsky and Salerno, "Financiamiento e inversión," 11.
13. Pablo Gerchunoff and Lucas Llach, *El ciclo de la ilusión y el desencanto: Un siglo de políticas económicas argentinas* (Buenos Aires: Ariel, 1998), 68–74.
14. Salaberry's draft in *DSCD*, 2, June 24, 1919, 466–69 and Molina's reform in *DSCD*, 8, February 5, 1920, 826–29 and Caravaca, "Estado, economía," 55–57.
15. In 1923, the average wage for male workers in the city of Buenos Aires was less than 150 pesos per month, that is, 1,800 pesos per year. Unskilled labor and women earned less than that, and wages in the interior were substantially lower. Thus, as late as 1930, a policeman in the province of La Rioja received 60 pesos per month. The figures in Julio Godio, *Historia del movimiento obrero argentino: 1870–2000* (Buenos Aires: Corregidor, 2000), 349 and Joel Horowitz, *Argentina's Radical Party and Popular Mobilization, 1916–1930* (University Park: Pennsylvania State University, 2008), 84, 198. Of course, in the case of families in which both spouses earned salaries, incomes might climb to the minimum set by the law. However, in addition to family allowances, in Molina's final version of the tax, a married taxpayer might deduct from their taxable income 1,000 pesos.
16. Gerchunoff and Aguirre, *Economía argentina*, 51.
17. Caravaca, "Estado, economía," 54.
18. Tulio Halperin Donghi, *Vida y muerte de la república verdadera (1910–1930)* (Buenos Aires: Ariel, 2000), 156–57.
19. "El impuesto sobre la renta I. Significado de esta reforma," *La Prensa*, June 9, 1917.
20. "El impuesto sobre la renta III. ¿Obedecerá a una reforma orgánica?," *La Prensa*, June 13, 1917.
21. See their opinions in *La Nación*, September 4–6, 1918.
22. *REA*, June 1919, 474–75.
23. See Rock, *Politics in Argentina*, 125–200 and Rock, "Lucha civil en la Argentina: La Semana Trágica de enero de 1919," *Desarrollo Económico* 11, nos. 42/44 (1971–1972): 165–215.
24. The Radical governments tried to pass (sometimes successfully) many measures concerning social insurance, minimum wages, the extension of the eight-hour day, and the mandatory rest day for all workers. They also show a limited support for trade unions and even some strikes, arousing the annoyance of economic elites, which accused the government of encouraging social unrest for the sake of electoral benefits. See Horowitz, *Argentina's Radical Party*, 115–47.

25. Eduardo Zimmermann, *Los liberales reformistas: La cuestión social en la Argentina, 1890–1916* (Buenos Aires: Editorial Sudamericana/ Universidad de San Andrés, 1995) and Caravaca, "Estado, economía," 26.
26. *REA*, September 1918, 295.
27. Ibid., 356.
28. "El impuesto sobre la renta II. La reforma en Italia," *La Prensa,* June 11, 1917.
29. *La Nación,* September 10, 1918. See also Caravaca, "Estado, economía," 63–64 and Sánchez Román, "El poliedro de la igualdad: Nociones de justicia impositiva en el Brasil y la Argentina en las décadas de 1920 y 1930," *Boletín del Instituto de Historia Argentina y Americana Dr. Emilio Ravignani 28* (2005): 14.
30. *REA*, September 1918, 338.
31. Salvador Oria, one of the defenders of the new tax, acknowledged some of these problems, REA, September 1918, 32–23. See the critics in *REA*, September 1918, 339; *La Nación,* September 5–6, 1918.
32. CACIP, "Impuesto a la renta. Su inoportunidad y peligros," *Estudios de Problemas Nacionales,* 5, December 1918, 12.
33. Ramm Doman, Llobet, José Etchevery, president of the Cereal Stock Market of Buenos Aires, and the CACIP shared this opinion. See *La Razón,* September 3, 1918 and CACIP, "Impuesto a la renta," 14.
34. *REA*, September 1918, 356.
35. See, for example, *REA*, September 1918, 296 and *La Nación,* September 5, 1918.
36. *La Nación,* September 13, 1918.
37. Rock, *Politics in Argentina,* 110.
38. Horowitz, *Argentina's Radical Party,* 65. In fact, due to economic circumstances, Yrigoyen was forced to cut 20 percent in public expenditure, mostly in public investments. His successor, Alvear, was more fortunate, and he could expand public outlays. Nonetheless, Alvear's administration did not spend more in proportion to population than previous Conservative rulers had done, at least until 1927. See Gerchunoff and Aguirre, *Economía argentina,* 58–62.
39. Regalsky and Salerno, "En los comienzos del Estado empresario: la inversión pública en ferrocarriles y obras sanitarias entre 1900 y 1928," *Anuario del Centro de Estudios Históricos "Profesor Carlos S. A. Segretti"* 5, no. 5 (2005): 251.
40. *DSCD,* 5, September 24–25, 1928, table 8.
41. Regalsky and Salerno, "Financiamiento e inversión," 3.
42. CACIP, "Impuesto a la renta," 17.
43. Letter of the UIA to the Chamber of Deputies of the Nation, December 5, 1918, reproduced in CACIP, "Impuesto a la renta," 24.
44. U.K. Department of Overseas Trade, *Report on the Financial and Economic Condition of the Argentine Republic,* by Mr. H. O. Chalkley, (Commercial Secretary to H. M. Legation Buenos Aires) 1921, 9.

45. Between 1920 and 1930, public expenditures increased by 100 percent. Gerchunoff and Llach, *Ciclo de la ilusión,* 469.
46. Regalsky and Salerno, "Comienzos del Estado," 252. See also Díaz Fuentes, *Políticas fiscales,* 52 and *DSCD,* 5, September 24–25, 1928, 453–54.
47. Regalsky and Salerno, "Comienzos del Estado," 250–53.
48. "El impuesto sobre la renta II" and "El impuesto sobre la renta III."
49. Proceedings of the first Annual University Congress of La Plata University, November 5, 1923, published in *REA*, July 1924, 89.
50. Díaz Fuentes, *Políticas fiscales,* 123.
51. Montequín, "Sector público," 150.
52. Department of Overseas Trade, *Report on the Financial* 1921, 8.
53. See a detailed analysis in the quoted works of Regalsky and Salerno.
54. Robert Potash, *El ejército y la política en la Argentina, 1928–1945: De Yrigoyen a Perón* (Buenos Aires: Editorial Sudamericana, 1971), 36–37.
55. To some extent, Argentine fragmentation of authority resembled the United States pattern, although in the latter, the interaction between regional politics and cumbersome Congress arrangements produced a much more complex outcome. See Sven Steinmo, *Taxation and Democracy: Swedish, British, and American Approaches to Financing the Modern State*, (New Haven, CT: Yale University Press, 1993), 72.
56. See, for instance, *DSCD,* 6, September 30, 1927, 436.
57. *La Nación,* September 17, 1924.
58. Department of Overseas Trade, *Report of the Financial* 1923, 7.
59. *DSCD,* 5, January 16, 1930, 713.
60. In 1926, Alejandro Bunge wrote about a "financial dictatorship" consequence of "the inaction of the Congress that has given up its most elemental rights and duties." *REA*, June 1926, 486.
61. *DSCD,* 8, December 16, 1926, 45 and 6, September 30, 1927, 454.
62. *La Razón,* November 22, 1918.
63. Caravaca, "Estado, economía," 30.
64. Héctor Diéguez, "Crecimiento e inestabilidad del valor y el volumen físico de las exportaciones en el período 1864–1963," *Desarrollo Económico* 12, no. 46 (1972): 333–49 and Gerchunoff and Llach, *Ciclo de la ilusión*, 466.
65. On Bunge and the *Revista de Economía Argentina,* see Jorge Pantaleón, "El surgimiento de la nueva economía argentina: El caso Bunge," in *Intelectuales y expertos: La constitución del conocimiento social en la Argentina*, ed. Federico Neiburg and Mariano Plotkin (Buenos Aires: Paidós, 2004), 183–88; Caravaca and Plotkin, "Crisis, ciencias sociales y elites estatales: La constitución del campo de los economistas estatales en la Argentina, 1910–1935," *Desarrollo Económico* 47, no. 187 (2007): 401–28. On Bunge's political influence, see Claudio Belini, "El grupo Bunge y la política

económica del primer peronismo, 1943–1952," *Latin American Research Review* 41, no. 1 (2006): 30–31; Mark Falcoff, "Economic Dependency in a Conservative Mirror: Alejandro Bunge and the Argentine Frustration, 1919–1943," *Inter-American Economic Affairs* 35, no. 4 (1982): 57–75. On Bunge's ideas see José Luis de Imaz, "Alejandro E. Bunge, economista y sociólogo," *Desarrollo Económico* 14, no. 55 (1974): 545–67 and María Cristina Lucchini, Teodoro V. Blanco, and Ángel Cerra, "El pensamiento industrialista argentino en el período de entreguerras-el estudio de un caso: La influencia de List en Bunge," *EIAL* 11, no. 2 (2000): 151–70.

66. Caravaca, "Estado, economía," 41–42.
67. Most of the associations signing the CACIP's manifesto represented agrarian or commercial interests; among them: the SRA, the Buenos Aires Stock Market, the Cereal Stock Market of Buenos Aires; and many local rural societies. CACIP, "Impuesto a la renta."
68. Ibid., 25.
69. Bunge, "Nueva orientación de la política económica argentina. Introducción al estudio de la industria nacional," *REA*, June 1921, 451.
70. Ibid., 478.
71. In addition to the many articles published in the *REA*, see, for example, "La ley aduanera," *La Nación*, July 13, 1921, or "Intereses de la industria," *La Razón*, July 20, 1921.
72. "Informe de la Confederación Argentina del Comercio, de la Industria y de la Producción, sobre la actual situación económica y perspectivas, elevado a la Comisión de Presupuesto y Hacienda de la Honorable Cámara de Diputados de la Nación," *REA*, January 1922, 78.
73. Ibid., 83.
74. They even considered acceptable a tax on absentee landowners. See CACIP, "Reforma impositiva. Informe elevado a la Comisión de Presupuesto y Hacienda de la Hon. Cámara de Diputados de la Nación," *Estudios de Problemas Nacionales* 14, January 10, 1922, 13.
75. Jèze gave several conferences at the University published by the *Revista de Economía Argentina*. On Jèze's influence see, Caravaca, "Estado, economía," 74–76.
76. Jèze, "La reforma de los impuestos nacionales de la Argentina," *REA*, October-November 1923, 271.
77. In fact, Wagner supported Chancellor Bismarck's authoritarian reformism and later on would join the first anti-Semitic parties in Germany. On Wagner's ideas, see D. E. Schremmer, "Taxation and Public Finance: Britain, France and Germany," in *The Industrial Economies: The Development of Economic and Social Policies*, ed. Peter Mathias and Sidney Pollard, vol. 8, *The Cambridge Economic History of Europe* (Cambridge: Cambridge University Press, 1989), 360–62.
78. On Gaston Jèze economic and fiscal ideas, see Olivier Dard, "Économistes, juristes, technocrates et publicistes face aux questions

fiscals, de l'entre-deux-guerres aux années soixante," in *L'impôt en France aux xix et xx siècle*, ed. Comité pour l'Histoire Économique et Financière de la France (Paris: Ministère de l'Économie, des Finances et de l'Industrie, 2006), 49–54.

79. See, for example, *La Vanguardia*, May 19, 1923, and May 25, 1923.
80. *REA*, August 1923, 138.
81. *REA*, February 1932, 147. The secretary of this commission was the young economist Raúl Prebisch. See also Sánchez Román, "Shaping Taxation: Economic Elites and Fiscal Decision-Making in Argentina, 1920–1945," *Journal of Latin American Studies* 40 (2008): 83–108.
82. Yet, for the minister, the calling of interest group associations to discuss public policy was embarrassing since it contradicted the Radical Party's and Argentine liberal-democratic credo. Thus, he offered a confused apology for the existence of the advisory commissions saying that the new policy respected "those democratic principles based on the respect of individual wellbeing, the individual interest, and individual aspiration... To say individual interests is also to say every single corporation through which modern societies are organized," Rafael Herrera Vegas, "Participación del trabajo, la producción, las industrias y el comercio en los problemas económicos y financieros de la nación," *REA*, June 1923, 469.
83. When Herrera Vegas announced his reform, several banking, commercial, and industrial associations met at the Buenos Aires Stock Market and launched a campaign against the new taxes. Revealingly enough, the three most important interest associations did not participate in the meeting, and most of the participants who were involved in commerce or finance were foreigners. The SRA, the UIA, and the CACIP had been called by the government and probably hoped to obtain important gains from their negotiation with the state. Willing Spencer, Chargé d'Affaires ad Interim to the Secretary of State, August 17, 1923, Buenos Aires, *Records of the Department of State Relating to the Internal Affairs of Argentina, 1910–1929,* M 514, 835.512/37, NARA.
84. The Socialist newspaper *La Vanguardia* stated with irony: "Taking advantage of parliamentary holidays, the finance minister has decided to create a second national congress" and warned that the Rural Society had become a "co-legislative power," (July 14, 1923 and August 8, 1923). *Aréopago* was the Superior Tribunal of Ancient Athens.
85. *REA*, August 1923, 149.
86. Words of Víctor Valdani, representative of the UIA in the Commission of Tax Regime of the Ministry of Finance, sessions of August 10 and 24, 1923, *BUIA,* September 15, 1923, 7, 11.
87. CACIP, "Reforma impositiva," 10.
88. *BUIA,* September 15, 1923, 7.

89. Even *La Vanguardia,* always prone to denounce "capitalist interference," admitted that "Thanks to the prodigious diligence of the Super Technocrat Alejandro Bunge, the *Areópago* still has some functions to carry out," *La Vanguardia,* August 22, 1923.
90. *La Vanguardia,* November 7, 1923.
91. *BUIA*, November 15, 1923, 3, and *La Nación,* September 23, 1924.
92. A more extended analysis of these issues in Sánchez Román, "Shaping Taxation," 87–93.
93. Argentine *ad valorem* tariff was based on a scheme of official valuations in lieu of the actual prices of the world market. These valuations had been fixed in 1906, but they had been left behind by the rise in international prices that resulted from wartime inflation in Europe. To catch up with the actual world market prices, the Congress increased the *avalúos* in 1923: see Carl Solberg, "The Tariff and Politics in Argentina, 1916–1930," *HAHR* 53, no. 2 (1973): 275.
94. Department of Overseas Trade, *Report on the Financial,* September 1923, 12–26.
95. *BUIA*, December 15, 1923, 10.
96. Ibid., 5. The conservative daily *La Nación,* which adopted a proindustrialist stance in the 1920s, supported the UIA's complaints. See June 30, 1924 or September 21, 1924.
97. Solberg, "Tariff and Politics," 276.
98. On the industrialists' concern about tariffs and their lobbying activity, see, for example, UIA, *Texto del Memorial con que la Unión Industrial Argentina respondió a la consulta que le formulara la Comisión de Presupuesto y Hacienda de la H. Cámara de Diputados sobre el actual estado económico del país* (Buenos Aires, 1922), 56–57. On the importance of Congress for the design of the tariff, see Fernando Rocchi, "El imperio del pragmatismo: Intereses, ideas e imágenes en la política industrial del orden conservador," *Anuario IEHS* 13 (1998): 103 and Solberg, "Tariff and Politics," 264–47.
99. *DSCD*, 1, May 15, 1923, 244 and 4, June 27, 1923, 381.
100. *DSCD*, 4, June 27, 1923, 381.
101. Ibid., 395.
102. Caravaca, "Estado, economía," 84.
103. This paragraph and the following ones draw largely on Sánchez Román, "Economic Elites," 253–83.
104. *DSCD*, 1, June 9, 1920, 655.
105. *DSCD*, 2, June 22, 1920, 183. The minister defended himself by arguing, "As far as the taxes are concerned, one had to follow circumstances' advise," 188.
106. UIA, *Impuesto a la renta. Proyecto del P. E. y observaciones formuladas por la Unión Industrial Argentina* (Buenos Aires: Talleres Gráficos Caracciolo y Plantié, 1925).
107. *DSCD*, 2, June 20, 1924, 15.

108. UIA, *Impuesto a la renta.*
109. Martin Daunton, *Just Taxes: The Politics of Taxation in Britain, 1914–1979* (Cambridge: Cambridge University Press, 2002), 138.
110. Charles S. Maier, *Recasting Burgeois Europe: Stabilization in France, Germany, and Italy in the Decade after the World War First* (Princeton, NJ: Princeton University Press, 1977), 466–67 and *DSCD*, 4, August 27, 1924, 5–6.
111. Sánchez Román, "Shaping Taxation," 89–90.
112. *ASR*, September 15, 1925, 891.
113. Nonetheless, 1919 was an exceptional year. In fact, prewar figures were recovered already in 1922. The figures are drawn from the Montevido Oxford Latin American Economic History Database http://oxlad.qeh.ox.ac.uk (accessed October 9, 2011) and Roy Hora, *The Landowners of the Argentine Pampas: A Social and Political History, 1860–1945* (Oxford: Oxford University Press, 2001), 167.
114. Ibid., 163–75 and Peter H. Smith, *Politics and Beef in Argentina: Patterns of Conflict and Change* (New York: Columbia University Press, 1969), 86–107.
115. Hora, *Landowners,* 171.
116. Ibid., 156.
117. Richard J. Walter, *The Province of Buenos Aires and Argentine Politics, 1912–1943* (Cambridge: Cambridge University Press, 1985), 74–77.
118. *DSCD*, 1, April 18, 1932, 673–75.
119. UIA, *Impuesto a la renta.*
120. Ibid., 38.
121. Ibid., 39.
122. *REA*, November 1928, 407.
123. UIA, *Impuesto a la renta*, 56–57.
124. *DSCD,* 2, June 20, 1924, 10–14.
125. Ibid., 44. See also *La Nación,* September 21, 1924 and September 23, 1924.
126. Nota de la Unión Industrial Argentina al Señor Ministro de Hacienda de la Nación, Dr. Víctor M. Molina, May 2, 1924, Documento: Economía 187, Biblioteca Tornquist.
127. *DSCD,* 2, June 20, 1924, 8.
128. In fact, the industrialists devoted most of their efforts during 1924 to a more immediate threat: the approval of the Pension Law no. 11.289. See Joel Horowitz, "Cuando las élites y los trabajadores coincidieron: La resistencia al programa de bienestar patrocinado por el gobierno argentino, 1923–1924," *Anuario IEHS* 16 (2001): 109–28.
129. UIA, *Impuesto a la renta,* 30.
130. On the fiscal transformation of an interior province after the 1890's crisis, see Sánchez Román, "Tucumán y la industria azucarera ante la crisis de 1890," *Desarrollo Económico* 41, no. 163 (2001): 467–94.

131. Luis Colombo, "La protección a las industrias propias," *La Nación*, January 7, 1928.
132. *REA*, June 1927, 501.
133. See María Esther Rapalo, "De la Asociación del Trabajo a la revista Criterio: Encuentros entre propietarios e ideólogos, 1919–1929," in *La derecha argentina: Nacionalistas, neoliberales, militares y clericales*, ed. D. Rock et al. (Buenos Aires: Ediciones B, 2001).
134. *DSCD*, 7, February 1920, 831.
135. *REA*, January 1928, 54.
136. Spencer to the Secretary of State, August 17, 1923, Buenos Aires, *Records of the Department of State Relating to the Internal Affairs of Argentina, 1910–1929,* M 514, 835.512/37, NARA.
137. *REA*, June 1926, 491.
138. Article 67, however, was ambiguous enough for a more willing executive or congress to pass the law. The mentioned article stated that the Chamber of Deputies had the right to "impose direct taxes for a predetermined period that was proportionally equal in all the territory of the Nation, as far as the defence, common security and general welfare of the State demands it." *Constitución de la Nación Argentina* (Buenos Aires: Bibliográfica Argentina, 1961), 24.
139. "La unificación de los impuestos internos. Informe elevado al Ministro de Hacienda por el Director General de Impuestos Internos, Dr. Diógenes Taboada, 5 de agosto de 1925," *REA*, September 1925, 193. Bunge, in spite of being favorable to the unification of the domestic taxes, also underlined the rigor of the measure: "This, in spite of the excellent objective pursued, means to declare the national boycott to the provinces," *REA*, August 1925, 107.
140. *DSCD,* 6, September 24, 1924, 822.
141. The Governors' Conference reminded the participants of the former League of Governors, which held a decisive political grip in the construction of the Argentine state in the nineteenth century.
142. "La Conferencia de Gobernadores. Conclusiones aprobadas," *REA*, August 1926, 95.
143. "Los problemas de los impuestos internos." Letter of Benjamín Villafañe to Alejandro Orfila, August 18, 1926, published in *REA*, April 1927, 373.
144. *DSCD*, 7, January 27, 1926, 13.
145. *DSCD,* 3, August 10, 1926, 721.
146. A list of approved investments in *DSCD*, 3, August 10, 1926, 721.
147. See *DSCD,* 3, August 10, 1926, 806–08.
148. Ibid., 750.
149. Villafañe, "Los problemas de los impuestos," 373.
150. *DS* Senado, 3, August 10, 1926, 750.
151. *DS Senado,* 1, August 12, 1926, 461–62.
152. *DS Senado,* 1, July 22, 1926, 227.

153. On the position of the executive see *DS Senado*, 1, July 22, 227.
154. *DS Senado*, 1, July 1, 1926, 10–25.
155. *Constitución*, 28.
156. *DSCD*, 4, August 13, 1926, 246–47.
157. Gerchunoff and Llach, *Ciclo de la ilusión*, 97–98.
158. Ibid., 98.
159. Department of Overseas Trade, *Report on the Financial, October 1928*, 17.

2 Economic Elites, Legitimacy, and Progressive Taxation (1930–1945)

1. On these topics, see Margaret Levi, *Of Rule and Revenue* (Berkeley: University of California Press, 1988), chap. 3 and Martin Daunton, *Trusting Leviathan, The Politics of Taxation in Britain, 1779–1914* (Cambridge: Cambridge University Press, 2001), chap. 1.
2. On the impact of world depression in Argentina, see Pablo Gerchunoff and Lucas Llach, *El ciclo de la ilusión y el desencanto: Un siglo de políticas económicas argentinas* (Buenos Aires: Ariel, 1998), 112–20.
3. Díaz Fuentes, *Crisis y cambios estructurales en América Latina: Argentina, Brasil y México durante el período de entreguerras* (México: FCE, 1994), 318.
4. Gerchunoff and Llach, *Ciclo de la ilusión*, 114.
5. Gerardo Della Paolera and Alan Taylor, *Straining at the Anchor: The Argentine Currency Board and the Search for Macroeconomic Stability, 1880–1935* (Chicago, IL: University of Chicago Press, 2001), 196.
6. Díaz Fuentes, *Las políticas fiscales latinoamericanas frente a la Gran Depresión: Argentina, Brasil y México* (1920–1940) (Madrid: Instituto de Estudios Fiscales, 1993), 52.
7. Peter Alhadeff, "The Economic Formulae of the 1930s: A Reassessment," in *The Political Economy of Argentina, 1880–1946*, ed. Guido di Tella and D. C. M. Platt (Oxford: Macmillan, 1986), 108–09.
8. See, among others, Tulio Halperin Donghi, *Vida y muerte de la república verdadera (1910–1930)* (Buenos Aires: Ariel, 2000), 234–71; David Rock, *Politics in Argentina, 1890–1930: The Rise and Fall of Radicalism* (London: Cambridge University Press, 1975), 260–64; Luciano de Privitelio, "La política bajo el signo de la crisis," in *Crisis económica, avance del Estado e incertidumbre política (1930–1943)*, ed. Alejandro Cattaruzza, vol. 7 of *Nueva Historia Argentina* (Buenos Aires: Editorial Sudamericana, 2001), or María Inés Tato, *Viento de Fronda: Liberalismo, conservadurismo y democracia en la Argentina, 1911–1932* (Buenos Aires: Siglo XXI, 2004), 157–82. On Uriburu's military regime and the coup, see Halperin

Donghi, *La república imposible (1930–1945)* (Buenos Aires: Ariel, 2004), 25–56, and on his ideological trascendance, see Federico Finchelstein, *Fascismo, liturgia e imaginario: El mito del general Uriburu y la Argentina nacionalista* (Buenos Aires: FCE, 2002).

9. Ernesto Malaccorto, interview by Leandro Gutiérrez, August 1971, Proyecto Historia Oral ITDT, Buenos Aires, 3–8.
10. See a complex account for the European case in Maier, "Between Taylorism and Technocracy: European Ideologies and the Vision of Industrial Productivity in the 1920s," *Journal of Contemporary History* 5, no. 2 (1970): 27–61.
11. Jimena Caravaca, "Estado, economía y economistas: El caso del impuesto a la renta en la Argentina, 1890–1932" (master's thesis, FLACSO-Buenos Aires, 2008), 93.
12. Mateo Magariños, *Diálogos con Raúl Prebisch* (México: FCE, 1991), 68–69.
13. *REA*, February 1932, 150–54.
14. Ibid., 158–59.
15. Prebisch attempted to exonerate his cooperation with Uriburu's reactionary regime and with Uriburu himself in his interviews with Mateo Magariños: "It meant to make the tax reform in Argentina. To make those who earn more pay more...Of course the income tax had political color! It meant a slap in the face of the oligarchy." At the same time, it claimed that the income tax was a sort of dangerous word in Argentina in 1930 (Magariños, *Diálogos*, 67–69). Yet, as we have seen, this was far from accurate. Malaccorto's words reveal his attempt at presenting his past actions as always committed to social justice. But in fact, social justice was not the main concern of Mallaccorto or Prebisch when they designed the income tax : "We also had a clear-cut idea that the large majority of taxes of our country were regressive; we did not use that word yet...but we were perfectly aware that the tax system in our country did not take into consideration the capacity of payment of the taxpayer" (Malaccorto, interview by Leandro Gutiérrez, 3–4).
16. Magariños, *Diálogos*, 67.
17. José F. Uriburu, *Mensaje del Presidente provisional de la Nación al pueblo de la república: La obra del gobierno y la administración del 6 de septiembre al 6 de septiembre de 1931* (Buenos Aires: Cámara de Diputados, 1931).
18. The *Review of the River Plate,* a publication linked to British interests in Argentina, welcomed the income tax as the solution to Argentine fiscal problems and noticed that the "numerous congratulations received from abroad show only too plainly the relief that is felt at the news that emission has not been, and will not be, contemplated." See "Taxation: The Safe if Stony Path to Prosperity," *RRP*, January 22, 1932, 11. There is a long discussion about the orthodoxy or heterodoxy of Argentine governments

during the 1930s and of the consequences of public policies as far as economic recovery and even the development of a process of industrialization were concerned. However, most scholars would agree with the idea that up to 1934 or 1935, fiscal orthodoxy characterized the economic policy of the national government. See Díaz Fuentes, *Crisis y cambios*, 138–46; Alhadeff, "Economic Formulae," 57; Aldo Ferrer, *La economía argentina: Etapas de su desarrollo y problemas actuales* (México: Fondo de Cultura Económica, 1963), 230–34; Carlos Díaz Alejandro, *Essays on the Economic History of the Argentine Republic* (New Haven, CT: Yale University Press), 96, and Paolera and Taylor, *Straining at the Anchor*,188–96.

19. Deputy Antelo, *DSCD,* 1, April 16, 1932, 274.
20. *DSCD,* 1, April 23, 1932, 641–42.
21. Ibid., 189.
22. Ibid., 643–44.
23. Ibid., 644.
24. *DSCD,* 7, December 28, 1932, 760.
25. Ibid., 769.
26. Ibid., 765.
27. *La Vanguardia,* January 23, 1932, 1; February 15, 1932, 5, or February 23, 1932, 6.
28. *La Vanguardia*, February 23, 1932, 6. See also "Las organizaciones sindicales protestan contra el impuesto al trabajo," *La Vanguardia,* January 26, 1932, 5.
29. Deputy Ruggieri, *DSCD,* 1, April 19, 1932, 655.
30. In March 1932, the Socialists called the workers to "make their voice heard" and to "force the constitutional government to renounce the tax," *La Vanguardia,* March 13, 1932, 1.
31. *La Vanguardia,* February 4, 1932, 5; February 7, 1932, 5; February 8, 1932, 5; February 18, 1932, 5, or February 19, 1932, 8.
32. *La Vanguardia,* April 2, 1932, 1. In Spanish, the term income tax was originally translated as the *impuesto a la renta* or *réditos. Renta* is an ambiguous word in Spanish meaning both profit or income and also rent, such as the land rent denounced by the Socialists as the main source of privilege in Argentina.
33. Joel Horowitz, *Los sindicatos, el estado y el surgimiento de Perón, 1930–1946* (Buenos Aires: Universidad Nacional Tres de Febrero, 2004), 105–06.
34. *RRP,* February 5, 1932, 7–9.
35. White to the Secretary of State, February 12, 1932, Buenos Aires, General Conditions of the Argentine Republic/74, M1230, R3, 835.00, 15.NARA.
36. White to the Secretary of State, March 23, 1932, Buenos Aires, General Conditions of the Argentine Republic/77, M1230, R3, 835.00,18.NARA. According to Prebisch, the opposition of *La*

Prensa to many of the economic measures taken by the conservative governments of the 1930s was due to an old-fashioned laissez-faire ideology, Magariños, *Diálogos*, 92–93.

37. "Torturas e impuestos," *La Vanguardia*, February 26, 1932, 1. See also "Los impuestos de la dictadura," *La Vanguardia*, March 13, 1932, 1.
38. Deputy J. H. Martínez, *DSCD*, 1, April 19, 1932, 648.
39. Ibid., 673.
40. White to the Secretary of State, February 25, 1932, Buenos Aires, General Conditions of the Argentine Republic/75, M1230, R3, 835.00, 15–20, NARA.
41. Carlos Nino, *Un país al margen de la ley: Estudio de la anomia como componente del subdesarrollo argentino* (Buenos Aires: Emecé, 1992), 63–64.
42. *La Vanguardia*, May 23, 1932, 9, and May 24, 1932, 9.
43. Bliss to the Secretary of State, September 23, 1932, Buenos Aires, General Conditions of the Argentine Republic/90, M1230, R4, 835.00, NARA.
44. *BUIA*, November 1932, 19.
45. Note sent to Congress by the UIA, *DSCD*, 7, December 1, 1932, 145.
46. *The Buenos Aires Herald*, September 16, 1933, stated: "The tax on transactions. A comparative failure. Forty-five percent of merchants decline to pay." See also *La Nación*, September 9, 1933. Commercial associations all over the country continued sending protests to Congress during 1933. See for example, *DSCD*, 1, May 11, 1933, 126; 1, May 12, 1933, 151; 3, August 31, 1933, 643 or 4, and September 6, 1933, 70.
47. "Memorial de la Comisión Popular Pro Derogación de los Impuestos a las Transacciones y Réditos Comerciales," sent to Congress, *DSCD*, 1, May 12, 1933, 168–69. The list of associations belonging to the Commission is on pages 173–74.
48. Ibid., 171.
49. Ibid.
50. Ibid., 172.
51. Weddel, to the Secretary of State, November 3, 1933, Buenos Aires, General Conditions of the Argentine Republic/120, M1230, R4, 835.00, NARA.
52. *The Buenos Aires Herald*, September 16, 1933 and also *DSCD*, 7, December 1, 1932, 145.
53. *DSCD*, 6, September 29–30, 1934, 605–08. The government acknowledged that the pressure of small and medium retailers was behind the decision to abolish the *impuesto a las transacciones*: "The difficulties...in the application of the tax on transactions due to its impact on retail commerce are the origin of the conception of the sales tax." *DSCD*, 7, December 19, 1934, 776.
54. *La Nación*, September 9, 1933.

55. Facundo Alvaredo, "The Rich in Argentina over the Twentieth Century, 1932–2004," in *Top Incomes: A Global Perspective*, ed. A. B. Atkinson and T. Piketty (Oxford: Oxford University Press, 2010), 259–60.
56. Gerchunoff and Llach, *Ciclo de la ilusión*, 115–18.
57. Gerchunoff and Llach, *Ciclo de la ilusión*, 116, and Roberto Cortés Conde, *La economía política de la Argentina en el siglo XX* (Buenos Aires: Edhasa, 2005), 92–94.
58. Cortés Conde, *Economía política*, 101–05. Prebisch claimed to have designed this mechanism as well; see Magariños, *Diálogos*, 92.
59. These figures come from Gerchunoff and Llach, *Ciclo de la ilusión*, 132; Cortés Conde, *Economía política,* 114–15, and figure 2.1.
60. The figures are based on the statistics published by the *Memoria* of the DGIR between 1933 and 1945. In Britain, the standard rate (without the surtax) of income tax was already close to 30 percent. See Daunton, *Just Taxes*, 14.
61. *DSCD,* 3, August 24, 1933, 501–02.
62. *DSCD,* 3, August 16, 1933, 502.
63. Argentina. Ministerio de Hacienda de la Nación, *Memoria correspondiente al año 1932.*
64. Guillermo Ahumada, "Impuesto sobre la renta: Nociones e ideas sobre el impuesto," *Revista de la Universidad Nacional de Córdoba* (May–June 1934): 50.
65. *DSCD,* 4, September 15, 1933, 486.
66. *The Buenos Aires Herald,* September 16, 1933.
67. DGIR, *Memoria año 1935*, 15 and *Memoria año 1937*, 30.
68. DGIR, *Memoria año 1935*, 14.
69. DGIR, *Memoria año 1935*, 37.
70. *DSCD,* 8, December 20, 1934, 13–14.
71. Although in 1940, the DGIR began to monitoring nonregistered taxpayers as well. See DGIR, *Memoria año 1940*, 7.
72. Alvaredo, "Rich in Argentina," 290. The director of the DGIR, Ernesto Malaccorto, was proud of the fact that in five years (between 1933 and 1938) all the big *frigoríficos* (meat packers) had been inspected. See Malaccorto, interview by Leandro Gutiérrez, 39.
73. DGIR, *Memoria Año 1942*, 10.
74. Ibid., 45–46.
75. DGIR, *Memoria Año 1943*, 18–19.
76. As argued by Caravaca and Plotkin, "Crisis, ciencias sociales," 401–28. The development of a more interventionist state in the 1930s was shaped to some extent by this group of economists.
77. Halperin Donghi, *República imposible*, 134.
78. Caravaca and Plotkin, "Crisis, ciencias sociales," 417–19. Juan Domingo Perón, later on, would refer to this group as "*la trenza de Prebisch*" (literally, "Prebisch's braid," but its meaning was closer

to Prebisch band or gang), Malaccorto, interview by Leandro Gutiérrez 51.

79. Caravaca, "Estado, economía," 95.
80. Malaccorto, interview by Leandro Gutiérrez, 19.
81. Ibid., 21.
82. Ibid., 22.
83. In Ibid., 10, Malaccorto boasted of the "modern" traits of the Argentine tax regime. In Britain, even if the system of retention at source for some kind of incomes was already implemented in the nineteenth century, the so-called "PAYE," ("pay as you earn") system was not enforced until 1942, due to the resistance of workers, employers, and even the Inland Revenue. See Daunton, *Just Taxes,* 113, 179–80. In the United States, the system of "collection at the source" had been employed under dire circumstances such as the Civil War between 1913 and 1916, but it was abandoned afterwards. In 1943, President Roosevelt's proposal of withdrawing the income tax from the payroll was finally enacted, although with much resistance and without including dividends and bond interests in the system of collection at the source. See W. Elliot Brownlee, "Tax Regimes, National Crisis, and State Building in America," 92, and Carolyn C. Jones, "Mass-based Income Taxation: Creating a Taxpayer Culture, 1940–1952," 129–31, both in *Funding the Modern American State, 1941–1995*, ed. Brownlee (Cambridge: Cambridge University Press, 1996).
84. Argentina. Ministerio de Hacienda de la Nación, *El presupuesto general de 1932 y el estado presente de las finanzas nacionales* (Buenos Aires: Imprenta de la Honorable Cámara de Diputados de la Nación, 1932), 46–67.
85. Alhadeff, "Economic Formulae," 102.
86. *BUIA,* April 1932, 55.
87. *AUIA*, July 1934, 55–57.
88. *AUIA*, July 1936, 21.
89. DGIR, *Memoria año 1942,* 54. On the improvements in the collection of stamp duties, licences, and land tax, see *Caras y Caretas,* January 14, 1933.
90. *DSCD*, 7, December 28, 1932, 769.
91. Hora, *Landowners,* 201.
92. See María Inés Barbero and Rocchi, "Industry," in *New Economic History* (see note 23, introduction), 272.
93. *ASR,* June 1937, 429–30 and October 1937, 663.
94. *ASR,* March 1940, 199.
95. DGIR, *Memoria Año1938*, 20.
96. DGIR, *Memoria Año 1936*, 36.
97. DGIR, *Memoria Año 1941*, 44.
98. DGIR, *Memoria Año 1941,* 14.

99. Jorge Macon, *Las finanzas públicas argentinas: Período 1950–1980* (Buenos Aires: Macchi, 1985), 107.
100. DGIR, *Memoria Año 1942*, 32.
101. Ricardo Sidicaro, *Los tres peronismos: Estado y poder económico 1946–55/ 1973–76/ 1989–99* (Buenos Aires: Siglo XXI, 2002), 29–30. The Rural Society asserted that the law creating the *Junta Nacional de Carnes* was the *ley madre* (mother-law) and as such "must be considered by every rancher," *ASR*, June 1939, 490.
102. Bolsa de Comercio de Buenos Aires, *Memoria correspondiente al año 1933*, 29–30.
103. Bolsa de Comercio de Buenos Aires, *Memoria correspondiente al año 1936*, 9–10. In 1938, the Rural Society celebrated the intervention of the government in the meat market and claimed with enthusiasm: "We have the invaluable privilege of having the determined support of the government," *ASR*, January 1938, 10.
104. On "selective incentives" see Levi, *Rule and Revenue*, 64.
105. DGIR, *Memoria Año 1935*, 19.
106. *AUIA*, December 1934, 43–44.
107. Unión Industrial Argentina a Manuel Fresco, Presidente de la Cámara de Diputados de la Nación, 25 October 1934, Buenos Aires, Archivo Justo, Caja 43, Doc. 38, AGN.
108. DGIR, *Memoria Año 1938*, 64.
109. Deputy Bustillo, *DSCD* 7, December 19, 1934, 779.
110. *DSCD,* 8, December 20, 1934, 27–30.
111. *DSCD,* 8, December 27–28, 1934, 527–28.
112. Gerchunoff and Llach, *Ciclo de la ilusión*, 48–50.
113. Alvaredo, "Rich in Argentina," 268.
114. *DSCD,* 1, April 19, 1932, 650.
115. *REA*, March 1932, 201.
116. *DSCD,* 7, November 28–29, 1934, 94–95.
117. *DSCD,* 7, December 19, 1934, 741.
118. Deputy Pueyrredón, ibid., 740.
119. Ibid.
120. Cox to the Secretary of State, January 4, 1936, Buenos Aires, General Conditions of the Argentine Republic, M 1230, R 20, 835.5123/26,NARA.
121. The DGIR began to warn in 1940 about the growing problems to maintain collection due to the economic difficulties caused by war. See DGIR, *Memoria año 1940,* 7 and 10. However, the fall of customs revenues was the main concern for the Treasury: See República Argentina, Ministerio de Hacienda, *Memoria correspondiente al año 1940,* 1, 184–85.
122. As Sidicaro, *Tres peronismos*, 43, has pointed out, this fiscal device was a clear antecedent of the program of control of rural exports under the IAPI, created by Perón.

123. *DSCD,* 1, May 30, 1941, 82; 1, June 11, 1941, 399; 1, June 2, 1941, 896.
124. *DSCD,* 1, June 6, 1941, 357 and 1, June 25, 1941, 714.
125. The Buenos Aires Stock Market, the SRA, the UIA, and the CACIP together signed the pamphlet "Consideraciones sobre los proyectos financieros e impositivos a estudio del Honorable Congreso de la Nación," *ASR,* September 1942, 716. I have analyzed this conflict in Sánchez Román, "Shaping Taxation," 98–106.
126. Argentina. Ministerio de Hacienda de la Nación, *Modificación de leyes impositivas y creación de nuevos gravámenes* (Buenos Aires, 1944).
127. DGIR, *Memoria Año 1942*, 32–33.
128. "Consideraciones sobre los proyectos," 745.
129. DGIR, *Memoria Año 1942*, 27.
130. Ibid., 30.
131. "Consideraciones sobre los proyectos," 717.
132. *ASR*, February 1942, 151.
133. Caravaca and Plotkin, "Crisis, ciencias sociales," 414.
134. Ibid., 424.
135. In 1935, Argentine GDP attained 1929 levels. The second wave of the international depression affected Argentina in 1937 as well, although not as deeply as did the first one. Della Paolera and Taylor, *Straining at the Anchor*, 201–18 and Gerchunoff and Llach, *Ciclo de la ilusión*, 139–40.
136. See Laura Ruiz Jiménez, "Peronism and Anti-imperialism in the Argentine Press: 'Braden or Perón' was also 'Perón is Roosevelt'," *Journal of Latin American Studies* 30, no. 3 (1998): 551–71.
137. See Sánchez Román, "Poliedro de la igualdad," and chap. 1 of this book.
138. José Abel Verzura, *Impuesto progresivo a inmuebles de 10.000 hectáreas o más: Antecedentes legislativos y reglamentarios de la Ley N° 4834 vigente en la provincia de Buenos Aires* (Buenos Aires: Guillermo Kraft Ltda., 1943), 34–35.
139. Americo Ghioldi and Romulo Bogliolo, *Los socialistas, los gastos públicos, las cuestiones impositivas* (Buenos Aires, 1942), 31.
140. Ibid., 41.
141. The motives behind the military coup are beyond the scope of this study. To sum up a very complex process, the army withdrew their support of an unpopular government that had been tainted with the stain of the electoral fraud. Moreover, the growing influence of "nationalist"—many of them pro-Axis—officers within the army, who feared that the government had decided to break Argentine neutrality in favor of the Allies in World War II, encouraged the movement. See Halperin Donghi, *República imposible*, 267–68 and 290–92 and Potash, *Ejército y política*, 263–88.

142. "Conferencia pronunciada por el Presidente del Consejo de la Dirección General del impuesto a los Réditos, Sr. José P. Hernández, el día 6 de junio del corriente año en la exposición de la obra realizada por el gobierno de la revolución del 4 de junio de 1943," in DGIR, *Boletín Informativo*, May–June 1944, 10.
143. This was in fact a general strategy of a government that was bereft of social supporters and was anxious to establish solid relationships with relevant sectors of civil society. Thus, between June 1943 and December 1944, the UIA was required to participate in 33 official boards and committees, and at the end of 1943, the government heeded to a traditional petition of the manufacturers' association and created the Secretariat of Industry and Commerce: see Horowitz, "Industrialists and the Rise of Perón, 1943–1946: Some Implications for the Conceptualization of Peronism," *The Americas* 4, no. 2 (1990): 201.
144. Louise Doyon, "El crecimiento sindical," in *La formación del sindicalismo peronista*, ed. Juan Carlos Torre (Buenos Aires: Legasa, 1988), 171.
145. Workers participated in other committees created by the military government, which discussed important issues, such as pensions and wages. However, this participation began in 1944, when Perón was establishing his power base as the Secretary of Labor. See Horowitz, "Industrialists," chap. 9.
146. *ASR*, September 1942, 715, 718.
147. To some extent, the economic elites continued to identify themselves without referring to class notions such as capital versus labor, etcetera. However, most Argentineans realized by the mid-1940s that their society was firmly anchored to class cleavages: see Halperin Donghi, *La larga agonía de la Argentina peronista* (Buenos Aires: Ariel, 1994), 27.
148. "Consideraciones sobre los proyectos," 721–22.
149. Argentina. Gobierno de la Nación, *Dictamen de la Comisión Honoraria Asesora del Gobierno Nacional para el estudio de los problemas fiscales* (Buenos Aires, 1944), 26.
150. Ibid., 26.
151. Ibid., 175.
152. Ibid., 28.
153. Ibid., 1.

3 Taxation and Peronism (1946–1955)

1. Juan Carlos Torre, "Introducción a los años peronistas," in *Los años peronistas (1943–1955)*, ed. Torre, vol. 8 of *Nueva Historia Argentina* (Buenos Aires: Editorial Sudamericana, 2002), 2–27.
2. Juan Carlos Torre and Elisa Pastoriza, "La democratización del bienestar," in *Los años peronistas* (see note 1), 267–69.

3. Pablo Gerchunoff and Lucas Llach, *El ciclo de la illusion y el desencanto: Un siglo de políticas económicas argentinas* (Buenos Aires: Ariel, 1998), 181–82. Nonetheless, the increased share of wages and salaries in the national product was mainly due to the migration of workers from low productive/rural areas from the interior to the urban/industrial areas of the littoral. Torre and Pastoriza, "Democratización del bienestar," 279.
4. Facundo Alvaredo, "The Rich in Argentina over the Twentieth Century, 1932–2004," in *Top Incomes: A Global Perspective*, ed. A. B. Atkinson and T. Piketty (Oxford: Oxford University Press, 2010), 264, 272.
5. Torre and Pastoriza, "Democratización del bienestar," 282.
6. Peter Ross, "Justicia social: Una evaluación de los logros del peronismo clásico," *Anuario del IEHS* 8 (1993): 108; Torre and Pastoriza, "Democratización del bienestar," 288–90; and Horacio Gaggero and Alicia Garro, "La política de seguridad social peronista," in *Sueños de bienestar en la Nueva Argentina: Estado y políticas públicas durante el peronismo 1946–1955,* ed. Patricia Berrotarán, Aníbal Jáuregui, and Marcelo Rougier (Buenos Aires: Imago Mundi, 2004).
7. Torre and Pastoriza, "Democratización del bienestar," 291–92.
8. Ibid., 295–99.
9. On the economic evolution during the period, see, among others Gerchunoff and Llach, *Ciclo de la ilusión*; Gerchunoff and Damián Antúnez, "De la bonanza peronista a la crisis de desarrollo," in *Los años peronistas* (see note 1); Díaz Alejandro, Carlos Díaz Alejandro, *Essays on the Economic History of the Argentine Republic* (New Haven, CT: Yale University Press, 1970); Di Tella and Roger Dornbusch, *The Political Economy of Argentina, 1946–1983* (Oxford: Macmillan Press, 1989); Roberto Cortés Conde, *La economía política de la Argentina en el siglo XX* (Buenos Aires: Edhasa, 2005).
10. Ibid., 191.
11. Mario S. Brodersohn, "Fiscal Policy and the Composition of Government Purchases, the Case of Argentina," *Public Finance/Finances Publiques* 19, no. 3 (1964): 230.
12. Cortés Conde, *Economía política*, 188, and *BDGI*, May 1956, 411. Here, social security taxes are excluded. In fact, the total tax burden—including social security—increased during Perón's government and, in the early 1950s, fiscal deficit was one of the lowest in Argentine history. See Gerchunoff and Antúnez, "Bonanza peronista," 175.
13. Argentina. Ministerio de Hacienda de la Nación, *Memoria correspondiente al año 1946*, 74.
14. *La Nación*, June 8, 1947.
15. *DSCD*, 5, September 26, 1947, 656–60.
16. *DSCD*, 2, August 10–11, 1950, 1732.
17. Oscar Oszlak, "Inflación y política fiscal en la Argentina: El impuesto a los réditos en el período 1956–1965" (Documento de Trabajo,

Instituto Torcuato di Tella, Buenos Aires, 1970), 34, and Stanley S. Surrey and Oliver Oldman, "Report of a Preliminary Survey of the Tax System of Argentina," pt. 1, *Public Finance/Finances Publiques* 16, no. 2 (1961): 164.

18. *The New Income Tax Laws of Argentina with their Regulations and a Complete Alphabetical Index* (Buenos Aires: La Facultad, 1949), 49.
19. *DSCD,* 2, August 10–11, 1950, 1734.
20. *DSCD,* 2, August 7–8, 1946, 397 and *DSCD,* 3, July 21, 1948, 1910.
21. DGIR, *Boletín Informativo,* February–March 1946, 5.
22. *DSCD,* 3, September 11, 1946, 2584–86 and *New Income Tax Laws,* 173.
23. Argentina. Ministerio de Hacienda de la Nación, *Modificación de las leyes nºs 11.682, 11.683 y decreto-ley nº 18.229/43. Creación del impuesto a las ganancias eventuales. Texto y comentario de las nuevas disposiciones* (Buenos Aires, 1946), 227.
24. As Minister Cereijo acknowledged: "Recurrence in difficult to establish (*la habitualidad es difícil de establecer*)", *DSCD,* 3, August 12, 1948, 2596. Therefore, the government introduced minor modifications in the law that were aimed at specifying its ultimate goal. Hence, in 1950, the government included among the profits subjected to the *ganancias eventuales* the bonus attached to the issues of shares. See Argentina. Ministerio de Hacienda de la Nación, *Boletín. Edición Semanal,* no. 188, January 1950, 46–47.
25. See *Pedro Rouspil v. Provincia de Buenos Aires,* 188, *Fallos* (1940), 242–43; *Satia v. Provincia de Buenos Aires,* 188, *Fallos* (1940), 39, or *María Sáenz v. Provincia de Buenos Aires,* 193, *Fallos* (1942), 373–74.
26. Segundo V. Linares Quintana, *El poder impositivo y la libertad individual: la causa constitucional del impuesto en el derecho fiscal constitucional argentino y comparado, especialmente a través de la jurisprudencia de la Corte Suprema de la Nación* (Buenos Aires: Alfa, 1951), 247.
27. In 1951, when the conservatives returned to power in Britain, they found marginal tax rates of 98 percent in the income tax and higher rates of 80 percent for the inheritance tax and launched a campaign for their removal, which was based more on the necessity of stimulating British economy than on a possible threat to private property. See Martin Daunton, *Just Taxes: The Politics of Taxation in Britain, 1914–1979* (Cambridge: Cambridge University Press, 2002), 229 and chap. 8.
28. See the complaints of the business peak associations in Argentina. Gobierno de la Nación, *Dictamen de la Comisión Honoraria,* 24.
29. On this issue Daunton, *Just Taxes,* 124, and "Churchill at the Treasury: Remaking Conservative Taxation Policy, 1924–29," *Revue Belge de Philologie et d'Histoire* 75, no. 4 (1997): 1070.

30. *DSCD,* 2, August 10–11, 1950, 1769.
31. Linares Quintana, *Poder impositivo,* 247.
32. *DSCD,* 4, n. d. 1950, 3989.
33. See this complain expresses in *La Nación,* December 26, 1948, or October 23, 1949.
34. Compare special deductions for first-category and for third-category incomes enacted in the income tax law of 1949. See *New Income Tax Laws,* 60–65, 169.
35. Hora, *Landowners,* 177 refers to Argentine landowners as a "embattle elite" since the 1920s.
36. *New Income Tax Laws,* 97.
37. See, for example, Enrique Dickmann, *Población y emigración* (Buenos Aires: Losada, 1946), 63, 86.
38. Argentina, Ministerio de Hacienda de la Nación. *Segunda Conferencia de Ministros de Hacienda* (Buenos Aires, 1947), 108.
39. Liliana Da Orden, "Recursos fiscales, Estado y sociedad: La provincia de Buenos Aires y el Gobierno Nacional durante el Peronismo, 1946–1952" (paper presented at 9 Jornadas de Historia Política, Mar del Plata, November 6–7, 2009) and SRA, *La Sociedad Rural Argentina ante los impuestos a la tierra en la provincia de Buenos Aires* (Buenos Aires, 1948), 38.
40. See, for instance, the debate on the tax reform of 1950 in *DSCD,* 2, August 10-11, 1950, 1742–44.
41. *La Nación,* August 9, 1950.
42. *La Nación,* August 11, 1950.
43. Of course, to obtain a clear picture of Peronist tax policies, we should look at the impact of provincial taxation as well, but this is very difficult to assess since we do not know much about provincial fiscal realities. Da Orden, "Recursos Fiscales," has shown that the governor of Buenos Aires, Domingo Mercante, a loyal collaborator of Perón, reformed provincial taxes and through changes in the land tax made the system more progressive, at least until 1950. Marcela Harriague, "Revisión de los aspectos tributarios del gobierno peronista, 1946–1955" (paper presented at 12 Jornadas de Historia Económica, Río Cuarto, September 22–24, 2010) notices a similar evolution in the federal and provincial tax schemes. In the provinces, direct taxes were more important in the early phase of the Peronist government, whereas indirect taxes became more significant as time went by.
44. This image of Perón's tax policies in Kent Eaton, *Politicians and Economic Reform in New Democracies: Argentina and the Philippines in the 1990s* (University Park: Pennsylvania State University Press, 2002), 144.
45. Ajay K. Mehrotra, "Envisioning the Modern American Fiscal State: Progressive-Era Economists and the Intellectual Foundations of the U.S. Income Tax," *UCLA Law Review* 52, no. 6 (2005): 1793–1866.

46. *DSCD*, 2, August 10–11, 1950, 1734.
47. Griziotti had visited Argentina in 1923 and gave several conferences in Buenos Aires about tax reform in the Latin American nation. See Benvenuto Griziotti, "Los problemas fundamentales de la economía y las finanzas de la República Argentina," *REA*, July 1923, 25–36.
48. *DSCD*, 2, August 10–11, 1950, 1734.
49. On this point, see Mehrotra, "Envisioning Modern American," and Sánchez Román, "Shaping Taxation," 277–78. See also D. J. Forsyth, *The Crisis of Liberal Italy: Monetary and Financial Policy*, 1914–22 (Cambridge: Cambridge University Press, 1993).
50. Linares Quintana, *Poder impositivo*, 229.
51. Juan Carlos Luque, "La obligación tributaria en el derecho argentino: Algunas consideraciones sobre su régimen constitucional," *Revista de Ciencias Económicas* (May–June 1953): 171.
52. Ibid., 191–94.
53. *Compañía Santafecina de Inmuebles y Construcciones v. Provincia de Córdoba*, 211, *Fallos* (1948), 1781. This sentence echoed others pronounced earlier, like *Sara Pereyra Iraola v. Provincia de Córdoba*, 206, *Fallos* (1946), 247 or *F. y R. Méndez Lynch v. Provincia de Córdoba*, 190, *Fallos* (1941), 316. Although aimed at protecting capital and property, that is accumulation of wealth, the doctrine emphasized the notion of confiscation for taxes on income or profits, which were flows and not stocks of wealth. For instance, in an October 1947 sentence, the Court stated: "The objection of confiscation is only admissible if it is proved that the tax absorbed more than the 33 percent of the current output of an economically speaking efficient rural estate," (quoted in SRA, *Sociedad Rural ante los impuestos*, 72).
54. In April 1947, the Senate dismissed the members of the Supreme Court, thus aiding Perón in establishing a firmer grip on the judicial power. Mariano Plotkin, *Mañana en San Perón: Propaganda, rituales políticos y educación en el régimen peronista (1946–1955)* (Buenos Aires: Espasa Calpe, 1993), 114 and Salvador Oría, *Finanzas*, vol. 1 (Buenos Aires: Editorial Guillermo Kraft, 1948), 656.
55. Sabatino A. Forino, *El desarrollo económico y la política fiscal: Las finanzas públicas nacionales y su participación en el desarrollo económico general y su planificación* (Buenos Aires: Macchi 1966), 100. Miranda became the second economics minister and was under Perón's personal protection. See Gerchunoff and Antúnez, "Bonanza peronista,"140.
56. Argentina. Ministerio de Hacienda de la Nación, *Tercera Conferencia de Ministros de Hacienda* (Buenos Aires, 1948), 127.
57. *BDGI*, May 1955, 562.
58. *BDGI*, May 1955, 569.
59. *DSCD*, 2, August 10–11, 1950, 1761.

60. Argentina. Ministerio de Hacienda de la Nación, *Sexta Conferencia de Ministros de Hacienda* (Buenos Aires, 1951), 147. For the opposition, however, the government was taking advantage of the exceptional circumstances of the international market. Once the market recovered, they feared that the sales tax on exports would be paid by Argentine producers. See Harriague, "Revisión."
61. For a discussion on the economic rationale behind Perón's export policies, see Jorge Fodor, "Perón's Policies for Agricultural Exports 1946–1948: Dogmatism or Common Sense?" in *Argentine in Twentieth Century*, ed. Rock (Pittsburgh, PA: Pittsburgh University Press, 1975).
62. Ministerio de Hacienda, *Tercera Conferencia*, 127.
63. Ministerio de Hacienda, *Sexta Conferencia*, 148.
64. *DSCD*, 6, 27–28 September, 1948, 4518–19.
65. Harriague, "Revisión." In fact, some luxury items, such as jewelry or furs, were taxed by these duties during Peronism. See Da Orden, "Recursos fiscales."
66. *DSCD*, 3, September 11, 1946, 2502–03.
67. Ministerio de Hacienda, *Sexta Conferencia*, 145.
68. Ibid., 1815.
69. Despite this measure, share prices kept falling until 1952. On the market failure of 1949, see Rougier and Martín Fiszbein, "De *Don Derrochín a Maese Ahorrín*: El fomento del ahorro durante la economía peronista," in *Sueños de bienestar* (see note 6), 119–22, 136–37.
70. *DSCD*, 2, August 10–11, 1950, 1735.
71. Brokers celebrated Argentine legislation as being one of the most favorable in the world. See Rougier and Fiszbein, "De Don *Derrochín*," 140.
72. The opposition claimed that the main beneficiaries of the measure were the businessmen represented in the stock market. Ironically, a Radical deputy referred to "that *descamisado*" ("shirtless," the name that popular supporters of Perón received) José Hernández, president of the Stock Market, *DSCD*, 3, September 19, 1951, 1985. For Eugenio Blanco, who was economics minister in 1956, the problem was not only the regressive character of that policy but its spurious objectives: "This 1950's fiscal reform allowed that the increases of patrimony without justification would be legalized...through a disguised operation of buying and selling capital shares. The immorality of the system is apparent." *BDGI*, October 1956, 319.
73. For example, Cortés Conde, *Economía política*, 191, and Jorge Macon, *Las finanzas públicas argentinas: Período 1950–1980* (Buenos Aires: Macchi, 1985), 1985, 107–08.
74. Ibid., 104 and Alvaredo, "Rich in Argentina," 260.
75. Federico Herschel and Samuel Itzcovich, "Fiscal Policy in Argentina," *Public Finance/Finances Publiques* 12, no 2–3 (1957): 110–12.
76. Gerchunoff and Antúnez, "Bonanza peronista," 173–78.

77. Daunton, *Just Taxes*, 195.
78. Carolyn Webber and Aaron Wildavsky, *A History of Taxation and Expenditure in the Western World* (New York: Simon and Schuster, 1986), 475.
79. Ibid., 548. On the traditional French resistance against income taxation, see Jean-Pierre Gross, "Progressive Taxation and Social Justice in Eighteenth-Century France," *Past and Present,* 140, (August1993): 79–126.
80. Webber and Wildavsky, *History of Taxation*, 523, 548.
81. See the minister's report on the Budget for 1953 and 1954 in Argentina. Ministerio de Hacienda de la Nación, *Boletín. Edición Semanal*, no. 293, July 1952, 909.
82. Alvaredo, "Rich in Argentina," 262–63.
83. In 1954, more than 5 million Argentineans were wage earners who worked in the factories or in the service sector. See Doyon, *Perón y los trabajadores: Los orígenes del sindicalismo peronista, 1943–1955* (Buenos Aires: Siglo XXI, 2006), 245. This was an important number, but because the total number of tax units were around 10 million, many potential taxpayers were not filling in their returns.
84. Argentina. Ministerio de Hacienda de la Nación, *Boletín. Edición Semanal*, no. 217, August 1950, 1440 and *BDGI*, January 1955, 27.
85. In Britain, those in the highest income tax bracket in 1945 were taxed at 97 percent, whereas those in the United States were taxed at 90 percent. In Sweden, the highest tax bracket was taxed at around 46 percent, which was closer to the Argentine rate. Steinmo, *Taxation and Democracy*, 25, 118.
86. Ibid., 41.
87. Steinmo refers to the American system after World War II as "loophole madness" (ibid., 142).
88. Ibid., 101.
89. See Carolyn Jones, "Mass-based Income Taxation." According to one study, Australia, during World War II, was able to transform the income tax into a mass tax, whereas Argentina lagged behind. See Andrew Mitchell, "Institutions or Factor Endowments? Income Taxation in Argentina and Australia" (paper presented at the 14th International Economic History Congress, Helsinki, August 21–25, 2006).
90. Torre and Pastoriza, "Democratización del bienestar," 275–76.
91. Donna Guy, *Women Build the Welfare State: Performing Charity and Creating Rights in Argentina, 1880–1955* (Durham and London: Duke University Press, 2009).
92. Argentina. Ministerio de Hacienda de la Nación, *Boletín. Edición Semanal*, no. 327, May 1953, 359.
93. *BDGI*, January 1954, 16 or November 1954, 65.
94. *BDGI*, November 1954, 65.
95. Surrey and Oldman, "Report of a Preliminary," pt. 1, 174–75.

96. This is known among economists as the "Olivera-Tanzi effect." See Vito Tanzi, "Inflation, Real Tax Revenue, and the Case for Inflationary Finance: Theory with an Application to Argentina," *International Monetary Fund Staff Papers* 25, no. 3 (1978): 417–51.
97. Surrey and Oldman, "Report of a Preliminary," pt. 1, 173.
98. Brodersohn, "Elasticidad-ingreso del impuesto a la renta en la Argentina," *Desarrollo Económico* 3, no. 4 (1964): 580.
99. Jorge J. Peire, *Evasión impositiva* (Buenos Aires: 1959), 13.
100. *BDGI*, January 1955, 44–45.
101. See Radical Deputy Frondizi's statement, *DSCD*, 2, August 10–11, 1752.
102. Ibid.
103. Argentina. Ministerio de Hacienda de la Nación, *Memoria correspondiente al año 1949*, 96.
104. Argentina. Ministerio de Hacienda de la Nación, *Boletín. Edición Semanal*, no. 222, September 1950, 1615–16.
105. *DSCD*, 2, August 10–11, 1950, 1740.
106. Cortés Conde, *Economía política*, 155.
107. Gerchunoff and Llach, *Ciclo de la ilusión*, 195–99.
108. Because the social security system ran a surplus due to the situation of full employment and the age structure of the Argentine population, the government sold bonds to the pension funds.
109. Cortés Conde, *Economía política*, 190.
110. Macon, *Finanzas públicas*, 104. Alternative figures can be found in Alvaredo, "Rich in Argentina," 260, but they do not alter the general picture. To sum up, social security contributions were around 6 percent of the GDP during the whole period, whereas the income tax reached 4 percent, but since 1952, it began a dramatic decline. The faster growth of social security contributions—as compared to other taxes—might be a Latin-American phenomenon. In Chile, tax revenues stalled between 1935 and 1956, but social security taxes increased in proportion to the GDP and rose from 2.8 percent to 5.9 percent. See José Pablo Arellano, *Políticas sociales y desarrollo: Chile 1923–1984* (Santiago de Chile: Corporación de Investigaciones Económicas para Latinoamérica, 1985), 40.
111. Macon, *Finanzas públicas*, 152.
112. Hector L. Diéguez and Alberto Petrecolla, "La distribución funcional del ingreso y el sistema previsional en la Argentina, 1950–1972," *Desarrollo Económico* 14, no. 55 (1974): 434–39.
113. Dino Jarach, being quoted in Daniel Lvovich: "Sindicatos y empresarios frente al problema de la seguridad social en los albores del peronismo," in *Las políticas sociales en perspectiva histórica*, ed. Lvovich and Juan Suriano (Buenos Aires: Prometeo-Universidad Nacional de General Sarmiento, 2005), 165.
114. Ministerio de Hacienda, *Tercera Conferencia*, 129.
115. Ibid., 128.

116. Ibid., 127.
117. Ibid., 128.
118. Ibid., 128.
119. Argentina. Ministerio de Hacienda de la Nación, *Primera Conferencia de Ministros de Hacienda* (Buenos Aires, 1946), 339.
120. *DSCD,* 2, August 10–11, 1950, 1732. It is noteworthy that in the statistics collected by the DGI, the capital gains tax was lumped together with the income tax and the extraordinary profit tax as taxes on profits, whereas death duties were labelled taxes on capital.
121. R. C. Whiting, "Ideology and Reform in Labour's Tax Strategy, 1964–1970," *The Historical Journal* 41, no. 4 (1998): 1123.
122. In fact, industrialization was conceived as part of Perón's social policies. See Berrotarán, "La planificación como instrumento: políticas y organización en el Estado peronista (1946–1949)," in *Sueños de bienestar* (see note 6), 19.
123. On the conflicts between Perón and the UIA, see Jorge Schvarzer, *Empresarios del pasado: la Unión Industrial Argentina* (Buenos Aires: CISEA, 1991), chap. 5. The relationship between entrepreneurs and Perón has been diversely interpreted as ranging from cooperation to straightforward hostility. See Cristina Lucchini, *Apoyo empresarial en los orígenes del peronismo* (Buenos Aires: Centro Editor de América Latina, 1990); Paul H. Lewis, *Crisis of Argentine Capitalism,* chap. 8; Dardo Cuneo, *Comportamiento y crisis de la clase empresaria* (Buenos Aires: Pleamar, 1967); Graciela Swiderski, "La UIA: ¿sustitución de importaciones o mercado externo?," in *Economía e Historia: Contribuciones a la Historia Económica argentina,* ed. Mario Rapoport (Buenos Aires: Tesis, 1988); James P. Brennan, "Industriales y bolicheros: La actividad económica y la alianza peronista, 1943–1976," *Boletín del Instituto de Historia Argentina y Americana Dr. Emilio Ravignani* 15 (1997): 101–41; and Brennan, "El empresariado: La política de cohabitación y oposición," in *Los años peronistas* (see note 1).
124. Ibid., 105.
125. *RUIA*, July 1946, 76.
126. In June 1944, the military administration issued Decree no. 14630/44, thus creating the regime of "industries of national interest" (*industrias de interés nacional*), which established the bases of protection of some key sectors, including favorable tax policies. Belini, "Estado y política industrial durante el primer peronismo (1946–1955)," in *Sueños de bienestar* (see note 1), 76.
127. Nonetheless, these expectations were not entirely realistic. On the external constraints of the Argentine economy, see Fodor, "Perón's Policies."
128. *DSCD*, 3, September 11, 1946, 2586–87.
129. Ministerio de Hacienda, *Memoria 1946,* vol. 2, 858.
130. See, Belini, "Estado y política industrial," 80.

131. Argentina. Ministerio de Hacienda de la Nación, *Boletín. Edición Semanal,* no. 301, September 1952, 1237.
132. In some cases, these exemptions were part of the program of "industries of national interests," and together with tax allowances, firms obtained import privileges and cheap credit. On the meaning and implementation of this policy, see Belini, "Estado y política industrial," 88–90.
133. *DSCD,* 2, August 10–11, 1950, 1730. Oil imports were one of the main origins of the external trade deficit that repeatedly affected Argentina. See Cortés Conde, *Economía política,* 147. On sugar exemption, see DGIR, *Boletín Informativo,* April 1946, 18. On the allowances for tobacco producers see: *DSCD,* 1, May 10, 1949, 44.
134. Argentina. Ministerio de Hacienda, *Memoria 1949,* 163.
135. *DSCD,* 2, August 10–11, 1950, 1737.
136. Ministerio de Hacienda de la Nación, *Boletín. Edición Semanal,* no. 190, February 1950, 129.
137. SRA, *Sociedad Rural ante los impuestos,* 8–9.
138. Ibid., 14–15.
139. Ibid., 14.
140. Ibid., 17.
141. Ibid., 46.
142. It was a question of political opportunity rather than of political sympathy that moved Radicalism toward agrarian advocacy. The Radicals found in the Argentine countryside a field that allowed them to criticize the government for neglecting a key factor in the nation's development. See Marcela García Sebastiani, *Los antiperonistas en la Argentina peronista: Radicales, Socialistas en la política argentina entre 1943 y 1951* (Buenos Aires: Prometeo, 2005), 91.
143. Words of Radical deputy Rudy, *DSCD,* 2, August 10–11, 1950, 1743.
144. Ibid.
145. As mentioned above, the decree 15,921 of June 1946 was addressed to manufactures. However, rural producers took advantage of a loophole in the income tax law that included, in the third-category income, those profits that came from agricultural activities and were carried out along with manufacturing, and therefore maintained that they were entitled to enjoy the same deductions that applied to factories. See *New Income Tax Laws,* 64 and Ministerio de Hacienda de la Nación, *Boletín. Edición Semanal,* no. 301, September 1952, 1238.
146. *BDGI,* September 1955, 204.
147. Ibid., 205–06.
148. Thus, Perón became, for the Peronist collective image, *el primer trabajador* ("the first worker." See Plotkin, *Mañana es San Perón,* chap. 4.
149. *BDGI,* June 1956, 533.
150. *La Nación,* August 11, 1950, 4.

151. *BDGI*, January 1955, 27.
152. Ibid., 27.
153. My own estimation, based on Diéguez and Petrecolla, "Distribución funcional," 433.
154. *BDGI*, May 1957, figures 12 and 14.
155. *DSCD*, 3, September 19, 1951, 1970.
156. Ibid.
157. This is the theme of Torre, *La vieja guardia sindical y Perón.*
158. Patrick Renshaw, "Organized Labor and the United States War Economy, 1939–1945," *Journal of Contemporary History* 21, no. 1 (1986): 17.
159. Steinmo, *Taxation and Democracy*, 63. Revealingly enough, Spain remained neutral during World War I and, although the government attempted to introduce the income tax in the 1920s, the tax was not implemented until the return of democracy in the 1970s. The absence of international wars and the persistence of authoritarian and exclusionary politics could have deterred the transformation of the Spanish tax regime.
160. Presidencia de la Nación. Secretaría de Informaciones, *Perón habla a los trabajadores argentinos sobre el 2º Plan Quinquenal* (Buenos Aires, 1953), 59.
161. Marcos Giménez Zapiola and Carlos M. Leguizamón, "La concertación peronista de 1955: El Congreso de la Productividad," in *La formación del sindicalismo peronista* (see note 144, chap. 2).
162. *BDGI*, March 1955, 367.
163. Ibid., 368.
164. The CGE was Perón's last attempt at unifying business associations in a single—and responsive to the government—peak organization. Despite its origins, the CGE was far from being obsequious to Peronist guidelines. On CGE constitution and evolution, see Brennan, "Industriales y bolicheros."
165. Zapiola and Leguizamón, "Concertación peronista," 337.
166. *BDGI*, April 1955, 467.
167. Ibid., 467.
168. Ibid., 467.
169. The literature is abundant. See, among others, the articles included in Philippe C. Schmitter and Gerhard Lehmbruch, eds., *Trends Toward Corporatist Intermediation* (London and Beverly Hills: SAGE, 1979), and those included in Suzanne Berger, ed., *Organizing Interests in Western Europe* (Cambridge: Cambridge University Press, 1981). On the key role of wage bargaining in these arrangements, see Charles S. Maier, "Preconditions for Corporatism," in *Order and Conflict in Contemporary Capitalism*, ed. John H. Goldthorp (Oxford: Oxford University Press, 1984).
170. Whiting, "Ideology and Reform," 1124, and Maier, "Preconditions," 50–51.

171. As Webber and Wildavsky, *History of Taxation*, 533 put it, while referring to Western European countries such as Denmark: "Supporters of the social-welfare state are in the uncomfortable position of choosing a progressive income tax, which they probably cannot raise sufficiently to pay for what they want, or regressive Social Security and sales tax."
172. Torre and Pastoriza, "Democratización del bienestar," 288–90.
173. Gaggero and Garro, "Política de seguridad social," 180.
174. Ibid., 182.
175. Lvovich, "Sindicatos y empresarios," 166.
176. Camila Arza, "Distributional Impacts of Pensions Policy in Argentina," *Journal of Economic History* 66, no. 2 (2006): 468.
177. Ross, "Justicia social," 108–09 and Plotkin, *Mañana es San Perón*, 219–22.
178. Lvovich, "Sindicatos y empresarios," 135–36, 155. The author emphasizes that the creation of a "universal" system is an exception rather than the norm. Actually, the universalization of social security and other benefits was historically more important for Social-democratic parties, which had to reach voters beyond their working-class constituencies, than it was for trade unions themselves, which looked upon universalism with suspicion. Besides, Argentine unions' reluctance to give up particular funds was not an exception. Similar examples can be found in other countries, such as Germany, Denmark, or Sweden, where, despite the development of universal welfare states, unions resisted the transfer of some of their funds, such as sickness or unemployment funds. See Gosta Esping-Andersen, *The Three Worlds of Welfare Capitalism* (Cambridge: Polity Press, 1990), 24–25, 68.
179. See Gerchunoff and Llach, *Entre equidad y crecimiento.*
180. Ibid., 68.
181. Giménez Zapiola and Leguizamón, "Concertación peronista," 337–41; Doyon, "La organización del movimiento sindical peronista (1946–1955)," in *Formación del sindicalismo* (see note 144, chap. 2), 191–94; and Daniel James, *Resistance and Integration: Peronism and the Argentine Working Class, 1946–1976* (New York: Cambridge University Press, 1988), 55–57.
182. James, *Resistance and Integration*, 89–90.
183. Gaggero and Garro, "Política de seguridad social," 184.
184. Overall, the ideas on equity and justice that guided Peronist tax policies had almost Paretian features. Any tax was fair, as long as it did not worsen any particular situation; it did not create winners or losers. See the analysis (and criticism) of Pareto's and utilitarian ideas on equality in A. K. Sen, *Collective Choice and Social Welfare* (San Francisco: Holden-Day, 1970), 22–26, and John Rawls, *A Theory of Justice* (Cambridge, MA: Harvard University Press, 1971), 103–04.

185. Thus, in 1949, the government had to implement a "bonus" of 40 percent to 88 percent for all pensions in order to adjust retirees' incomes to price risings. They did this by diverting funds from the sales tax. See *La Nación,* December 26, 1948.
186. Harold G. Moulton, *La nueva filosofía de la deuda pública. (Con un estudio preliminar sobre la nueva filosofía de la deuda pública en Argentina, por Dino Jarach)* (Buenos Aires: Instituto Argentino de Investigaciones y Estudios Económicos, 1947), 21.
187. David Ricardo, *Principles of Political Economy and Taxation* (London: Dent, 1974), 161–63. Nonetheless, for Ricardo, the equivalence was only quantitative and not qualitative or moral, because loans, unlike taxes, encourage waste in lieu of parsimony.
188. Moulton, *Nueva filosofía*, 16. The Radical leader Frondizi dismissed with irony in the chamber the "Peronist doctrine" on domestic public debt and at the same time criticized the tax increases of 1950: "I cannot understand why the government's men who in this Chamber develop a new theory of the domestic public debt—by saying that a government that owes [money] to national creditors in truth it does not owe anything because it owes it to itself—do not resort to the issue of bonds in lieu of raising taxes. If that financial theory about the public debt was right, they should continue issuing bonds." *DSCD,* 2, August 10–11, 1950, 1758.
189. Inflation rates in Gerchunoff and Llach, *Ciclo de la ilusión,* 470.
190. Cortés Conde, *Economía política*, 186.
191. Surrey and Oldman, "Report of a Preliminary," pt. 1, 175.
192. *DSCD,* 2, August 10-11, 1950, 1758.
193. Harriague, "Revisión."
194. Ibid.
195. Plotkin, *Mañana es San Perón*, 231–2.
196. See the suggestive analysis of Halperin Donghi, *Larga agonía*, 26.
197. Surrey and Oldman, "Report of a Preliminary," pt. 1, 163, 168.
198. Ibid., 170.
199. "Comentarios impositivos. Los dictámenes de las Comisiones Asesoras y la reciente reforma impositiva," *Revista de Ciencias Económicas,* 44 (March–April 1956): 144.
200. Total nondeclared income in 1952 meant 49 percent and 51 percent in 1955. Since economic elites' incomes represented a substantial portion of the country's total taxable income, their contribution to evasion was not negligible. Surrey and Oldman, "Report of a Preliminary," pt. 1, 175.
201. Gerchunoff and Llach, *Ciclo de la ilusión*, 185.
202. Doyon, "La formación del sindicalismo peronista," in *Los años peronistas* (see note 1), 375.
203. On this point, see Hora, *Landowners*, 212–18 and Halperin Donghi, *Larga agonía*, 32–33. The reform of the tax on land was also resented by middle and small owners. See Da Orden, "Recursos fiscales."

204. Argentina. Ministerio de Hacienda de la Nación, *Boletín. Edición Semanal*, no. 327, May 1953, 309.
205. *BDGI*, January 1954, 12.
206. *BDGI*, August 1954, 12.
207. *BDGI*, August 1954, 12.
208. In nineteenth-century Britain, taxpayers—mainly local notables—fulfilled an important role as far as collection of the income tax was concerned. In that way, the government tried to gain public acceptance of the tax and presented itself as less intrusive. Daunton, *Trusting Leviathan*, 197–204.
209. Doyon, "Formación del sindicalismo peronista," 376–77.

4 Into the Labyrinth (1955–1976)

1. Carlos Díaz Alejandro, *Essays on the Economic History of the Argentine Repiblic* (New Haven, CT: Yale University Press), 129.
2. In Argentina and Brazil, these "developmental" ideas are associated with the policies of presidents Arturo Frondizi and Juscelino Kubitschek. See Katryn Sikkink, *Ideas and Institutions: Developmentalism in Brazil and Argentina* (Ithaca & London: Cornell University Press, 1991). Nonetheless, I will use here the word *desarrollismo* in a wider though less accurate sense, in trying to capture the widespread "obsession" with economic development and big industry. See Juan Caros Korol and Hilda Sabato, "Incomplete Industrialization: An Argentine Obsession," *Latin American Research Review* 25, no. 1 (1990): 7–30.
3. On the fiscal goals and strategies of "developmental" governments, see Bird and Oldman, eds., *Readings on Taxation in Developing Countries* (Baltimore, MD: Johns Hopkins University Press, 1967).
4. Ricardo Aroskind, "El país del desarrollo posible," in *Violencia, proscripción y autoritarismo (1955–1976)*, ed. Daniel James, vol. 9 of *Nueva Historia Argentina* (Buenos Aires: Editorial Sudamericana, 2003), 83–89; Pablo Gerchunoff and Lucas Llach, *Entre la equidad y el crecimiento: Ascenso y caída de la economía argentina, 1880–2002* (Buenos Aires: Siglo XXI, 2004), 76–88 and Díaz Alejandro, *Essays*, chap. 7. A theoretical exploration of the stop-and-go cycle is found in Oscar Braun and Leonard Joy, "A Model of Economic Stagnation: A Case Study of the Argentine Economy," *The Economic Journal* 78, no. 312 (1968): 868–87.
5. The literature on the political processes of the period is now a vast one. See among many others: James, ed., *Violencia, proscripción* (see note 4); James, *Resistance and Integration*; Marcelo Cavarozzi, *Autoritarismo y democracia (1955–2006)* (Buenos Aires: Ariel, 2006); Robert A. Potash, *The Army and Politics in Argentina, 1962–1973: From Frondizi's Fall to the Peronist Restoration* (Stanford, CA: Stanford University Press, 1996); Halperin Donghi, *Larga*

agonía de la Argentina peronista (Buenos Aires: Ariel, 1994); or Guillermo O'Donnell, *Bureacratic Authoritarism: Argentina 1966—1973, in Comparative Perspective* (Berkeley: University of California Press, 1988).

6. Gerchunoff and Llach, *Ciclo de la ilusión*, 321. Good introductions to Argentine inflation are Richard D. Mallon and Juan Sourrouille, *La política económica en una sociedad conflictiva: El caso argentino* (Buenos Aires: Amorrortu, 1973), chaps. 6 to 8 and Díaz Alejandro, *Essays*, 362–90.
7. Inflation rates in Gerchunoff and Llach, *Ciclo de la ilusión*, 470–71.
8. Among others, see Oscar Oszlak, "Inflación y política fiscal en Argentina: el impuesto a los réditos", (Documento de Trabajo, Instituto Torcuato di Tella, Buenos Aires, 1970); Mario Brodersohn, "Elasticidad-ingreso del impuesto a la renta en Argentina", *Desarrollo Económico* 3, no. 4 (1964): 573–83; Javier Villanueva, "Argentina's Inflationary Experience (1943–1962)," in *Inflation and Growth in Latin America,* ed. Werner Baer and Isaak Kerstnetzky (Homewood, IL: Richard D. Irving, 1964). In an epoch of inflation in both developed and underdeveloped countries, this was a global concern. See Amotz Morag, *On Taxes and Inflation* (New York: Random House, 1965).
9. This was not a marginal opinion. A mainstream economist like Morag, *On Taxes*, 8, argued: "The economic choice is always at the margin and it is conceivable that at a certain level of taxation the marginal social sacrifice of some deficit financing would be lower than the marginal social sacrifice of further taxation. This is usually the case when the economy is underemployed, since the marginal social sacrifices of deficit financing are quite low and may even be negative if indirect "multiplier benefits" are deducted from them. But even when deficit financing means inflation, the social costs of *some* inflationary deficit financing and *more* taxation should always be compared."
10. Nicholas Kaldor, "Fiscal and Financial Policies," in *Inflation and Growth* (see note 8), 486.
11. See Federico Herschel and Julio Rossi, "Distribución de la carga tributaria en Argentina," *Desarrollo Económico* 5, no. 17/19 (1965): 89 or Federico Herschel, "Fiscal and Financial Policies," in *Inflation and Growth* (see note 8), 505.
12. Ibid., 508.
13. Ibid., 505–507.
14. Henry Bloch, "Fiscal and Financial Policies," in *Inflation and Growth* (see note 8), 487–92.
15. Jorge M. Mayer, *El impuesto a los réditos y la destrucción de la clase media* (Buenos Aires: Librería del Colegio, 1962), 19.
16. Juan A. Vega, "Comentario" (working paper, Cuadernos 40, Facultad de Ciencias Económicas, Universidad Nacional de Cuyo, 1969), 18.

17. Nicolás J. Scotti, "El impuesto a los réditos sobre las rentas del trabajo personal y la inflación," *Derecho Fiscal* 17b (January 1968): 585–86.
18. Mayer, *Impuesto a los réditos*, 82.
19. Villanueva, "Argentina's Inflationary Experience," 357–58.
20. Mallon and Sourrouille, *Política económica*, 246.
21. Oszlak, "Inflation," 24. Nonetheless, when prices were momentarily under control, as in the early phases of the stabilizations plans in 1959–1960 or in 1966–1967, revenues increased due to the reversal of the Olivera-Tanzi effect.
22. Hugo González Cano, "Estimación de las rentas no declaradas que deberían tributar el impuesto a los réditos" (working paper, Documentos CITAF-OEA, Buenos Aires, 1968), 5.
23. Fernando V. Tow, "Una contribución al estudio de la evasión del impuesto a los réditos personales en la Argentina," in *Finanzas Públicas: Terceras Jornadas* (Buenos Aires: Macchi, 1971), 74.
24. González Cano, *Estimación de las rentas*, 5.
25. Nonetheless, many Latin American countries had a weaker performance than Argentina's. Thus, Mexican taxes in 1959 only amounted to 9.9 percent of the GDP, and taxes in Uruguay in 1960 only reached 13 percent of the GDP. Bloch, "Fiscal and Financial," 492 and Azar et all, *¿De quiénes?*, 95.
26. Marcelo R. Lascano, "El impuesto al valor agregado en la república Argentina. Antecedentes y experiencias resultantes de su implantación," *BDGI*, May 1975, 606.
27. *BDGI*, June 1974, 795.
28. Most OECD countries experienced increases in their collections. Between 1965 and 1975, tax revenues went from 22 percent to 26 percent in Australia; from 28 percent to 40 percent in Denmark; and from 25 percent to 29 percent in the UK. Tax revenues stagnated in countries such as the United States, where they remained around 21 percent. In countries such as Italy, tax revenues fell from 16 percent to 14 percent. See OECD, *Revenue Statistics* (Paris: OECD, 2000), 69.
29. Aroskind, "País del desarrollo," 93. Compared to other countries, Argentina's public expenditure was relatively small. From 1974 to 1976, the OECD average public expenditure was 41 percent. Western European countries' public expenditure was usually over 40 percent and that of the United States and of Australia were well over 30 percent. See Webber and Wildavsky, *History of Taxation*, 495.
30. Mallon and Sourrouille, *Política económica*, 304–05.
31. Argentina. Ministerio de Hacienda de la Nación, *Memoria correspondiente al año 1962*, 201.
32. Gerchunoff and Llach, *Ciclo de la ilusión*, 470–71.
33. Roberto Cortés Conde, *La economía política de la Argentina en el siglo XX* (Buenos Aires: Edhasa, 2005), 260.
34. Ibid., 263, 266, 269.

35. Ignacio C. Tandeciarz, "Comentario," *Desarrollo Económico* 5, no. 17/19 (1965): 113 posed this question in 1965: "Is the tax system regressive or is evasion shaping it in that fashion?"
36. Oszlak, "Inflation," 31 and Gerchunoff and Llach, *Ciclo de la ilusión*, 470. Vito Tanzi, "Inflation, Real Tax Revenue and the Case for Inflationary Finance: Theory with an Application to Argentina," *International Monetary Fund Staff Papers*, 25: no. 3 (1978): 417–51 reached similar conclusions to Oszlak, noticing that in a situation in which tax elasticity was low and the lag in tax payment significant, the stabilizer effect of the income tax was dubious. With high inflation, a decrease in real revenues was a more obvious outcome.
37. Mallon and Sourrouille, *Política económica*, 246.
38. All the figures on progressive and regressive taxes during the period come from *BDGI*, October 1969, 416 and June 1974, 799.
39. Oszlak, "Inflation," 24.
40. See a critique of the whole system of revaluation of assets in Oszlak, "Inflation," 57–60, 66.
41. Ricardo Carciofi, *La desarticulación del pacto fiscal: Una interpretación sobre la evolución del sector público argentino en las dos últimas décadas* (Buenos Aires: CEPAL, 1990), 5.
42. Herschel and Rossi, "Distribución carga tributaria," 93.
43. Jorge Macon, *Las finanzas públicas argentinas: Período 1950–1980* (Buenos Aires: Macchi, 1985), 104.
44. Herschel and Rossi, "Distribución carga tributaria," 107. See chapter 3 of this book. In the discussions on the possible suppression of income tax for fourth-category taxpayers, the defenders of this idea argued that wage earners suffered from double taxation since they have to pay both the personal income tax as well as social security taxes. See, for example, the words of Deputy Giordano Echegoyen in *DSCD,* 8, November 10–11, 1961, 5093. See also Ted Reutz, "Ilusiones fiscales, dimensión y método de financiamiento del déficit fiscal del gobierno, 1928–1972," *Ciclos* 1, no. 1 (1991): 131 or Macon, *Finanzas públicas*, 103–04.
45. Ibid., 104.
46. *La Prensa*, March 13, 1962, 24.
47. *La Prensa,* March 19, 1962, 8.
48. Ibid.
49. *DSCD*, 8, November 15–16, 1961, 5300.
50. The case of Denmark is revealing. The attempt at replacing Social Security contributions with revenue coming from the income tax made the income tax system so burdensome that it caused a major tax revolt. Therefore, social security taxes survived—until today—as one of the main fiscal tools in Denmark. However, Denmark stood—and still stands—for progressive welfare policies. See the discussion in Webber and Wildavsky, *History of Taxation*, 532.

51. Belnicoff was hailed by demonstrators in Buenos Aires and became the main speaker in the gathering of March. See *La Prensa,* March 13, 1962, 24.
52. Carciofi, "Desarticulación," 11.
53. Herschel and Rossi, "Distribución carga tributaria," 95.
54. Cortés Conde, *Economía política,* 253.
55. Ibid., 258.
56. Ibid., 252.
57. Herschel and Rossi, "Distribución carga tributaria," 102–05. The distributive impact was probably greater than what this discussion on prices assumed. As Pablo Gerchunoff and Lucas Llach, *Entre equidad y crecimiento,* demonstrated, the Argentine export economy was associated with growing inequalities, whereas an industrial and protected economy, despite its inefficiency, was strongly correlated to an increase in equality. This means, however, that in order to obtain greater levels of equality, the most productive sector had to be attacked. See chapter 3 of this book.
58. Sabatino A. Forino, *El desarrollo económico y la política fiscal: Las finanzas públicas nacionales y su participación en el desarrollo económico general y su planificación* (Buenos Aires: Macchi, 1966), 194, stated in 1966 that Argentine tax system was overall regressive, but it had some progressive elements, particularly the income tax.
59. Oszlak, "Inflación," 1.
60. The figures come from Consejo Técnico de Inversiones, *La economía argentina* (Buenos Aires: Consejo Técnico de Inversiones, 1964–1976).
61. Brodersohn, "Elasticidad-ingreso," 580. For Albert O. Hirschman, *Journeys toward Progress. Studies of Economic Policy-Making in Latin America* (Boulder, CO: Westview Press, 1993), 189; budgets based upon direct taxes are more vulnerable to inflation due to "a greater lag in collection." This might be a powerful stimulus to shift from direct to indirect taxation during a long period of growing prices.
62. Argentine income tax income-elasticity was 0.77 percent, whereas Britain's was 2.0 percent and that of the United States, 1.6. Nonetheless, Argentina resembled other Latin American countries. Chile's income tax income-elasticity was 0.46. Brodersohn, "Elasticidad-ingreso," 578–79. (In simple words, an income-elasticity of 1 means that an increase of overall national income of 1 unit would cause an increase in the income tax collection of 1 unit. An income-elasticity over 1 means that the income tax collection is highly sensitive to variations in the national income, whereas an income-elasticity under 1 indicates that income tax collection does not respond adequately to income variations).
63. Tanzi, *Inflation and the Personal Income Tax: An International Perspective* (Cambridge: Cambridge University Press, 1980), 98.

64. Macon, *Finanzas públicas*, 104. Here, Argentina was clearly falling behind the industrialized countries. Between 1965 and 1980, income tax revenues, as a percentage of the GDP, kept growing in the most developed nations. In Sweden—an exceptional case—they reached over 15 percent; in Britain and the United States, they were around 10 percent. See Steinmo, *Taxation and Democracy*, 28.
65. A discussion of these topics for the Argentine case can be found in Oszlak, "Inflación."
66. Tanzi, *Inflation and Income Tax*, 3.
67. See the above-mentioned works by Vega or Mayer.
68. See the discussion in Oszlak, "Inflación," 33.
69. Ibid., 36–37.
70. Herschel, "Algunas observaciones críticas con respecto a la estructura del impuesto a los réditos," in *Finanzas Públicas: Segundas Jornadas* (Buenos Aires: Macchi, 1969), 562.
71. *BDGI*, December 1973, 883, and April 1975, 585.
72. Oszlak, "Inflación," 45–46, emphasized that personal and family allowances did not follow price movements since 1950. However, Oszlak's analysis ended in 1966 and did not take into consideration the increase of allowances of 1967, which raised the nontaxable income from 72,000 pesos to 192,000 pesos. Nonetheless, Oszlak's remark is relevant because the losses caused by inflation are not easily compensated in the future, and therefore they caused a traumatic and lasting discontent among the victims.
73. The best critique to this inequity in favor of fourth-category taxpayer is Oszlak, "Inflación," 46–51.
74. This phenomenon is well reflected by the fact that between 1955 and 1961, wage earners climbed from 13 percent to 19 percent of the total taxable income, whereas their participation in the national income fell by 7 points. See Oszlak, "Inflación," 25.
75. Sergio A. Vernier, "Una explicación de la evasión del impuesto a los réditos," (working paper, Cuadernos 40, Facultad de Ciencias Económicas, Universidad Nacional de Cuyo, 1969), 2.
76. Herschel, "Algunas observaciones," 560.
77. Ibid., 567.
78. These problems were common to most Latin American republics. The peculiarities of dealing with corporations and the existence of nonbearable shares represented important challenges to the tax administration in the region. See Carlos Vattuone, "Problemática tributaria derivada de la existencia de las sociedades por acciones" (working paper, Documentos CITAF-OEA, Buenos Aires, 1971).
79. Herschel, "Algunas observaciones," 561.
80. Ángel L. Boccia, "Las utilidades de sociedades anónimas y la base del impuesto personal al rédito," in *Finanzas Públicas: Segundas Jornadas* (see note 70), 380–81.

81. Tow, "Contribución al estudio," 77–78. This was a long-run tendency. According to data provided by the *Consejo Nacional de Desarrollo* (National Council for the Development), wages and salaries received in 1952 47.8 percent of the national income. In 1961, that percentage had decreased to 39.4. See Argentina. Consejo Nacional de Desarrollo, *Cuentas Nacionales de la República Argentina: Resumen de los resultados provisionales de la primera parte del programa de investigación CONADE-CEPAL sobre 'Distribución del Ingreso en la República Argentina'* (Buenos Aires: CONADE, 1964), 44–45.
82. Tow, "Contribución al estudio," 76, 78.
83. Ibid., 74, 80.
84. Vega, "Comentario," in *Finanzas Públicas: Terceras Jornadas* (see note 23), 90.
85. Ibid., 90.
86. Ozslak, "Inflación," 26.
87. Claudio Belini and Marcelo Rougier, *El Estado empresario en la industria argentina: conformación y crisis* (Buenos Aires: Manantial, 2008), 209–10.
88. Díaz Alejandro, *Essays*, 250 and Adolfo Dorfman, *Cincuenta años de industrialización argentina, 1930–1980: Desarrollo y perspectivas* (Buenos Aires: Solar, 1983), 352. Between 1955 and 1966, bank credit represented a diminishing portion of the financing of many companies. These enterprises resorted to increasing their debts to other companies, to the social security system, and to the DGI, taking advantage of the inflation. See Belini and Rougier, *Estado empresario*, 219–20.
89. Herschel and Rossi, "Distribución carga tributaria," 93.
90. This complex process and the different alternatives have been analyzed in detail by Belini and Rougier, *Estado empresario*, 222.
91. César Tcach, "Golpes, proscripciones y partidos políticos," in *Violencia, proscripción* (see note 4), 43.
92. *BDGI*, November 1963, 9.
93. Ibid., 11.
94. Paul H. Lewis, *The Crisis of Argentine Capitalism* (Chapel Hill: The University of North Carolina Press, 1990), 326. One of the most important cases affected SIAM, one of the biggest Argentine firms. On the details of the tax debt of SIAM and its relationships with the DGI, see Belini and Rougier, *Estado empresario*, 222.
95. Lewis, *Crisis of Argentine Capitalism*, 326.
96. "Disertación por L.S. 82 T.V. Canal 7, efectuada el día 19 de marzo de 1964, por el Director General de la DGI, Alberto María Caletti, con motivo de la inauguración del ciclo anual 'Impositiva Informa'," *BDGI*, March–April 1964, 267.
97. For a detailed account of this process, see Lewis, *Crisis of Argentine Capitalism*, 326–28.

98. See article 1 of the law, quoted in Rougier, *Industria, finanzas e instituciones en la Argentina: La experiencia del Banco Nacional de Desarrollo*, 1967–1976 (Buenos Aires: Universidad Nacional de Quilmes, 2004), 115 and an insightful analysis of this policy, in pages 112–16.
99. See Guillermo Walter Klein interviewed by Luis Alberto Romero, Mayo 31, 1973, Proyecto Historia Oral ITDT, Buenos Aires, 2–3.
100. Aroskind, "País del desarrollo," 92.
101. *BDGI*, October 1966, 326.
102. Belini and Rougier, *Estado empresario*, 209.
103. Rural producers were also part of the story. If Díaz Alejandro is right and cost-push factors are more important than monetary ones in the explanation of Argentine inflation, then the dynamic of wage increases and devaluation that characterized the cycle of stop-and-go and pushed prices up was also a dynamic of transfers of income (and conflict) from urban to rural and vice versa. See Díaz Alejandro, *Essays*, 373, 379.
104. This "political" interpretation of inflation is found—among many others—in Hirschman, *Journeys*, 162, 213–16 and 222–23; Hirschman, "Reflections on the Latin American Experience," in *The Politics of Inflation and Economic Stagnation*, ed. Leon Lindberg and Maier (Washington: Brooking Institution, 1985), or Maier, *In Search of Stability: Explorations in Historical Economy* (Cambridge: Cambridge University Press, 1987), 206–07. For the Argentine case see Cavarozzi, *Autoritarismo y democracia*, 115–16. Keynes, in the interwar period, had already delved into some of these political aspects of inflation. See John Maynard Keynes, *The Collective Writings of John Maynard Keynes*, vol. 4, *A Tract on Monetary Reform* (London: Macmillan/St. Martin Press, 1971), 17–29.
105. Tanzi, *Inflation and Income Tax*, 54.
106. Alberto T. López, "Los sistemas fiscales como generadores de deshonestidad," *Revista de Ciencias Económicas* (January–March 1957): 48.
107. Ibid., 48. Aneurin Bevan was a British politician from the Left wing of Labour Party who favored socializing policies. He was health minister in the 1940s and labor minister in the 1950s, Martin Daunton, *Just Taxes: The Politics of Taxation in Britain, 1914–1979* (Cambridge: Cambridge University Press, 2002), 225.
108. Yet, as I tried to demonstrate, Peronism was a striking attempt at guaranteeing social justice without dramatically increasing taxation.
109. López, "Los sistemas fiscales," 48–50.
110. Ibid., 52–54.
111. *Panorama de la Economía Argentina*, November 1957, 98.

112. Mayer, *Impuesto a los réditos*, 38.
113. *BDGI*, September 1963, 355.
114. Confederación General del Trabajo de la República Argentina, *La CGT en marcha hacia el cambio de estructuras* (Buenos Aires: CGT, 1965), 21.
115. Ibid., 21. Of course, and beyond these coincidences, the CGT was not portraying the "middle classes" as the victims of high taxes and the politics of social justice.
116. *RUIA*, July–September 1963, 12.
117. Letter of the UIA to Anselmo Marini, Speaker in the Chamber of the UCRP, 20 November, 1961, published in *DSCD*, 9, January 26, 1962, 6400.
118. Letter of the UIA to Manuel Rapoport, Dirección General Impositiva, 17 November, 1961, published in *DSCD*, 9, January 26, 1962, 6401.
119. Ibid., 6402.
120. *BDGI* (1961), Cuadro 13.
121. *DSCD*, 9, January 26, 1962, 6402.
122. Letter of the Argentine Chamber of Commerce to the National Congress, published in *DSCD*, 9, January 26, 1962, 6399.
123. Ibid. 6396.
124. Mayer, *Impuesto a los réditos*, 29–30.
125. Ibid., 17.
126. Ibid.
127. Ibid., 47, 78.
128. The discussion on adversarial and cooperative tax states in Lieberman, *Race and Regionalism*, 59–60.
129. Quoted in Mayer, *Impuesto a los réditos*, 16.
130. Political violence was becoming endemic. In addition to the permanent intervention of the military in politics, since the late 1960s, Peronist and Left-wing guerrillas appeared in an already turbulent scenario. See Mónica Gordillo, "Protesta, rebelión y movilización: De la resistencia a la lucha armada, 1955–1973," in *Violencia, proscripción* (see note 4).
131. Manuel Rapoport, *Historia económica, social y política de la Argentina (1880–2003)* (Buenos Aires: Ariel, 2006), 533, 568.
132. Aldo Ferrer, *La economía argentina: Desde sus orígenes hasta principios del siglo XXI* (Buenos Aires: FCE, 2004), 256.
133. The idea of an impending fiscal crisis in the mid-1970s was widespread in many Western countries. See a Marxist interpretation in James O'Connor, *The Fiscal Crisis of the State* (New York: St. Martin Press, 1973).
134. For Carciofi, *Desarticulación*, 51, this process of collapse unfolded between the end of the 1970s and the hyperinflationary crisis of 1989. See also Cavarozzi, *Autoritarismo y democracia*, 65.

5 Searching for Solutions: the VAT

1. Perón was prevented from being the "Justicialist" candidate in the elections of March 1973 by a rule that forced the would-be candidates to be in the country before August 1972. Nonetheless, the Peronist candidate, Héctor Cámpora, obtained a landslide victory. The return of Perón to Argentina in June 1973 made Cámpora's government unsustainable, and after fresh elections in September, Perón was elected president of the Republic. On this complex process, see Juan Carlos Torre, *El gigante invertebrado: Los sindicatos en el gobierno, Argentina 1973–1976* (Buenos Aires: Siglo XXI, 2004), 49–50.
2. Torre, *gigante invertebrado*, 25 and Maristella Svampa, "El populismo imposible y sus actores, 1973–1976," in *Violencia, proscripción* (see note 4, chap. 4).
3. Torre, *Gigante invertebrado*, 33.
4. See, for example, Minister Alsogaray's attempt in 1962 to create a national advisory council and the reaction of different business associations in Jorge Niosi, *Les entrepreneurs dans la politique argentine 1955–1973* (Montreal: Les Presses de l'Université de Québec, 1976), 128–30.
5. Confederación General Económica de la República Argentina, *Sugerencias del empresariado nacional para un programa de gobierno* (Buenos Aires: CGE, 1973), 22.
6. Ibid., 79.
7. Ibid., 23.
8. Ibid., 20.
9. Ibid., 23.
10. The same document proposed a "national plan of development." Planning, national development, and corporatist arrangements formed an ideological construction that is difficult to simplify as an anti interventionist program. See ibid., 24.
11. Svampa, "Populismo imposible," 397 and Guido Di Tella, *Perón-Perón, 1973–1976* (Buenos Aires: Editorial Sudamericana, 1983), 150–52.
12. Luis Osvaldo Roggi, comp., *Argentina: Confederación General del Trabajo, 1965. Documentos y reacciones de prensa*, Dossier 3 (Cuernavaca: Centro Intercultural de Documentación, 1967), 49.
13. Ibid.
14. CGT, *CGT en marcha*, 50.
15. Ibid., 21.
16. See Pablo Gerchunoff and Lucas Llach, *Entre la equidad y el crecimiento: Ascenso y caída de la economía argentina 1880–2002* (Buenos Aires: Siglo XXI, 2004).
17. CGT, *CGT en marcha*, 21.
18. Ibid., 22–26.

19. See also Niosi, "Les entrepreneurs," 12.
20. CGT, *CGT en marcha*, 26.
21. Esping-Andersen, *The Three Worlds*, 176–78, Tanzi, *Inflation and Income Tax*, 130, and Maier, *In Search of Stability*, 166–68.
22. Torre, *Gigante invertebrado*, 31–36.
23. Ibid., 54–55 and 60. This was an important symbolic triumph. However, as Juan Carlos Torre noticed, the lack of technical personnel meant that the trade unions could not derive as much power from their new prerogative.
24. Torre, *Gigante invertebrado*, 79.
25. See the details of this process in ibid., 89–124.
26. Di Tella, *Perón-Perón*, 152–53. Wages' share in the national income reached its maximum, 46 percent, under the first Peronist administration. In 1971, it had dropped to 38 percent. See Svampa, "Populismo imposible," 399.
27. *BDGI*, June 1974, 743–47.
28. Marcelo Rougier and Martín Fiszbein, "De *Don Derrochín a Maese Ahorrín*: El fomento del ahorro durante la economía peronista," in *Sueños de bienestar en la nueva Argentina: Estado y políticas públicas durante el peronismo 1946–1955*, ed. Patricia Berrotarán, Aníbal Jáuregui, and Marcelo Rougier (Buenos Aires: Imago Mundi, 2004), 139–40.
29. *BDGI*, June 1974, 749, 765.
30. Carlos Leyba, *Economía y política en el tercer gobierno de Perón* (Buenos Aires: Biblos, 2003), 110–11.
31. However, the most important tax collected by DGI, the income tax, dropped constantly as a proportion of the GDP, from 3.8 percent to 0.8 percent between 1950 and 1975. See Jorge Macon, *Las finanzas públicas argentinas: Período 1950–1980* (Buenos Aires: Macchi, 1985), 104.
32. Marcelo R. Lascano, "El impuesto al valor agregado en la República Argentina. Antecedentes y experiencias resultantes de su implantación," *BDGI*, May 1975, 606.
33. Nevertheless, the sales tax had some features of the VAT. When the raw materials employed by the industry were already taxed (for instance by an excise) the taxpayer—the firm—only had to pay the added value on the final product. In fact, the sales tax was an improvement on the original cascading tax that had been implemented between 1932 and 1934.
34. Raúl Prebisch, *Informe preliminar acerca de la situación económica* (Buenos Aires: Secretaría de Prensa y Actividades Culturales de la Presidencia de la Nación, 1955), 83–84.
35. Federico Herschel, "Política fiscal y desarrollo económico en la República Argentina," *Revista de la Universidad de Buenos Aires* (January–March 1962): 91. That year, from a different ideological perspective, Jorge M. Mayer, *Impuesto a los réditos y la destrucción*

de la clase media (Buenos Aires: Librería del Colegio, 1962), 81 proposed among others a progressive tax on sales as an alternative to the income tax.

36. *RUIA*, October–December 1965, 62.
37. *BDGI*, February 1963, 331.
38. Arnold Harberger, "Fiscal and Financial Policies," in *Inflation and Growth* (see note 8, chap. 4), 502.
39. Carl Shoup, "The Value Added Tax and Developing Countries," *The World Bank Research Observer* 3, no. 2 (1988): 140.
40. The *BDGI* followed the international debates on the VAT and often published articles translated from foreign journals. For example, in September 1969, the *BDGI* published the article by Marcel Piquemal, "El valor agregado financiero y sus amputaciones," translated from the *Revue de Sciencie Financière* of Paris; in August 1972, Edwin S. Cohen, "La experiencia extranjera con el impuesto al valor agregado," originally published in the *National Tax Journal,* appeared in the BDGI; "Impuesto al valor agregado en Inglaterra," a report presented to the British Parliament by the Chancellor, was translated and republished in November 1972; or "Impuesto al valor agregado a prueba de simplificación," published in December 1972, from an original of the *Revue de la Direction Générale des Impôts.*
41. Consejo Federal de Inversiones, *Política fiscal en la Argentina* (Buenos Aires: CFI, 1965), 159–69.
42. *Macon,* "Impuesto a las ventas", *BDGI, June 1967,* 487–88.
43. See the minister's justification for the introduction of the VAT in Cámara de *Sociedades Anónimas, Reforma impositiva 1967, Ley 17.196* (Buenos Aires: 1967), 5–6.
44. For instance: automobiles would attract 10 percent; TV sets, air-conditioned devices or photographic cameras, 15 percent; and champagne, cards, gold, silver, and jewelry, 20 percent. *Primera Plana,* May 9–15, 1967, 25.
45. *Primera Plana,* May 9–15, 1967, 25.
46. Macon, "Impuesto a las ventas," 487–88. All the figures are from this source.
47. Raúl E. Cuello, "Política fiscal e inversión privada. Conferencia impartida en la Bolsa de Comercio de Buenos Aires, el 4 de abril de 1968, a invitación de la Cámara Argentina de Sociedades Anónimas," *BDGI*, May 1968, 432.
48. *BDGI*, January 1970, 7.
49. Sociedad Rural Argentina, *Memoria* (Buenos Aires: SRA, 1971), 78.
50. Lascano, "Impuesto al valor agregado," 606. ACIEL stands for Coordinating Associations of Free Business Institutions. This association was created in 1958 by the Stock Market, the SRA, and the UIA with the aim of tackling the leverage of the CGE and of offering support to the more free-trade oriented entrepreneurs. It became

a sort of political speaker for these business associations. See Niosi, *Les entrepreneurs*, 179.

51. J. A. Ballotta, "Operación y administración del IVA en la Argentina," *BDGI*, December 1974, 754.
52. Ricardo Lumi, "La reforma tributaria. Herramienta de política de desarrollo y de distribución del ingreso," *BDGI*, June 1974, 784–85, and María A. Allegretti de Salgado, *El impuesto al valor agregado en la República Argentina* (Buenos Aires: DGI, 1974), 5.
53. *DSCD*, 1973, 4.516.
54. "Explicó el contador Ballotta los alcances del nuevo impuesto al valor agregado (I.V.A.)," *Boletín Semanal del Ministerio de Economía*, May 31, 1974, 6. The secretary of finance, Ricardo Lumi, spoke of a "policy of development and income distribution," Lumi, "La reforma tributaria," 784. See also Allegretti de Salgado, *Impuesto al valor agregado*, 2–3. This author, advisor to the Ministry of Economy, stated: "The V.A.T. is conceived as a mere tool for collection... the possibility of using it as an instrument of selective policy has been discarded for the sake of simplicity... exemptions have been minimized and there will be only two rates."
55. CGE, *Sugerencias del empresariado*, 24.
56. Macon and Pedro F. J. Pavesi, *Un impuesto al valor agregado para Argentina* (Buenos Aires: El Ateneo, 1973), 124. Years later, Macon insisted on the lack of progressiveness of the Argentine tax system. See Macon, *Finanzas públicas*, chap. 6.
57. Lascano, "Impuesto al valor agregado," 604.
58. Macon and Pavesi, *Impuesto al valor agregado*, 124.
59. Lascano, "Impuesto al valor agregado," 611.
60. Ibid. 602.
61. Macon and Pavesi, *Impuesto al valor agregado*, 124–25.
62. The momentousness of the reform was apparent for the bureaucrats. The VAT was accompanied by a fiscal amnesty, which was referred to as "*borrón y cuenta nueva*" ("let's make a fresh start") by the DGI's publicity. See Ballotta, "Operación y administración del IVA en la Argentina," *BDGI*, December 1974, 749.
63. Ballotta, "Principios generales que inspiran la reforma tributaria," *BDGI*, June 1974, 787.
64. Oscar Cetrángolo and Juan Pablo Jiménez, *Política fiscal en Argentina durante el régimen de convertibilidad* (Buenos Aires: CEPAL, 2003), 79.
65. Edward Ames and Richard T. Rapp, "The Birth and Death of Taxes: A Hypothesis," *Journal of Economic History* 37, no. 1 (1977): 161–78.
66. A publication of the Radical Party of 1989 linked the "fiscal crisis of the state" to the collapse of the industrialization led by the substitution of imports. See Roberto L. Esteso and Héctor M. Capraro, *La cuestión federal en Argentina: Características de la*

relación nación-provincias y rasgos de la localización productiva (Buenos Aires: Fundación Arturo Illia para la Democracia y la Paz, 1989), 11.

67. E. V. K. Fitzgerald, "ECLA and the Theory of Import Substituting Industrialization in Latin America," in *Industrialization and the State in Latin America: The Postwar Years*, vol. 3, of *An Economic History of Twentieth-Century Latin America*, ed. Enrique Cárdenas, José Antonio Ocampo, and Rosemary Thorp (New York: Palgrave/ Macmillan, 2000), 89, notices that this process was particularly acute in Argentina and Chile. Nonetheless, the crisis of (income) taxation was general. In the mid-1970s, unable to deal with inflation and the indexation problem, the Uruguayan military government decided to suppress the income tax altogether. See Tanzi, *Inflation and the Income Tax*, 6 and Azar et al., *¿De quiénes?*, 109.
68. See on Menem's reforms Cetrángolo and Jiménez, *Política fiscal*; Carlos H. Acuña, Sebastián Galiani, and Mariano Tommasi, "Understanding the Political Economy of Structural Reform: the Case of Argentina," in *Understanding Market Reforms in Latin America: Similar Reforms, Diverse Constituencies, Varied Results*, ed., José María Fanelli (New York: Palgrave/Macmillan, 2007), and Gerchunoff and Torre, "La política de liberalización económica en la administración de Menem," *Desarrollo Económico* 36, no. 143 (1996): 733–67.

Conclusions

1. Rawls's *A Theory of Justice* was originally published in 1971.
2. Luis Alberto Romero, *Breve historia contemporánea de Argentina* (Buenos Aires: FCE, 1994). This interpretation of Romero's book in Hora, "La calma y la tormenta: Comentario al libro de Luis Alberto Romero: *Breve historia contemporánea de Argentina*," *Desarrollo Económico* 35, no. 140 (1996): 667–71.
3. This interpretation can be found, among many other works, in two influential recent essays: Tulio Halperin Donghi, *Larga agonía de la Argentina peronista* (Buenos Aires: Ariel, 1994), and Pablo Gerchunoff and Lucas Llach, *Entre la equidad y el crecimiento: Ascenso y caída de la economía argentina 1880–2002* (Buenos Aires: Siglo XXI, 2004).
4. See Carlos H. Acuña, Sebastian Galiani, and Mariano Tommasi, "Understanding Reform in Latin America," (working Papers 88, Universidad de San Andres, Departamento de Economia).
5. Marcelo S. Bergman, *Tax Evasion and the Rule of Law in Latin America: The Political Culture of Cheating and Compliance in Argentina and Chile* (University Park: The Pennsylvania State University Press, 2009), 603.

6. Oscar Cetrángolo and Juan Pablo Jiménez, *Política fiscal en Argentina durante el régimen de convertibilidad* (Buenos Aires: CEPAL, 2003), 78–79.
7. Acuña, Galiani and Tommasi, "Understanding Reform," 54–55.
8. On these reforms see Cetrángolo and Jiménez, *Política fiscal*, 34.
9. This is Gerchunoff and Llach's suggestive hypothesis. See Gerchunoff and Llach, *Entre equidad y crecimiento,* 95–98.
10. ECLAC, *Economic Survey of Latin America and the Caribbean 2001–2002*, (Santiago de Chile: ECLAC, 2002), 102–03.
11. Roberto Cortés Conde, "La crisis Argentina de 2001–2002," *Cuadernos de Economía* (Santiago de Chile) 40, no. 121 (2003): 764–66.
12. ECLAC, *Economic Survey 2001–2002*, 102.
13. Oscar Cetrángolo and Juan Carlos Gómez Sabiani, *Política tributaria en la Argentina: Entre la solvencia y la emergencia* (Buenos Aires: CEPAL, 2007), 34.
14. Ibid., 15 and 28–32.
15. Martin Daunton, *Just Taxes: The Politics of Taxation in Britain, 1914–1979* (Cambridge: Cambridge University Press, 2002), 282–95.
16. *La Nación*, March 7, 2006.
17. Ibid.
18. Ibid.
19. Herwig Immervoll et al., "The Impact of Brazil's Tax-Benefits System on Inequality and Poverty" (discussion Paper 117, Ibero-America Institute for Economic Research, 2005), 21.

Index